# IN RE ALGER HISS
*Volume II*

# IN RE ALGER HISS

## Volume II

### EDITED BY EDITH TIGER

 HILL AND WANG  NEW YORK
*A division of Farrar Straus Giroux*

Library of Congress Cataloging in Publication Data
Main entry under title: In re Alger Hiss: a petition
for a writ of error coram nobis.
1. Hiss, Alger. 2. Trials (Perjury)—New York (City)   I. Tiger, Edith.
KF224.H57T53   345'.73'0234   78–26085
ISBN 0–8090–5808–1   ISBN 0–8090–0143–8 pbk.

# CONTENTS

For this publication, the entire text has been numbered consecutively on the outside top corner of each page. These are the page numbers referred to above. The original pagination of each document appears at the foot of the page.

# EDITOR'S NOTE

*In Re Alger Hiss, Volume II,* is a facsimile reproduction of the Memorandum and exhibits in support of Alger Hiss's petition for a writ of error *coram nobis* prepared by Victor Rabinowitz of Rabinowitz, Boudin, Standard, Krinsky and Lieberman for the National Emergency Civil Liberties Foundation, Inc. This Memorandum, a legal brief, is a companion to *In Re Alger Hiss* (Hill and Wang, 1979), a facsimile reproduction of Hiss's petition to the Federal District Court to set aside his 1950 conviction for perjury as unconstitutional. Mr. Rabinowitz's brief, reproduced herein, expands and clarifies the allegations presented in the original petition, presents extended legal argument and additional documentary evidence that Hiss's conviction was obtained in violation of fundamental constitutional rights, and demands that the conviction therefore be set aside. It is a document of major historical and legal significance, dealing as it does with one of the most widely disputed political trials of the century, and providing the most complete discussion of the law of *coram nobis* available.

Going back over thirty years, the Hiss conviction set in motion a controversy about Hiss's guilt or innocence which remains unresolved to this day. Fifteen books about the case have been published and others are in preparation; a major documentary film of the Hiss trials has been released; and there have been countless newspaper and magazine articles. The background of the case in brief is this:

Hiss was a former high-level State Department official who had accompanied President Franklin D. Roosevelt to the Yalta conference of Allied leaders toward the end of World War II, and later served as Secretary-General of the founding conference of the United Nations in 1945. At the time of his indictment in December 1948, he was president of the Carnegie Endowment for International Peace.

The chief protagonist against Hiss—and on many issues the sole witness—was Whittaker Chambers, a senior editor at *Time* magazine, and a self-styled former courier for Soviet espionage agents in the United States.

A federal grand jury indicted Hiss for perjury in denying under oath that he had given copies of classified State Department documents to Whittaker Chambers. A first trial opened in May 1949 and resulted in a hung jury in July 1949. A second trial, begun in November 1949, ended with a conviction in January 1950. Appeals to higher courts were unavailing.

The trials were conducted in an atmosphere of national confusion and fear. Hiss became a special target for those forces which had been hostile to both the Roosevelt New Deal and the concept of the United Nations. The case is generally credited with launching the cold war of the 1940's and 1950's, and was one of the great state trials of our history. The adverse effect of the conviction on the exercise of First Amendment rights cannot be overstated. Among other things, the case marked the beginning of the political rise of Richard M. Nixon, a member of the House Committee on Un-American Activities, who was serving his first term in Congress at the time of Hiss's indictment.

Because of this highly charged atmosphere, many observers felt that the Hiss verdict could never be overturned, but Supreme Court Justice William O. Douglas took a different view in his memoir, *Go East, Young Man* (Random House, 1974). Writing about the Supreme Court's refusal to accept the Hiss case for review in 1951, Douglas noted that two justices—Stanley F. Reed and Felix Frankfurter—had disqualified themselves from the deliberations because they had been character witnesses for Hiss. Douglas wrote: "If either Reed or Frankfurter had not testified at the trial, we doubtless would have had [enough votes] to grant [certiorari]; and in my view no court at that time could possibly have sustained the conviction."

Hiss himself has never yielded in his belief that he would ultimately achieve vindication and he has never ceased in his struggle to that end. After his release from prison he reaffirmed his innocence and wrote a book to argue his case. Disbarred and unable to practice law (the Massachusetts bar readmitted him in 1975), Hiss eked out a precarious living primarily as a salesman for a printing and stationery company; but he never halted his quiet campaign to establish his innocence. The present proceeding is the culmination of that campaign.

In March 1975, the National Emergency Civil Liberties Foundation, Inc., acting on behalf of Hiss, began efforts, under the Freedom of Information Act, to obtain documents regarding the Hiss case from government agencies. In October 1976, Foundation attorneys at Rabinowitz, Boudin, Standard, Krinsky and Lieberman brought a successful lawsuit to speed up the process. Since then voluminous files—many heavily censored—have been turned over to Hiss. Based to a large extent on this new information, on July 27, 1978, Hiss's attorneys petitioned the Federal District Court in New York to overturn his 1950 conviction. The petition requested relief in the form of a rarely used writ of error *coram nobis,* which in layman's language is an order of the court declaring that fundamental constitutional errors have been committed in a previous trial and correcting the earlier judgment. (*In Re Alger Hiss* has a scholarly introduction by Yale Law School professor Thomas I. Emerson which sets forth the historical origins and uses of *coram nobis.*)

The petition asserts that the perjury conviction—for which Hiss served forty-four months—violated Hiss's Fifth and Sixth Amendment rights because the government had used an informer within the legal camp of the defense; permitted perjurious testimony to be presented; made serious misrepresentations to the judge, the jury, and the defense; and withheld evidence exculpatory to the defendant. On October 31, 1979, Hiss's attorneys amended the *coram nobis* petition to assert that the government had also used wiretaps on Hiss's home telephone, and other surveillance in violation of the Fourth Amendment, to obtain Hiss's conviction.

In November 1979 and March 1980, the United States Attorney for the Southern District of New York filed an answer and two legal briefs in opposition to Hiss's *coram nobis* petition and moved the Federal District Court to deny the petition. Mr. Rabinowitz's Memorandum and accompanying exhibits were filed on July 8, 1980, to answer the government's opposition and to demonstrate Hiss's entitlement to relief.

Except as noted below, the Memorandum and the exhibits to the Memorandum are reproduced herein exactly as they were submitted to the United States District Court for the Southern District of New York. Reproduced in the appendix is a facsimile of the amendment to the original *coram nobis* petition.

For the most part, the exhibits, like those filed with the original *coram nobis* petition, consist of documents released to Hiss's attorneys under the Freedom of Information Act by the Justice Department and the Federal Bureau of Investigation. In many cases the exhibits, as submitted to the court, are multi-paged documents or groups of documents, and the brief for petitioner relies on only a few of these pages. To avoid excessive bulk, we have in such cases reproduced only the first page of the document or documents in question, and the pages which are relied upon in the brief. The unabridged exhibits are on file with the clerk for the United States District Court, Southern District of New York.

For the convenience of the reader, certain exhibits, or portions of exhibits, which are difficult to read because they were reproduced from poor photostats supplied by the government, have been transcribed. In such cases, the transcription is included on the page adjacent to the illegible reproduction of the government copy.

Mr. Rabinowitz is responsible for the brief and its contents, but it could not have been written without the hard work, the legal analysis, and the exhaustive research of many persons. I would particularly like to acknowledge the considerable contributions of Gordon J. Johnson, Ellen J. Winner, James M. Pruitt, Susan Davis, Jeffrey Kisseloff, Anne Winslow, Larry Vogelman, and William H. McDavid.

E.T.

# THE MEMORANDUM

UNITED STATES DISTRICT COURT
SOUTHERN DISTRICT OF NEW YORK

- - - - - - - - - - - - - - - -x

                         :

                         :       78 Civ. 3433 (RO)

       In Re           :

       ALGER HISS,      :

           Petitioner.  :

- - - - - - - - - - - - - - - -x

MEMORANDUM IN SUPPORT OF PETITIONER'S
MOTION TO GRANT WRIT OF CORAM NOBIS
OR, IN THE ALTERNATIVE, TO GRANT TO
PETITIONER AN EVIDENTIARY HEARING AND
TO PERMIT DISCOVERY IN AID THEREOF.

RABINOWITZ, BOUDIN, STANDARD,
  KRINSKY & LIEBERMAN
30 East 42nd Street
New York, N. Y. 10017
(212) 697-8640

Attorneys for Petitioner
Victor Rabinowitz, Esq.
Gordon J. Johnson, Esq.
Ellen J. Winner, Esq.
  James M. Pruitt (Applicant for Admission
                      to the New York Bar)
  Susan Davis (Third Year Law Student)

Dated:  July 8, 1980
      New York, N. Y.

# TABLE OF CONTENTS

i

UNITED STATES DISTRICT COURT
SOUTHERN DISTRICT OF NEW YORK

- - - - - - - - - - - - - - - - - - - - - X
                                          :
         In Re                            :
                                          :
    ALGER HISS,                              78 Civ. 3433 (RO)
                                          :
         Petitioner.                      :
                                          :
- - - - - - - - - - - - - - - - - - - - - X

MEMORANDUM IN SUPPORT OF PETITIONER'S
MOTION TO GRANT WRIT OF <u>CORAM NOBIS</u>
OR, IN THE ALTERNATIVE, TO GRANT TO
PETITIONER AN EVIDENTIARY HEARING AND
TO PERMIT DISCOVERY IN AID THEREOF.

This memorandum is written in support of petitioner's motion that the writ of error <u>coram nobis</u> for which he sues be granted or, in the alternative, that the government's motion be denied and that an evidentiary hearing be ordered, to be preceded by such discovery as is necessary to permit full presentation at such a hearing.

INTRODUCTION

A petition for a writ of error <u>coram nobis</u> is intended to correct a manifest injustice arising from the fact that petitioner did not get a fair trial. It is a vehicle whereby the courts can "act in doing justice if the record makes plain a right to relief." <u>United States v. Morgan</u>, 346 U.S. 502, 505 (1954). Such relief should be granted against a judgment of conviction where there are circumstances compelling such action to achieve justice. <u>Id</u>. at

-1-

411. Otherwise, "a wrong may stand uncorrected which the available remedy would right."[1] Id. at 512.

The courts have granted coram nobis writs in a large variety of cases; a list of the circumstances in which the writ is available is as long as the list of the ways in which constitutional rights can be denied. The dimensions of coram nobis relief can no more be sketched than the dimensions of habeas corpus. Although the government would restrict use of the writ to a limited number of cases, there is no legal basis for such restriction. Constitutional errors appropriate for consideration in coram nobis proceedings include the prosecution's failure to turn over Brady materials, U.S. v. Keogh, 391 F.2d 138 (2d Cir. 1968), selective prosecution, United States v. Danks, 357 F.Supp. 193 (D. Haw. 1973), the failure to allow the defendant to appear

---

[1]    See, Palmentere v. United States, 351 F.Supp. 167, 176-77 (W.D. Mo. 1972):

> A system of law which permits the
> correction of its past denials of
> fundamental rights to particular individuals
> is one which is consistent with the declaration in the Preamble which states that our
> constitution was ordained and established
> to 'establish justice. . .and to secure
> the blessings of Liberty to ourselves
> and our Posterity.' It is a system of
> law which is based upon the premise that
> justice required that a wrong be remedied;
> not concealed and forgotten.

pro se, United States v. Plattner, 330 F.2d 271 (2d Cir. 1964),
and the knowing use of perjured testimony, Garrison v. United
States, 154 F.2d 106, 107 (5th Cir. 1946), in addition to the
cases cited by the government.  Government Memorandum in
Opposition to Petitioner's Application, hereinafter Govt. Memo,
38, 39.  We can predict with some confidence that should a new
and compelling set of facts be presented which require relief
by coram nobis, our legal system will be flexible enough to
provide a remedy.

Coram nobis, of course, will not be available to
give relief in all cases.  The government cites several cases
in which the facts were held to be insufficient to merit relief.[2/]
The listing of such cases will provide no help in determining
the instant application for a writ, however, for here there is
an almost unprecedented array of errors of constitutional
dimension.

The petition herein presents extended argument and
evidence in support of petitioner's contention that his trial
was unfair.  It shows that the Department of Justice and the FBI
utilized the services of an informer in the camp of petitioner's
counsel; that it concealed evidence in its files which would
have been exculpatory; that it suffered witnesses to commit

2/      See, e.g., U.S. v. Wolfson, 558 F.2d 59, 65-66 (2d
Cir. 1977); U.S. v. Garguilo, 324 F.2d 795, 796 (2d Cir. 1963),
U.S. v. Re, 372 F.2d 641, 643 (2d Cir.), cert. denied, 388 U.S.
912 (1967).  Contrary to the impression created by the government, the claims raised in all three cases are susceptible to
relief through post-conviction collateral attack.

perjury, and that it engaged in extensive prosecutorial misconduct designed to convict petitioner in one of the most important
political trials of the time. In support of his petition the
petitioner presented over eighty exhibits, most of them recently
discovered from FBI files. */

Petitioner has, without doubt, presented sufficient
evidence of governmental misconduct ot overcome the presumption
that "the proceedings were correct." United States v. Morgan,
supra, 346 U.S. at 512, and "to put on the government the
burden of coming forward with proof" that such misconduct did
not occur. United States v. Keogh, 440 F.2d 737, 741 (2d Cir.
1971). Cf., Mitchell v. United States, 482 F.2d 289, 295-97
(5th Cir. 1973); Palmentere v. United States, supra, 351 F.Supp.
at 169-171; Farnsworth v. United States, 232 F.2d 59, 64-65 (D.C.
Cir. 1956). The government has sorely failed to meet its burden
of rebutting this showing of extensive governmental misconduct.

Although petitioner was convicted almost thirty years
ago, he is not precluded from seeking relief at this time.
United States v. Morgan, supra, 346 U.S. at 507; United States
v. Cariola, 323 F.2d 180, 183 (3d Cir. 1963). The government's suggestion that a higher standard of proof must be
offered due to the lapse of 29 years is simply without merit.

---

*/ Textural and footnote references to "CN Ex. 1," etc. through
"CN Ex. 84" are to exhibits annexed to the petition for writ of
error coram nobis submitted to the Court on July 26, 1978
(hereinafter "petition"). References to "CN Ex. 85," etc. are
to exhibits annexed to this memorandum and are submitted to
the Court herewith.

Both cases relied upon by the government for this proposition make clear that the defendant has a heavier burden of proof only if he unreasonably delays seeking relief. United States v. Cariola, supra, 323 F.2d at 183; United States v. Morgan, 222 F.2d 673, 675 (2d Cir. 1955). Here, as was the case in Morgan, the petitioner evidenced marked diligence from the moment when he discovered the government's trial misconduct; as the FOIA documents were not received until very recently, 3/ there were "sound reasons existing for failure to seek appropriate earlier relief." 4/ United States v. Morgan, supra, 346 U.S. at 512.

---

3/      The government's suggestion that the petition must be denied due to Hiss' reliance on these documents, Govt. Memo at 36, must be dismissed summarily. As is abundantly clear, the writ is not being used to introduce newly discovered evidence on matters which were litigated at trial, but, instead, to raise constitutional claims of which Hiss had no knowledge at trial or on appeal. Compare, United States v. Carter, 319 F.Supp. 702 (M.D.Ga. 1969), aff'd, 437 F.2d. 444 (5th Cir. 1971).

4/      It should be noted that numerous coram nobis actions involve a long lapse of time between the conviction and the collateral attack, and the attendant death of key witnesses and scattering of trial evidence. In not one case involving a good faith delay, however, is a heavier burden of proof imposed on the petitioner. See, e.g., United States v. Valentino, 201 F.Supp. 219 (E.D.N.Y. 1962)(approximately 30 years); United States v. Lavalle, 306 F.2d 216 (2d Cir. 1962)(19 years); Haywood v. United States, 127 F.Supp. 485 (S.D.N.Y. 1954)(Court Reporter's minutes and case files in United States Attorney's office, which were key elements of proof, "long since destroyed"); Waller v. United States, 432 F.2d 560 (5th Cir. 1970)(33 years).

The <u>Hiss</u> case was one of the great state trials in recent American history, and the government put its full resources to the task of convicting petitioner. The FBI and the Justice Department both considered the prosecution as having top priority. Scores of agents were assigned to the case for a period of many months, and J. Edgar Hoover took an immediate and personal interest in the matter, frequently giving direct and specific instructions to his subordinates. <u>See</u>, <u>e.g.</u>, CN Exs. 39, 85. Two grand juries took extensive evidence on the subject of the trial, even after petitioner's indictment. The Justice Department assigned one of its most skilled trial counsel to the case, and the motion for a new trial was argued by Myles Lane, then the U. S. Attorney for the Southern District.

Both trials were held against a background of extraordinary public interest. They were preceded by sensational stories coming from the House Committee on Un-American Activities; public interest continued through the post-trial motions.

Indeed, it may be said that at no time since the latter part of 1948 have the issues in the <u>Hiss</u> case dropped out of sight and, as this proceeding indicates, they are still very much alive. No case in recent United States jurisprudence has generated as much controversy among competent authorities as <u>United States</u> v. <u>Hiss</u>. The case has inspired over a dozen books and innumerable other writings by lawyers, historians and publicists who saw in the case the opening of an important era in the history of our country. Among the many who have analyzed the case in detail, there is sharp disagreement as to whether petitioner was guilty or not. But, whatever their conclusion, few of the commentators have concluded that the case was not close.

The government, nonetheless, maintains that the case was not a close one, and a full one-third of its memorandum is devoted exclusively to the argument that petitioner was guilty. This contention is embellished with numerous references to "immutable proof" of guilt; to the contention that "Hiss had unheard-of access to Chambers' testimony and the prosecution's documentary proof" [5/] and to a detailed analysis of a few items of "overwhelming proof" of the petitioner's guilt.

The government's assertions are entirely unsupported by the record. The mere fact that the first jury disagreed provides a clear indication that the case was a close one. As noted above, many of those who have written extensively on the case have agreed.

---

5/ This is sheer hyperbole. Every defendant who is tried for a second time after a jury disagreement has equally full access to the prosecution's evidence.

But we need not concern ourselves excessively with this problem. The Court of Appeals, after remand by the Supreme Court in United States v. Morgan, supra, said:

> To hold that this defendant can be re-
> lieved of an unconstitutional conviction
> only if he makes a showing of innocence
> (or a showing that he probably would be ac-
> quitted at a constitutionally conducted trial)
> would be to compound the unconstitutionality
> of his conviction, for it would shift to him
> the burden of proof, deprive him of the pre-
> sumption of innocence, and leave the determi-
> nation of his guilt or innocence to a judge,
> thus denying him of a jury trial. Surely
> one unconstitutional deprivation cannot
> justify still others. When a defendant is
> sent to jail without the semblance of a trial,
> his release does not depend on his establish-
> ing his innocence. No more does it here.

United States v. Morgan, supra, 222 F.2d at 674-675.

Hence, a detailed discussion of the guilt or innocence of the petitioner is irrelevant. Furthermore, detailed
response to the government's extended argument that petitioner
was clearly guilty would result in extensive discussion of the
trial evidence and we have no desire to write still another book
on the Hiss case. Furthermore, we regard all of the discussion
of the "overwhelming evidence" of guilt as a diversion to turn
the court's eyes away from the legal issues raised by the
petition.

Yet, in a larger sense, the question of petitioner's guilt or innocence cannot be shut out of our consciousness. If it were possible for petitioner to go into another trial, this time armed with the information he has received as a result of his FOIA proceeding, he would welcome that opportunity, but that is obviously impossible. He would welcome a new adversarial proceeding on the "immutable facts" or items of "overwhelming proof" upon which the government relies. But this, too, is not practical.

And so, we have set forth, in an appendix to this brief, a response to some of the principal arguments advanced by the government, necessarily truncated, but designed to present to the court enough to meet the charge that the case was not a close one and that the petitioner's guilt is clear. This will permit us to get on with the issues raised by the <u>coram nobis</u> petition without interruption to consider issues of guilt or innocence.

One additional observation is appropriate. If flight may be taken as some evidence of guilt, Hiss' conduct throughout this litigation has been that of a man sure of his innocence. From the beginning of the controversy he has himself sought out and has often secured the evidence which, ironically enough, has been used to convict him.

So, beginning with his challenge to Chambers to repeat his charges that Hiss had been a member of the Communist Party in a non-privileged arena, Hiss has consistently behaved as if full discovery of the truth would vindicate him. He did not have to issue such a challenge, nor to bring a libel suit when Chambers met the challenge. It is inconceivable that Hiss, if guilty, would have instituted the Baltimore libel suit knowing that if Chambers had retained the Baltimore documents, he would face serious charges. His insistence on appearing and testifying before the grand jury (though as an attorney he must have known of the danger of allegations of perjury)was consistent only with a consciousness of innocence.

When the Baltimore documents were produced, they were turned over to the Justice Department at Hiss' direction. It then became necessary to find standards for comparison of type-written manuscripts. Hiss cooperated fully with the FBI in searching for such standards and produced for the government two documents written on his typewriter. From the time of the production of the Baltimore documents, he conducted an extensive search for the missing typewriter, found it, and put it in evidence at the trial although, if he were guilty, production of the typewriter could only have done him harm. Failure to search for standards or failure to look for the typewriter could not have resulted in any criticism of his conduct and his pursuit of these items of evidence can be explained only by his certainty that they would prove him innocent.

Even after his conviction, petitioner has continued his struggle for vindication. He made an elaborate and expensive motion for a new trial at a time when his prison term had been half served. He wrote a book to argue his innocence when it might have seemed wiser had he let the matter rest. Now he has brought this proceeding which, if unsuccessful, can only cause him pain and suffering.

POINT I

PETITIONER WAS DEPRIVED OF THE EFFECTIVE ASSISTANCE
OF COUNSEL GUARANTEED TO HIM UNDER THE SIXTH AMEND-
MENT WHEN THE PROSECUTOR AND FBI AGENTS MET
REPEATEDLY WITH A PRIVATE INVESTIGATOR EMPLOYED BY
THE DEFENSE TO OBTAIN INFORMATION ON DEFENSE
ACTIVITIES AND TRIAL STRATEGY.

Horace Schmahl was a private investigator retained
by Edward McLean, Hiss' counsel, in connection with the <u>Hiss</u>
case. On an undisclosed number of occasions,[6/] Schmahl met
with the prosecutor and agents of the FBI to report on various
aspects of the defense investigation. Many of these meetings
occurred at "perhaps the most critical period of the proceedings" against petitioner -- from the time of the indictment "until the beginning of . . . trial, when consultation,
thoroughgoing investigation and preparation were vitally
important . . ." <u>Powell</u> v. <u>State of Alabama</u>, 287 U.S. 45,
57 (1932).

_____

6/  Despite Hiss' request under the Freedom of Information
    Act, the FBI has refused to release any of the FBI Field
    Office files pertaining to Schmahl and much information
    on Schmahl in the FBI headquarters files. Thus, the
    full extent of Schmahl's disclosures to the government
    is not yet known. The present discussion is based on
    evidence discovered in files which Hiss received to date,
    and the implications that arise therefrom.

The following information can be culled from FBI files:

On March 22, 1949, after indictment and before trial, Schmahl called Special Agent Shannon. He stated that he had information which he thought the FBI might be interested in "but that it was not too important." However, "he did not wish to make this information available over the telephone." Shannon told him that he should feel that "he was at liberty to drop into this office in the U.S. courthouse and make this information available to us." CN Ex. 4C. Schmahl may have taken advantage of this invitation and contacted Special Agents Shannon and Lee prior to June 1, 1949. CN Ex. 9. If so, we do not know the extent of the contact.

Some of the FBI personnel had reservations about speaking to Schmahl during the course of the trial, in view of Schmahl's employment by Hiss. But Assistant United States Attorney Murphy had no such inhibition. Schmahl reported to Murphy on at least two and probably three occasions during the first week of the first trial to "give information concerning the Hiss case." CN Exs. 10, 12. In one of the conversations Schmahl advised

-13-

Murphy of the efforts of Hiss' attorneys to secure an old Woodstock typewriter. CN Ex. 10. Murphy directed that the FBI inquire at the typewriter firm of Adam Kunze and learned that such a typewriter had in fact been acquired by McLean. CN Exs. 10, 11. This information was utilized by Murphy in cross-examining Hiss at the second trial, R. 2126-2128, and in his closing argument. R. 3253. */

Nor was this all. An FBI memorandum dated February 22, 1949 notes that Schmahl "turned over the results of his investigation [for Hiss] confidentially through Armand Chankalian, administrative assistant to the United States Attorney." CN Ex. 14. How extensive such reports were we do not know. There was, however, found in Murphy's files a six-page defense memorandum entitled "Outline of Investigation" which detailed the defense investigative strategy. This document was dated December 28th and was prepared by the Hiss lawyers during the time of Schmahl's employment. CN Ex. 13.

---

*/ References to "R" are to pages of the printed Case on Appeal from petitioner's conviction.

A defense file memorandum dated January 29, 1952 records a phone conversation in which a man named Morrow told Chester Lane, Hiss' lawyer at the time of the motion for a new trial, that "every report [Schmahl] made to the defense was turned over by him to the FBI." Petition at pp. 29-31.

The government does not deny these activities of Schmahl and defends on the following grounds:

(a) That Schmahl's contacts with the government were known to Hiss' attorneys and encouraged by them. Govt. Memo. at 32, 43, 50-52. But every incident the government cites of so-called "cooperation" with the FBI by Hiss' lawyers occurred before Hiss was indicted, at a time when Hiss was not even clearly the target of the grand jury investigation. See, CN Ex. 86. Once Hiss was indicted, however, the situation changed. The government fails to cite a single instance after the indictment in which the defense attorneys "encouraged" Schmahl to talk with either the FBI or Murphy. Contrary to the impression the government creates, the defense attorneys neither fostered nor condoned such actions by Schmahl. Indeed, apart from one conversation which Schmahl had with FBI Agent Kennedy on December 8, 1948, they had no knowledge that Schmahl was providing information to the government, even prior to indictment.

       (b)  That the FBI "diligently attempted to rebuff all offers of information." Govt. Memo. at 32, 52. Significantly, the government does not make a similar argument as to the Department of Justice. Murphy and Armand Chankalian evidently had continuing contact with Schmahl and did not "rebuff" but rather encouraged him.[7] Even the FBI had a strange way of "rebuffing" Schmahl. See, e.g., CN Ex. 5. Shannon invited him to come in any time he had information which might be useful. CN Ex. 4C. Shannon and Lee evidently both had

---

[7]    Donegan evidently had no concept at all as to his obligations. He advised on December 29th that an interview with Schmahl would not be of much value "at this particular time, as Schmahl had previously stated that he would keep the Bureau advised of any pertinent developments he might uncover." His understanding of Schmahl's status is curiously deficient. He felt "that there would be a duty placed upon SCHMAHL and also upon his attorney Mr. MC LEAN to advise the Government if any evidence came into their possession that would be pertinent to this criminal investigation." CN Ex. 8.

some contacts with Schmahl as late as May, 1949.  CN Ex. 9.

Schmahl's disclosure of defense activities, tactics and plans to both the FBI and the prosecutor deprived Hiss of the effective assistance of counsel guaranteed to him under Sixth Amendment.  Caldwell v. United States, 92 U.S.App.D.C. 355, 205 F.2d 879, 881 (D.C.Cir. 1953), cert. denied, 349 U.S. 930, reh. denied 349 U.S. 969 (1955); Coplon v. U.S., 89 U.S.App.D.C. 103, 191 F.2d 749, 759 (D.C.Cir. 1951), cert. denied 342 U.S. 926 (1952).

The government's assertion that Weatherford v. Bursey, 429 U.S. 545 (1977) mandates a contrary conclusion is clearly without merit.  Weatherford held that the Sixth Amendment is not violated where an informant does not communicate any information to the government. Id. at 558 It is fair to infer from the opinion that a Sixth Amendment violation will be found where information is actually disclosed.  Id. at 554, 556-557.  Accordingly, the court was careful to delineate the scope of its holding:

> . . . this is not a situation where the
> State's purpose was to learn what it
> could about the defendant's defense plans
> and the informant was instructed to in-
> trude on the lawyer-client relationship
> or where the informant assumed for
> himself that task and acted accordingly.

Id. at 557. Here, as Schmahl undisputedly communicated

information to the FBI and the prosecutor -- whether or

not he "assumed for himself that task," -- Weatherford

clearly does not preclude a finding of a Sixth Amendment

violation.

In Weatherford, moreover, the informer intruded

into the defense camp only to the extent that it was

necessary to be physically present at defense meetings

in order to preserve his cover. 429 U.S. at 557. The

court, concerned with the peculiar problems and dangers

inherent in the use of undercover agents, found that the

intrusion was neither wrongly motivated nor without ade-

quate justification. Id. Here, in contrast, Schmahl's

conduct cannot be justified by either "the unfortunate

necessity of undercover work" nor the "desirability and

legality of continued secrecy even after arrest." Id.

His intrusion into the defense camp can hardly be characterized as necessary to effective law enforcement. <u>Compare</u>, <u>United States</u> v. <u>Denno</u>, 221 F.2d 626, 628-29 (2d Cir. 1955). <u>See also</u>, <u>Caldwell</u> v. <u>United States</u>, <u>supra</u>, 205 F.2d at 879.

The government does not rest exclusively on the slim reed of the <u>Weatherford</u> case. It argues further that the petitioner failed to show that he suffered any prejudice by Schmahl's intrusion into the defense camp. A showing of such prejudice, argues the government, is required for relief. The cases cited by the government, however, stand for no such conclusion.

The law is clear enough. When an informant has passed information to the government, prejudice is presumed and petitioner need not show how great was that prejudice or put some mathematical value on it. [8/]   See. e.g.,

---

[8/]   The government's cases are all situations in which no information was passed on by the informant to the government. So, in <u>Weatherford</u> v. <u>Bursey</u>, the court said:

> At no time did Weatherford discuss with
> or pass on to his superiors or to the
> prosecuting attorney's staff any details

reason, the inquiry into prejudice must stop at the point where attorney-client confidences are actually disclosed to the government. See, United States v. Denno, supra, 221 F.2d at 631 (Frank, J., concurring).

The instant case is illustrative of how difficult, it not impossible, an attempt to measure the amount of prejudice a defendant suffered would be.

We know that Agents Lee and Shannon had conversations with Schmahl in reference to the Hiss case. CN Ex. 9. The FBI has not released memoranda concerning the substance of those conversations and an attempt to calculate the degree of prejudice suffered would require "unguided speculation." Holloway v. Arkansas, supra, 435 U.S. at 491. During the trial, on June 5th and 6th, 1949, Schmahl reported to Murphy to "give information concerning the Hiss case" and Schmahl told Agent Spencer that "an additional interview [with Murphy] was anticipated in the near future". CN Exs. 10 and 12. Again, as one can only speculate as to precisely what information was divulged and how Murphy used this information at trial, [9/] the probability of unfairness due to these

intrusions is incapable of realistic delineation. Accord,

United States v. Ripso, 460 F.2d 965, 976-977 (3d Cir.

1972). The dangers of speculating about possible pre-

judice are thus demonstrated most forcefully by the facts

of the instant case.

The government's attempts to calculate the

precise degree of prejudice suffered by Hiss lead to a

most disingenuous argument. In discussing the "Outline

of Investigation" found in Murphy's files, for example,

the government asserts that no actual prejudice to Hiss

of the magnitude required was caused. Govt. memo at 49.

As this document lists in detail specific leads to follow,

---

[9/] In one case relied on by the government, the court
read Weatherford to hold that "any use at all" by the
government of information gained through an intrusion
into the defense camp would constitute a Sixth Amendment
violation. Mastrian v. McManus, 554 F.2d 813, 821, n.10
(8th Cir.), cert denied, 433 U.S. 913 (1977). Here we
know that Murphy did make use of some of the information
he received from Schmahl. See Discussion at pp. 14 and
24 n. 10.

possible sources for specimens of Hiss' typewriting, and

numerous witnesses to be interviewed, the government's position

can hardly be taken seriously.[10/] As stated in a slightly

different context in In re Terkeltoub:

> At the heart of the job of 'thorough-
> going investigation and preparation' is the
> interviewing of prospective witnesses, hostile
> as well as friendly. And no lawyer, on any
> side of any case, would consider it salutary
> for his client that the opposition knew who
> was being interviewed and what was being said
> during such meeting. If vivid illustration were
> needed, it is supplied every day in this court-
> house by the Government's stout resistance
> to discovery efforts by defendants in
> criminal cases.

265 F.Supp. 683, 685 (S.D.N.Y. 1966).

Other information Schmahl provided to Murphy is

characterized by the government as information which "cannot

in a rational world be considered to have been a critical

---

10/      Even the failure of the defense to list areas of
relevant investigation would be most helpful to the prosecution.
         There was, however, an actual conveyance to and use
by the FBI of defense plans listed in the "Outline of
Investigation." In the holographic statement, CN Ex. 23,
Chambers stated: "Alger Hiss's defense obviously intends to
press the charge that I had homosexual relations with certain
individuals." That charge had yet to be made when Chambers
penned the words and, because the defense was not able to
substantiate the charge, was not used later. However, it is
apparent that the source of the intended defense plans was
CN Ex. 4B in which Schmahl was asked to investigate a statement
made by a "slightly drunk" reporter regarding an asserted
arrest of Chambers for homosexuality.

factor in convincing the jury of Hiss' guilt.[11] Govt. memo at 48.

No court has, to the best of our knowledge, ever applied such a "critical factor" test. The contrary is true. In O'Brien v. United States, 386 U.S. 345 (1967), the Supreme Court, relying on Black v. United States, 385 U.S. 26 (1966), vacated a judgment of conviction even though the only information before the Court was

---

11/ Any attempt to place the burden of showing prejudice on petitioner while simultaneously refusing discovery of the very material which would make that showing possible must be firmly rejected. Indeed, although ordinarily the burden of proof is borne by the party mounting a collateral attack on a conviction, United States v. Morgan, 346 U.S. 502, 512 (1954), the Second Circuit has indicated that on a motion for a new trial, the government bears the burden of proving that its intrusion into the defense camp did not prejudice the trial. United States v. Rosner, supra, 485 F.2d at 1224. Analogously, in a motion for coram nobis relief, once the defendant has established that an intrusion has occurred, the government should bear the burden of proving that the intrusion did not prejudice the trial. Cf. U.S. Ex. rel Chambers v. Maroney, 408 F.2d 1186, 1190 (3d Cir. 1969), aff'd on other grounds, 399 U.S. 42 (1970) (on § 2255 claim of ineffective assistance of trial counsel, once petitioner has made out a prima facie case by showing belated appointment, state must prove that lateness was not prejudicial.) Here, the government, through conclusory assertions, has not met its burden.

error occurs at trial and its scope is readily identifiable."
Holloway v. Arkansas, supra, 435 U.S. at 490. See also
U.S. v. Ripso, supra, 460 F.2d at 974. Here, the reprehen-
sible conduct consisted not of an isolated intrusion into
the defense camp, but instead of a yet unknown number of
intrusions where the government became privy to defense
tactics and strategy. The type of evidence obtained --
general investigative reports -- was not "easily identifiable"
and could clearly have been used by the government at
Hiss' second trial. For this reason, the fact that a new
trial was held was not sufficient to remedy the Sixth
Amendment violation and the error can by no means be
declared harmless. See, "Harmless, Constitutional Error:
A Reappraisal," 83 Harv.L.Rev. 814, 820-821 (1970).

Furthermore, contrary to the government's assertion,Gov.Mem.at 49,
the remedy for a Sixth Amendment violation is not limited
to the granting of a second trial. See, e.g., Massiah v.
United States, 377 U.S. 201 (1964) (Sixth Amendment violation remedied by reversal of conviction); United States v.

Levy, _supra_, 577 F.2d at 210 (where the trial has already taken place, the only appropriate relief is dismissal of the indictment); United States v. Morrison, _supra_, 602 F.2d at 533 (where challenged conduct is both inadequately justified and wrongly motivated, it is not amenable to relief through suppression or reversal of conviction and dismissal of the indictment is the proper relief); _see also_ Hoffa v. United States, 385 U.S. 293, 308 (1966).  Indeed, in United States v. Gartner, _supra_, 518 F.2d at 637 , this circuit recognized that the _per se_ rule of reversal[13/] has been applied where the government's intrusion into the defense camp has been "an offensive interference with the defendant's rights without any justification."[14/]  _See also_ U. S. v. Morrison

---

13/    The government's argument that the validity of the _per se_ rule of reversal is "highly questionable" in light of Weatherford must be dismissed summarily. Govt. memo at 47. Weatherford, as the Court found that the government's conduct did not even violate the Sixth Amendment, the question of the appropriate relief was not at issue.

14/    The court, citing U.S. v. Rosner, _supra_, 485 F.2d at 1228, stated that while the _per se_ rule of reversal had not yet been adopted in the Second Circuit, "if circumstances warranted it we would not shrink from such a result." 518 F.2d at 637.

_supra_, 602 F.2d 531-532. Here, even assuming _arguendo_
that Schmahl took it upon himself to report defense plans
to the prosecution, Murphy's eagerness to acquire this
information and his active cooperation with Schmahl can only
be characterized as an "offensive interference." Furthermore, there was no justification whatsoever for the repeated
intrusions.

The fatal flaw in the government's position -- _i.e._,
that the Sixth Amendment was remedied by the second trial --
becomes clear upon a cursory examination of cases in which
the granting of a new trial was held to be the appropriate
form of relief for a Sixth Amendment violation. In all
such cases, the second trial was ordered so that the potential
detrimental effects of the violation could be eliminated.
See, _e.g._, _Glasser_ v. _United States_, 315 U.S. 60 (1942)
(second trial ordered where defendant would be represented
by new attorney and conflict-of-interest problem could be
eliminated); _U.S._ v. _Ripso_, _supra_, 460 F.2d 965 (new trial
ordered where informer and "sham" defendant would not be

tried with defendant). Here, as Hiss was not aware of
the Sixth Amendment violation until recently, the second
trial in no way served to remedy the violation.

The purpose of remedying a Sixth Amendment violation by granting a new trial, as set forth in Black v. U.S.,
385 U.S. 26, 29 (1966) is to give the defendant an opportunity
to protect himself from the use of evidence gained from the
intrusion into the defense camp by excluding the evidence at
the second trial. Hiss, who did not learn about the government's conduct until long after the second trial had occurred,
had no chance to "protect himself" from the use of the
evidence which was wrongfully obtained. The second trial,
thus, did not serve to remedy the violation. For this
reason, the only appropriate relief at this point is the
granting of the writ of error coram nobis.

## POINT II.

### THE PROSECUTION'S FAILURE TO PRODUCE CHAMBERS' STATEMENTS DEPRIVED PETITIONER OF A FAIR TRAIL.

Thomas Murphy conceded in his opening statement to the jury the primacy of Whittaker Chambers' testimony to the prosecution's case:

> [I]f you don't believe Chambers, then we have no case....

Trial transcript, 1st Trial at p. 24.     Yet Hiss was deprived of the opportunity to test the credibility of this witness and his elaborate, chameleon-like testimony by the government's deliberate concealment of Chambers' pre-trial statements to FBI agents.  Had these statements, with their wealth of inconsistencies and exculpatory material, been made available to the defense, Hiss might well not be before this court today.

Chambers walked an exceedingly thin line in his testimony, trying to convince the jury that this time, finally, he was telling the truth. With Chambers' prior statements, deliberately suppressed by the prosecution, the defense would have been able to present to the jury the true Whittaker Chambers: a man whose story changed to fit the needs of the moment with no regard for the truth. This case presents government suppression of exculpatory evidence which, if it had been known to the defense at the time of trial, would have permitted them to decimate the prosecution's case and its star witness, Chambers.

The prosecution concealed the existence of three significant statements made by Chambers. 15/

The most extensive was a statement of 184 pages in length compiled from the stenographic notes of Chambers' statements made to FBI agents from January 3 through April 18, 1949. As the giving of the statement progressed day-to-day, Chambers was shown the typed transcript of previous days' statements. See CN Ex. 87. He read them carefully, and stenographers took his dictated corrections or clarifications, incorporated them into the drafts and, eventually, the final text of the statement. 16/

---

15/ The three were (a) the 184-page statement, dated May 11, 1949 (CN Ex. 21); (b) the five-page statement, dated March 28, 1946 (CN Ex. 22); and (c) the eight-page holographic statement relating to Chambers' homosexuality (CN Ex. 23).

16/ The government's assertion that the statement never was "adopted" or "approved" by Chambers--a statement which consisted of the corrected and edited stenographic transcript of his own words--displays, at best, total unfamiliarity with the FBI documents released pursuant to the FOIA request. See Govt. Memo at 57.

In sum, the 184-page statement was considered to be Chambers' definitive account of his activities and accusations.

The prosecution deliberately concealed the fact of the statement's existence from the trial court and the defense and refused to have Chambers sign the statement to facilitate such concealment.

The prosecutors were fearful that, if he did sign, "the Judge might allow defense attorneys to read the statement, which would probably result in some complications" (CN Ex. 20A). Therefore, in view of the prosecutors' "specific instructions... CHAMBERS, though entirely willing, was not asked to sign this statement." (CN Ex. 21). This course of action, expressly "contrary to the general [federal] Bureau [of Investigation] custom" (CN Ex. 20A), constituted a calculated fraud on the trial court and defense.

The second document, dated March 28, 1946 (CN Ex. 22), recorded Chambers' statements relating primarily to his alleged relationship with Hiss and the crucial issue of the date of his break with the Communist Party. The statement also records Chambers' response to FBI questioning that he had no documentary evidence to support his assertions regarding Hiss.

The third statement was a letter handwritten and
signed by Chambers, dated February 15, 1949, discussing his
homosexual activities from 1933 through 1938 and revealing his
own perception of his homosexuality.  The defense's motion to
present psychiatric evidence concerning Chambers' credibility
through an expert, Dr. Carl Binger, had been granted pre-trial.
United States v. Hiss, 88 F.Supp. 559 (S.D.N.Y. 1950).  This
signed statement of Chambers, the relevancy of which is described
below, was not even produced to the trial court.  The government now argues it was not produced because it was not requested.
Govt. Memo at 67.  As we discuss infra at pp. 40-42, it was
requested.

The prosecution's failure to disclose these statements
was in clear violation of the applicable law at the time
of trial, whether considered as a failure to produce a prior
statement for inspection, United States v. Krulewich, 145 F.2d
76 (2d Cir. 1942), or as a violation of the prosecution's due
process obligation to provide a defendant a fair trial by
revealing exculpatory evidence, Brady v. Maryland, 373 U.S. 83
(1963).  Furthermore, the prosecution's concealment was calculated and deliberate.  It surely was aware of its obligations,
since other documents produced by government agencies, which
were identical in form, were released by the trial judge to the

defense. The only difference between those released documents and these three statements is that the prosecution and FBI were able to hide the fact of the three statements' existence from the trial court and defense.

The government's assertion that only "signed statements" were produceable at the time of Hiss' trial is without support in law and was rejected by the trial court itself. Relying on United States v. Krulewich, supra, respondent argues that because in that case a signed statement was the pertinent written communication, only signed written statements were required to be produced. The court, however, did not limit the holding to signed statements.

The issue analyzed in Krulewich was not the form of the statement, such as whether it was sworn or signed, but whether it continued to maintain a privileged status as a communication to a prosecutor or investigating officer. Krulewich, supra, at 78-79. By virtue of the institution of criminal charges, the communication lost its confidentiality, id. at 79, and became presumptively competent, calling into play the normal rules of evidence regarding the use of prior inconsistent statements to impeach a witness.

The court makes no mention whatsoever in Krulewich

or any of the later cases cited by respondent of a necessity

that the "communications" be signed in order that production

of those written statement be required.  In <u>United States</u> v.

<u>Cohen</u>, 145 F.2d 82 (2d Cir. 1945), <u>cert</u>. <u>denied</u>, 323 U.S.

799 (1944), the court made no reference to "signed" statements,

and again used broad language which would have required the

production of the Chambers' statements.  Referring to <u>Krulewich</u>,

<u>supra</u>, the court stated:

> We held that when statements are taken by
> the prosecution which appear upon inspec-
> tion by the judge to contradict the
> testimony of the witness when he is called
> at the trial, the accused should be al-
> lowed to inspect them, since he cannot
> otherwise approach the witness.
> 17/

<u>United States</u> v. <u>Cohen</u>, <u>supra</u>, at 92.  In <u>United States</u> v.

<u>Simonds</u>, 148 F.2d 177, 179 (2d Cir. 1945), the written statement

in question was "a statement in question-and-answer form", no-
18/
where described as signed.

---

17/  Indeed, it appears that documents which might not have contained a witness' "statement" had been produced in <u>Cohen</u>.  <u>Id</u>. at
92 ("certain supposed statements" were inspected).

18/  The other cases cited by respondent do not support its contention either.  In <u>United States</u> v. <u>Ebeling</u>, 146 F.2d 254 (2d
Cir. 1944), the court held that the issue of the production of

(Fn. Cont'd)

Although petitioner does not seek retroactive application of the Jencks Act, 18 U.S.C. §3500, or <u>Jencks</u> v. <u>United States</u>, 353 U.S. 657 (1957), <sup>19/</sup> the Act's definition of "statement" is instructive. The Act defines statement "as any

---

<u>18</u>/  (Fn. Cont'd)

written statements had not been preserved procedurally for appellate review.  In <u>United States</u> v. <u>Cohen</u>, 148 F.2d 94 (2d Cir.), <u>cert</u>. <u>denied</u>, 325 U.S. 852 (1945), the majority relied on <u>Ebeling</u> and did not reach the issue.  However, Judge Frank, one of the judges on the <u>Cohen</u> panel, did reach the issue and found no prejudicial error based on a review of the reports, implicitly agreeing that the reports should have been produced. The written statement there consisted of an FBI agent's written notes relating to the defendant's statements to him.

<u>19</u>/ The government attempts to obscure its denial of due process by refuting an argument never made by the petitioner--that retroactive application of the Jencks Act or <u>Jencks</u> v. <u>United States</u> mandated disclosure of the Chambers' statements.  Govt. Memo. at 54.    Petitioner's claim, however, is that the prosecution deprived him of due process by failing to disclose exculpatory materials.  <u>See</u>, <u>Wiman</u> v. <u>Powell</u>, 293 F.2d 605, 607, n.2 (5th Cir. 1961) (distinguishing Jencks Act claim from allegation of unconstitutional suppression of witness statements).

written statement by a witness signed or otherwise adopted or
approved by him" or a "substantially verbatim recital. . .
recorded contemporaneously. . ." 18 U.S.C. §3500(e)(1)-(2)
(1957), manifesting Congress' concept of the policy it wished
to protect.  There is no doubt that the three statements meet
this definition and hence should have been divulged to the
defense at the time of trial.

The trial court, when faced with the "statement" issue,
adopted the defense's position and ordered the government to
produce recorded statements, signed or unsigned.  The defense
subpoenaed the notes of a conversation between Chambers and
Raymond Murphy, a State Department security officer, R. 307,
and, over the prosecutor's most vigorous objections, R. 307-
08, 370, 372, the trial court released the document, even though
not signed by Chambers, R. 371-72.  Similarly, the defense
requested notes of conversations between Chambers and Adolf
Berle, an Assistant Secretary of State.  Again the court
acceded to defense request, again over government protest. R. 415-16.

Chambers' statements dated May 14, 1942 and June 26,
1945 also were required to be produced to the court.  The prosecution argued that these two FBI report were not "statements
of the witness" and hence did not have been disclosed to defense

counsel, R. 360. The trial court disagreed and read portions
of the reports to the jury. The court also pointed out the
absence of references to Hiss' giving Chambers papers from
which a negative inference in favor of Hiss could be drawn,
R. 560-1. Hence, the prosecution was put on notice, if it
already was not aware, that not only recorded inconsistencies
pertinent to the examination of the witness, but also omissions
were probative and would require the release of documents.
See, Gordon v. United States, 344 U.S. 414, 421 (1953) (error
not to produce four prior statements not implicating defendant).

The government misrepresents the record when it
argues that Hiss' attorneys failed to request statements such
as these three. Govt Memo at 58-60. Prior to trial, the defense moved, inter alia, for the production of "[a]ll written
statements and affidavits, whether signed or not, made at any
time by Whittaker Chambers...." CN Ex. 20. That portion of
its motion was denied with leave to renew and the requests were
reserved at the first trial. See Petition ¶¶24-30.

At the second trial, the defense specifically asked
for "any statements of the FBI about their talks with Mr.
Chambers", R. 359. The prosecution responded by claiming that

"no statements were made by this witness", but admitted
possession of the two FBI reports of statements that had been
produced at the first trial, R. 360. The defense reasserted
its right to statements in the FBI reports, and the prosecution withdrew its objection. R. 361.

A short while later, the trial court, prosecution
and defense discussed the timing for reviewing the Murphy
statement. It was agreed that during the lunch break, the
prosecution would review the Murphy statement to redact one
particular paragraph which related to a man the State Department had asked remain confidential. R. 367. The defense
then asked that all FBI reports up to August 3, 1948, be produced after lunch as well. R. 368. The August 3, 1948, date
was not a limitation on the request as the government asserts,
but merely reflected the schedule for production of certain
of the requested documents. As the defense attorney put it,
"I just thought that I was helping out by suggesting that at
2:15 he may have these others". R. 368. The defense request
for "any statements" remained in full force.

The prosecution's response was an outright misstate-
ment designed to prevent the disclosure of these three state-

ments' existence.  The prosecutor, who already possessed the

Chambers' statements, claimed it was "[j]ust physically im-

possible" to check FBI indices and retrieve them.  R. 368.

The trial court advised the defense to give the prosecution

more time; but having misled  the court and defense, the

prosecution never produced the statement.  However, even if

the Chambers' statements were and are not considered "state-

ments" subject to the doctrine of Krulewich, supra, or had

not been requested, the prosecution nevertheless had an obli-

gation to reveal their existence under the prevailing law at

the time.  As the Second Circuit held in United States v.

Andolschek, 142 F.2d 503 (2d Cir. 1944):

> While we must accept as lawful [in civil
> cases] for deportment of the government
> to suppress documents, even when they will
> help determine controversies between
> third persons, we cannot agree that this
> should include their suppression in a
> criminal prosecution, bounded upon those
> very dealings to which the documents re-
> late, and whose criminality they will, or
> may, tend to exculpate.  So far as they
> directly touch the criminal dealings, the
> prosecution necessarily ends any confiden-
> tial character the documents may possess;
> it must be conducted in the open, and will
> lay bare their subject matter.

Id., at 506.  Indeed, even documents which relate but indirectly still must be produced by the prosecution:

> Nor does it seem to us possible to draw any
> line between documents whose contents bear
> directly upon the criminal transactions,
> and those which may be only indirectly rele-
> vant. Not only would such a distinction be
> extremely difficult to apply in practice,
> but the same reasons which forbid suppression
> in one case forbid it in the other, although
> not, perhaps, quite so imperatively.

Ibid. United States v. Coplon, 185 F.2d 629, 638-9 (2d Cir.

1950), cert. denied, 342 U.S. 920 (1952); see also, United

States v. Grayson, 166 F.2d 863, 870 (2d Cir. 1948); United

States v. Beekman, 155 F.2d 580, 584 (2d Cir. 1946); and

United States v. Krulewich, supra, at 79; in general,

United States v. Schneiderman, 106 F.Supp. 731 (S.D. Cal. 1952),

and cases cited therein.

The government's arguments that its obligation in

1950 to disclose favorable evidence, including that which im-

peached the credibility of a witness, was somehow less exact-

ing than it is today, and that Brady v. Maryland, 373 U.S. 83

(1963) is not retroactive, have no merit.

Long before the Supreme Court decision in Brady v.

Maryland 373 U.S. 83 (1963), courts had unequivocally acknowl-

edged that the prosecution is under an obligation to refrain

from suppressing evidence favorable to the accused as a
matter of due process.  As stated in United States v. Five
Persons, 472 F.Supp. 64, 66 (D.N.J. 1979):

> The principal of Brady was not new.  It was
> grounded on Mooney v. Holohan, 294 U.S.
> 103, 55 S.Ct. 340, 79 L.Ed. 791 (1935),
> Pyle v. Kansas, 317 U.S. 213, 63 S.Ct. 177,
> 87 L.Ed. 214 (1942) and two decisions in
> this circuit--United States ex rel. Almeida
> v. Baldi, 195 F.2d 815 (CA-3, 1952), and
> United States ex rel. Thompson v. Dye, 221
> F.2d 763 (CA-3, 1955)--both of which the
> Brady court agreed stated the constitutional
> rule.

Accord, Williams v. Dutton, 400 F.2d 797, 800 n.6 (5th Cir. 1968).

Numerous cases decided prior to Brady (including many
cases decided prior to Hiss) recognized the principle that an
allegation of prosecutorial suppression of favorable evidence
stated a due process claim even in situations where relief was
denied on factual grounds.  See, e.g., United States v. Andolschek, supra; Burns v. Lovett, 202 F.2d 335 (D.C. Cir. 1952),
aff'd sub nom. Burns v. Wilson, 346 U.S. 137 (1953); Woollomes
v. Heinze, 198 F.2d 577 (9th Cir. 1952), cert. denied, 344 U.S.
929 (1953); White Thunder v. Hunter, 149 F.2d 578 (10th Cir.
1945), cert. denied, 325 U.S. 889 (1945); Curtis v. Rives, 123
F.2d 936 (D.C. Cir. 1941); Jordon v. Bondy, 114 F.2d 599
(D.C. Cir. 1940); Soulia v. O'Brien, 94 F.Supp. 764 (D. Mass.

1950), <u>aff'd</u>, 188 F.2d 233 (lst Cir. 1951), <u>cert</u>. <u>denied</u>, 341 U.S. 928 (1951); <u>Pyle</u> v. <u>Amrine</u>, 159 Kan. 458, 156 P.2d 509 (1945), <u>cert</u>. <u>denied</u>, 326 U.S. 749 (1945).

The government's assertion that no court has ever held <u>Brady</u> to be retroactive, Govt. Memo at p. 55 , is misleading. Courts have, without exception, assumed <u>Brady's</u> retroactivity and have applied it without discussion to convictions which were final long before its date of decision. <u>See</u>, <u>e.g.</u>, <u>Link</u> v. <u>United States</u>, 352 F.2d 207 (8th Cir. 1965), <u>cert</u>. <u>denied</u>, 383 U.S. 915 (1966); <u>Thomas</u> v. <u>United States</u>, 343 F.2d 49, 53 & n.4 (9th Cir. 1965); <u>Barbee</u> v. <u>Warden</u>, <u>Maryland Penitentiary</u>, 331 F.2d 842, 844 n.3 (4th Cir. 1964); <u>United States ex rel. Meers</u> v. <u>Wilkins</u>, 326 F.2d 135 (2d Cir. 1964); <u>United States ex rel. Butler</u> v. <u>Maroney</u>, 319 F.2d 622 (3d Cir. 1963).

In fact, <u>Shuler</u> v. <u>Wainwright</u>, 491 F.2d 1213 (5th Cir. 1974) cited by the government in support of its position, stands for the opposite proposition. Although the <u>Shuler</u> court denied <u>habeas</u> relief because the evidence in question was not material to a determination of petitioner's guilt or innocence, <u>id</u>. at 1224, the court did in fact apply <u>Brady</u> retroactively,

and stated that "[s]ince the principle explicated in <u>Brady</u>
goes to the integrity to [sic] the fact finding process and
was foreshadowed by the decision in <u>Mooney</u> v. <u>Holohan</u>, 294
U.S. 103 (1935), we feel that if the statement was "favorable"
or "useful" or "exculpatory", to use the words variously appearing in the numerous decisions in this field since 1962,
then the prosecutor was bound by the principle even though he
could not be charged with anticipation of the case." <u>Id</u>. at
1220 n.22.

Such unquestioning application of the <u>Brady</u> doctrine
to prior convictions is completely understandable. The retroactivity of the constitutional interpretation it expressed is
beyond controversy under established Supreme Court precedent.

The suppressed documents were material and,
since their use at trial might have affected the verdict
(and in fact raise a reasonable doubt) the conviction must
be vacated. In <u>United States</u> v. <u>Agurs</u>, 427 U.S. 97 (1976),
the Court described three situations involving the discovery,
after trial, of information which was known to the prosecution
but was unknown to the defense. The first category includes
those instances in which the prosecution's case included
perjured testimony, of which the prosecution is charged with

knowledge. Id. at 103-04. The second situation is "characterized by a pre-trial request for specific evidence" with which the prosecution did not comply. Id. at 104. In both of these types of cases, the standard to be employed by the court in determining whether the conviction should stand is whether "the suppressed evidence might have affected the outcome of the trial." Id. at 104 (emphasis supplied).[20]

This case falls within the first two categories, because the prosecution deliberately concealed the statements which specifically had been requested by the defense both pre-trial and in the course of the trial.[21] Thus, this Court must examine

---

[20] The third category involves cases in which there is no request or only a general request for all "Brady material." In such situations, the proper standard of materiality is that the "omitted evidence creates a reasonable doubt that did not otherwise exist." United States v. Agurs, supra at 112.

[21] When there had been deliberate calculated suppression, "prophylactic considerations designed to deter future prosecutorial misconduct. . ." are properly before the court. U.S. v. Morell, 524 F.2d 550 (2d Cir. 1975); U.S. v. Pfingst, 490 F.2d 262, 277 (2d Cir. 1973), cert. den., 417 U.S. 919 (1974); see U.S. v. Keogh, 391 F.2d 138, 146-47 (2d Cir. 1968). Although Agurs suggests that when there has been no or only a general request for exculpatory material, the willfullness of the prosecutor is not relevant, in this case, we are dealing with first and second category situations which were not directly addressed by the Agurs court. Given the high standard imposed in these situations, some consideration of the prosecutor's willfullness--which is demonstrative of at least the materiality as perceived by the prosecutor--is appropriate.

the use to which the statements could have been put by the defense and determine whether the outcome might have been affected.

In making this determination, we must remember the centrality of Chambers to the prosecution case. See <u>United States v. Hiss</u>, <u>supra</u>, 88 F.Supp. at 559, where the court concluded "[i]t is apparent that the outcome of this trial is dependent to a great extent upon the testimony of one man - Whittaker Chambers. Mr. Chambers' credibility is one of the major issues upon which the jury must pass." If he was not believed, there was no case. As in <u>Giglio</u> v. <u>United States</u>, 405 U.S. 150, 154-55 (1972),

> The Government case depended almost entirely on [the witness'] testimony; without it there could have been no indictment and no evidence to carry the case to the jury. [His] credibility as a witness was therefore an important issue in the case. . .

Under such circumstances, suppressed evidence which goes toward the credibility[22/] of this witness must be evaluated carefully and with due consideration to its possible impact upon the jury. See <u>Du Bose</u> v. <u>Lefevre</u>, ___ F.2d ___, Slip Op. 2569 (2d Cir.

---

22/ Of course, evidence which is primarily useful on the issue of credibility is material, for often it is the discrediting of a prosecution witness which will mean the difference between conviction and acquittal. <u>Napue</u> v. <u>Illinois</u>, 360 U.S. 264, 269 (1959).

April 23, 1980).

CN Ex. 21 alone contained a wealth of contradictory and potentially exculpatory information which could have been used to search for inconsistencies in Chambers' testimony and hence to attack the prosecution's case.

The prosecution relied heavily in its closing on Chambers' testimony regarding the $400 loan, and in its present memorandum, refers to the loan as "literally overwhelming proof of Hiss' guilt." Govt. Memo. at 66. The inconsistency between Chambers' statement in CN Ex. 21, and his trial testimony, therefore goes not only to his credibility but to the substance of the government's proof on Count 2 of the indictment.

In his trial testimony, Chambers emphasized the precise amount of the loan, stating that it was $400, not $401 or $399, but $400, R. 626. But in CN Ex. 21, Chambers said the amount was $500, CN. Ex. 21, at p. 126, and gave the incredible story that the Hisses:

> . . .picked me up in their car somewhere in the northeast section of Washington and drove me to Baltimore. At that time they gave me the money.

Id.

Chambers also admitted in his statement that his "original recollection" was hazy and had to be told the date of the car purchase by the FBI. Id. at p. 127.

Had these comments been known to the defense, an effective cross-examination could have cast considerable doubt on his

story. The fact that his recollection was hazy and he had to be
told by the FBI agents interviewing him pertinent facts could
have suggested to the jury that he had been told the amount of the
asserted loan as well. Of course, his trial testimony was contradicted by his statement that the loan was $500, and his preci-
sion as to the amount of the loan would have been called into
question very effectively. It must be said that these matters
may have affected the jury's verdict.

The government suggests that this inconsistency was
unimportant because of an asserted "proof of borrowing [which]
was literally overwhelming." Govt. Memo. at 66. As set forth more
fully in the appendix, the proof was far from overwhelming, especially
in light of this and other documents discovered as a result of
Hiss' FOIA request. With CN Ex. 21, the asserted connection
between the purchase of the car and the withdrawal, relied upon
by the prosecution would have been placed in a much different
light.

Given the length and breadth of the CN Ex. 21 statement,
the number of inconsistencies and other material available for
cross-examination which, if properly released as exculpatory, could
have been used for development of evidence which would have
exculpated Hiss, is not surprising. Petitioner will mention but
a few more examples.

At the second trial, the relationship between Chambers and Wadleigh was a crucial issue. Wadleigh had admitted passing documents to Chambers and, as an employee in the Trade Agreements Division of the State Department, was in a position with potential access to the Baltimore documents. Chambers was asked on cross-examination about Wadleigh:

> Q. Did you mention him to the FBI?
> A. I did not, I believe.
> Q. You never mentioned Julian Wadleigh?
> A. I think not.

R. 402.

Wadleigh in fact was mentioned on thirteen of the 184 pages. See e.g., CN Ex. 21 at pp. 78, 87, 88, 93, 94, 95, 102, 103, 104, 105, 118, 129, 149.

Later in his cross-examination, Cross questioned Chambers about Wadleigh's membership in the Communist Party, R. 407-8:

> Q. You say that you don't remember whether you told Mr. Ray Murphy or Mr. Raymond Murphy about Wadleigh?
> A. That is right.
> Q. Even that he was a Communist?
> A. That is right.
> Q. And you know that you never told that to the FBI, or don't you?
> A. I don't believe I did.
> Q. You knew at the time that he was a Communist.
> A. I believed that he was. As a matter of fact, he wasn't.

In CN Ex. 21, however, not only did Chambers discuss Wadleigh -- a fact Chambers denied on the stand -- but in connection with Wadleigh's membership, the FBI discussed Wadleigh's own statements with Chambers:

> I have been told that WADLEIGH denied ever
> being a member of the Communist Party.  In
> this regard I cannot help but feel that he is
> mistaken.  My reason for so stating is that the
> question of Communist Party membership was one
> which was always asked and considered in recruiting
> individuals for underground work.  I might state that
> Party membership was the key to the reliability
> of the person and the key to the security.  Thus,
> if WADLEIGH had not been a Communist Party member,
> this situation would definitely cause me to have
> a feeling of reservation in my dealings with him
> as it was in the case of HARRY DEXTER WHITE.
> However, I never to my recollection had any such
> feeling of reservation regarding WADLEIGH.

CN Ex. 21 at p. 103.

Significantly, this particular paragraph in the statement was underlined and circled on the copy taken from government files provided petitioner.  It appears that this significant contradiction between Wadleigh -- who denied membership -- and Chambers was probably one of the reasons the prosecutors decided it was imperative to conceal the existence of this statement from the defense in the court.

At points in CN Ex. 21, the names of witnesses who gave statements contradicting Chambers were also incorporated.  Chambers was told what other persons had to say about certain matters, and then would either confirm or deny their statement.  One such person was Ludwig Lore, a journalist who had interviewed Chambers in 1941.  At that time, Lore reported that Chambers had told him, _inter alia_, that Chambers was obtaining government documents from two women, who were private secretaries to Assistant Secretaries of State and who made extra carbon copies of papers they typed in connection with their work to give to Chambers. CN Ex. 88. Chambers responded to Lore's charge in the statement, CN Ex. 21, at p. 144.

Had the statement been released, the defense would have learned of Chambers' prior inconsistent statement to Lore, and could have used that as a foundation for cross-examination. As we have described before, Chambers' denial of alternative sources for the Baltimore documents was a crucial issue at trial.

This also happened with reference to William Crane. Crane, who Chambers also called "Keith" and "Pete", was described in the first trial by Chambers as a photographer who copied documents at a Baltimore apartment, Transcript of first trial, p. 188; he also mentioned Crane at the second trial, R. 276. However, in the statement, he said:

> I have been told that WILLIAM EDWARD CRANE, who I knew as PETE and KEITH, has stated that he did photographic work for me in an apartment in Baltimore.
>
> . . . I would like to state that I have absolutely no independent recollection of CRANE having been in this apartment or having done photographic work there.

(CN, Ex. 21 at p. 102.) Other discrepancies between the two were revealed in his statement. See, e.g., CN Ex. 21 at pp. 68-70. Again, if the statement had been disclosed, the defense would have learned of this witness. 23/

23/ Indeed, Crane was at first looked upon as a major witness at the trial, CN Ex. 90, but apparently because of the extensive contradiction between him and Chambers, Crane was not called.

These witnesses disclosed by the statement demonstrated the ease with which Chambers changed his testimony to conform to his questioner's description of events. Given Chambers' credibility as the major issue for the jury and the factor which would make or break the government's case, these additional elements that could have been used in cross-examination would well have made the difference between conviction and acquittal.

So too, the March 26, 1946 statement, CN Ex. 22, is dismissed by the government as a merely cumulative recitation of Chambers' perjured statements to the FBI and others. Govt. Memo. at 65. In reality, this statement is much more dramatic, for it reveals that under intensive questioning by experienced FBI officers, Chambers had no recollection and no evidence, documentary or otherwise, of Communist Party membership of or espionage activity by Hiss. Unlike prior reports of interviews, this one reveals that Chambers was "grilled." He was asked repeatedly for his knowledge regarding Hiss, and repeatedly stated he had nothing. Indeed, Chambers actually qualified his previous statement of June, 1945 and stated that the implication in that statement that Hiss was a Communist Party member lacked proof:

> After preliminary discussion relative to information previously supplied by CHAMBERS concerning HISS, he related that his actual knowledge of HISS' activities concerned the period shortly preceding 1937 and he was unable to elaborate on any information concerning HISS' connection with the Communist Party. . . .He stated that <u>as a matter of fact he has absolutely no information</u> that would conclusively prove that

> HISS held a membership card. . . .or that he was
> an actual dues paying member of the Communist
> party even while [Chambers] was active [in the CP]
> prior to 1937.

CN Ex. 22 at 3 (emphasis supplied).

A second time he said he had no proof to support his

"belief":

> He indicated that he did not have any documentary
> or other proof to substantiate this belief and
> based it solely upon comments made by various
> Washington and New York newspaper writers.

CN Ex. 22 at 4.

Just to be sure, the FBI agents interviewing him <u>again</u>

asked Chambers to relate his "independent recollection" or

provide "documentary evidence," but he could not:

> . . . .CHAMBERS was again asked if in any
> of his past activities he had documentary evi-
> dence or any independent recollection that HISS
> was a dues paying member of the Communist Party.
> He again stated that he had no such information
> and that if he did have this information he would
> be more than glad to supply it to this Bureau.

CN Ex. 22 at 4.

Chambers' statement thus is not merely one of negative

inference, but an affirmative statement that he lacked evidence.

In this way, it is quantitatively and qualitatively different from

the other statements that were produced at the trial.  In this

suppressed statement, Chambers confesses that his entire tes-

timony is unsupported by even a scrap of actual evidence.  The impact of this confession on the jury surely would have been substantial.[24/]

It is probable that the Chambers' holographic statement, CN Ex. 23, would have been found highly relevant by the trial court and would have affected the trial's outcome. The court admitted evidence on similar matters regarding Chambers' mental state, a substantial issue at trial,[25/] over the prosecution's objection. For instance, the defense was permitted to question Chambers on his brother's suicide, R. 422-23, certainly a step more removed from Chambers' mental state than his own homosexuality. The prosecution objected, but the court permitted the questioning because of its connection to the psychiatric testimony to be presented later in the trial. R. 422. However, because the prosecution concealed this statement which was specifically requested by the defense, the trial court - closest to the case and most able to consider whether it should be admitted in evidence - was foreclosed from ever making the decision which was its to make.

---

24/        The report also demonstrates that Chambers "was receptive, cordial and cooperative" and that "if the Bureau decided to conduct an investigation of HISS' Communist activities that CHAMBERS will agree to anything within reason." CN Ex. 22 at 5. That evaluation could have been used to devastate Chambers' credibility just by itself.
        Also as discussed in Point III, infra, CN Ex. 22 contradicts Chambers' trial testimony regarding the date on which he left the Communist Party, a critical issue in the case.

25/        Prior to the start of trial, the trial court granted the defense's motion to permit the admission of psychiatric testimony regarding the credibility of Chambers. United States v. Hiss, 88 F.Supp. 559 (1950). See also, United States v. Partin, 493 F.2d 750 (5th Cir. 1974).

The holographic statement itself was relevant not because it contained admissions of Chambers' homosexuality <u>per se</u>, but because it revealed the effect of it upon his psyche. The statement powerfully illustrates the self-torture which Chambers' perception of his homosexuality caused him, and the impact this had on his relationships with individuals, including Hiss, which of course would have been pertinent to the psychiatric evaluation presented by Dr. Binger.[26]

Although in some cases the courts have ruled that based on the facts of the particular case, the admission of testimony regarding homosexuality is inappropriate, <u>see</u> Govt. Memo. at 69, but <u>see</u>, <u>Salgado v. United States</u>, 278 F.2d 830 (1st Cir. 1960), in the specific context of this case the statement would have been admissible. Given the enormous importance of Chamber's

---

[26] The statement also reveals a man obsessed at the time of trial with his crusade against Communism:

> I have said before that I am consciously destroying myself. This is not from love of self-destruction but because only if we are consciously prepared to destroy ourselves in the struggle can the thing we are fighting be destroyed.

CN Ex. 23. Chambers' own description of his role in the struggle and the admission that he would destroy himself to further the battle is a telling indicator of his bias and motivation, and surely would have had a signfiant impact upon the determination of his credibility. Although Binger had access to some of Chambers' descriptions of his "self-destruction," this one was significantly more potent and revealing.

credibility in this case, the degree to which his mental state was in issue, and the significance of the statement not on the issue of homosexuality per se, but the self-torture and admitted mental instability which his sexual feelings caused him, it was a clearly relevant piece of evidence. There is no question that Hiss had a right to challenge Chambers'

> . . .credibility with competent or relevant
> evidence or any mental defect or treatment
> at a time probatively related to the time
> period about which he was attempting to justify.

United States v. Partin, supra at 763.

Contemporary psychiatrists no longer regard homosexuality as a "mental defect," but the effect it had on Chambers' evaluation of himself cannot be denied and was relevant to the Hiss inquiry as to his credibility. Since the statement was relevant as to both his perception of his relationships in 1938, as well as his perception of his obligations in the "struggle" at the time of trial, the prosecution's deliberate suppression[27] deprived Hiss of his fundamental right to a fair trial.

---

27/ The government's assertion that the defense was "well aware of Chambers' homosexuality" is untrue. Govt. Memo. at 69. Ironically, in making this assertion, the government relies upon a defense memorandum found in the prosecution's files, CN Ex. 13. No reliable evidence of homosexuality was found — only rumors were heard — and hence the defense had nothing upon which to question Chambers at trial regarding that issue.

POINT III.

THE SUPPRESSION OF STATEMENTS AND
EVIDENCE REGARDING THE DATE OF
CHAMBERS' BREAK WITH THE COMMUNIST
PARTY DENIED HISS HIS FUNDAMENTAL
RIGHTS.

A crucial issue at the trial was the date of
Chambers' break with the Communist Party.  If Chambers had
left the Party before 1938, it was very unlikely, if not
impossible, that the Baltimore documents would have been
passed to him by Hiss.  In CN Ex. 22, Chambers said six
times that he left the Party in 1937.  This statement was
critical, for as described before, Chambers was questioned
intensively by the FBI when he gave the statement and took
care to clarify previous statements at the time.  Thus, when
he said he left the Party in 1937, CN Ex. 22, there was
every reason for the jury to give credence to that August,
1946 statement, rather than his contradictory trial testimony.

The date he left the Party was also tied in to the
date on which he received a translating assignment.  Chambers
testified that he had obtained a translation to perform from
Paul Willert, then of Oxford University Press.  This translation was received one month after he left the Party.  R.264-5.

In 1952, the defense discovered that Chambers received his translation from Willert prior to March, 1938, and that negotiations had been going on between the two for several months prior to that. Willert, in fact, affirmed that he had met Chambers "at the end of 1937 or at the very beginning of 1938." This new evidence was presented to the court in the motion for a new trial made in that year. Petition at ¶55. Hence, Chambers' testimony at trial regarding his break with the Party was severely undermined, but not enough, in the opinion of the court, to require a new trial.

The FOIA documents recently released to Hiss add a material element to this aspect of Chambers' story. They reveal that the FBI re-interviewed Chambers in February, 1952 in an attempt to reconcile the discrepancies between Chambers' testimony and the documentary evidence from Willert. Once again Chambers changed his testimony to fit the new facts:

> From documentary evidence presented by the defense in connection with its motion for a new trial, CHAMBERS now believes he must have been mistaken in this regard.

CN Ex. 30, p. 4. This latest change, however, was never made known to petitioner or the court.

At the argument on the motion for a new trial, the prosecution argued that Chambers' statement was "offhand", an argument which the court accepted. Petition at ¶6. The court was never informed that Chambers had admitted that his testimony at trial was false.  Furthermore, as both CN Ex. 21

and 22 reveal, Chambers' fixing of the sequence of dates just

before, at, and after his leaving of the Communist Party was

anything but offhand.  For instance, in CN Ex. 21, Chambers

said:

> After my break I moved with my
> family from 2116 Mt. Royal Ter-
> race to a house on Old Court
> Rd. on the outskirts of Balti-
> more where we lived in one room
> for about one month.
>
> Dr. Meyer Schapiro, whom I have
> previously mentioned in this
> statement, recommended me to one
> Paul Willert, an Englishman who
> was an officer in the Oxford
> University Press.  Willert was
> described by Schapiro as an ab-
> solutely reliable non-Communist.
> Willert got me a translation job
> through the firm of Longmans
> Green, which was an affiliate
> company of the Oxford Press.
> Willert also gave me an advance
> for this translation.

CN Ex. 21, p. 131.

Murphy also recorded Chambers' chronology similarly:

> Immediately after his defection
> in April of 1938 he went to New
> York and saw Dr. Meyer Shapiro
> [sic], informed him that he had
> broken away from the Party and
> was desirous of obtaining some
> translation work.

CN Ex. 33, p. 1.

The government argues that because Chambers had said on other occasions known to the defense that he had left the Party in 1937, these additional instances were merely "cumulative" and do not constitute a basis for relief. Because CN Ex. 21 and 22 both were very carefully prepared after intensive questioning, and CN Ex. 21 in particular was carefully reviewed and corrected by Chambers, these instances of contradictory statements take on a different character than his other statements. For instance, at trial, Chambers claimed that when he appeared before HUAC, he had not prepared his testimony carefully and was unaware of what exactly he would be asked. R. 597. The jury, upon learning of the circumstances under which Chambers had made the statements which the prosecution suppressed, might well have concluded instead that Chambers was telling the truth then, not when he testified at trial.

In particular, the government does not comprehend petitioner's argument with respect to their allegations regarding the motion for a new trial. In arguing against the motion, the prosecution had an obligation to bring before the court all the facts relevant to the issue that might lead to the conclusion that Chambers was lying on this critical

issue. The prosecution could not allow the court to consider what it knew to be false testimony or false facts
regarding the circumstances of Chambers' testimony. United
States v. Agurs, supra, 427 U.S. at 103-4.

Had these facts been before the trial court and
the jury, the outcome of the trial might have been acquittal even though the defense had other impeaching material available. See, e.g., United States v. Seijo, 514
F.2d 1357, 1364 (2d Cir. 1974), cert. denied, 429 U.S.
1043 (1977); United States v. Pacelli, 491 F.2d 1108,
1118-20 (2d Cir.), cert. denied, 419 U.S. 826 (1974);
United States v. Miller, 411 F.2d 825 (2d Cir. 1969).

POINT IV

THE PROSECUTION, BY SUPPRESSING RELEVANT
AND MATERIAL INFORMATION ABOUT THE
TYPEWRITER, WHICH IT ADOPTED, AND BY
PRESENTING A TRUNCATED AND DISTORTED
VERSION OF ITS EXPERT'S OPINION, DEPRIVED
PETITIONER OF A FAIR TRIAL.

Once Chambers unearthed the typewritten Baltimore
documents and claimed that they had been given to him by Hiss,
the defense began a search for the typewriter which had originally
belonged to the Fansler-Martin insurance partnership, had been
given to Priscilla Hiss by her father, Thomas Fansler, and was
present in the Hiss household at some time during the 1930's.
Petition ¶¶ 64, 67. The defense, knowing that the typewriter
had been disposed of by the Hisses prior to 1938, Petition ¶70,
and thus could not have used by the Hisses to type the Baltimore
documents, sought the typewriter in order to prove Hiss' innocence.
Finding what it believed to be that typewriter, the defense
innocently introduced it at trial, tracing it back through a
chain of custody to the sons of a former maid of the Hiss family,
to whom the typewriter was given in 1937. Petition, ¶¶ 70-71.
This Woodstock typewriter, which became Exhibit UUU, had the
serial number 230,099. Petition, ¶¶ 71, 77.

The FOIA documents now show that while the defense was

looking for the old typewriter which the Hisses had discarded, the FBI, too, set underway a major effort to locate the typewriter. Having access to sources of information[28] and resources[29] beyond the wildest dreams of the defense, the FBI began to compile a pro- file of the typewriter which the Hisses had received from Thomas Fansler. From authoritative sources, which were checked and rechecked, the FBI concluded that the Fansler-Hiss typewriter was a Woodstock, manufactured in 1927, with a serial number be- tween 145,000 and 204,500. Petition ¶¶ 85-94.

The FBI learned before trial that the defense had located Woodstock typewriter #230,099. While the significance

_____

28/ The government, for example, received information from North- western Life Insurance Company and the Woodstock Typewriter Company, both of whom refused to provide information to the defense. CN Exs. 35, 36. The defense could not locate Thomas Grady, the typewriter salesman, CN Ex. 34-A, but the government interviewed and reinterviewed him, CN Exs. 41, 42.

29/ See supra at 6.

of this serial number was lost on the defense, [30] the FBI knew

that it was impossible that this could be the correct machine,

as its serial number was much too high.   Petition, ¶¶ 96-98.

---

[30]   The government now alleges that the defense was aware at
trial of the highly questionable value of Exhibit UUU.   Govt.
Memo. at 34.   This is not the case.   Nothing in the defense files
suggests that defense counsel suspected that Woodstock 230,099
was not the Hiss machine prior to the motion for a new trial.
Although fleeting references to the dates of manufacture of
Woodstock typewriters appear in defense files, there is no indication that this information had any significance to the defense
lawyers at the trial.   The defense based its case on a showing
that the Hisses had given their Woodstock typewriter away prior
to the dates on which the Baltimore documents were typed. R3162-64.
It brought Ex. UUU into court as the Hiss Woodstock because this
typewriter appeared to be traceable all the way back through many
hands to the family of a maid to whose sons the Hisses had given
their Woodstock in 1937, R. 195.   The defense was so assured of
the seeming success of its search for the Hisses' typewriter,
that it ignored any indications which, if pursued, might have led
it before the end of the trial to an examination of the authenticity of 230,099.   The government's adoption of this exhibit
of course confirmed the defense's mistaken belief.   Doubts about
the authenticity of the typewriter did not surface in the defense
until Chester Lane was engaged after the conviction to prepare
a motion for a new trial.

The government's search for the typewriter, on the other
hand, which was undertaken by circularizing typewriter repair
shops and dealerships for the old machine, focused from the beginning on ascertaining what the serial number of the Hiss Woodstock would have to have been.   CN Exs. 38A, 45, 53.   Having
determined the range within which the Hiss typewriter would
necessarily fall, the government was immediately on notice that
230,099 was the wrong machine when it was discovered by the
defense.   CN Ex. 57.   The government also had access to critical
information about the typewriter which the defense did not have,
and which alerted it further to the serial number's significance.
See n. 28 at 65, supra.

The FBI redoubled its investigatory efforts,[31] but it was

never able to satisfactorily resolve this central discrepancy.

Petition ¶¶ 99-105.[32]

The government badly needed corroboration of Chambers'

testimony that Hiss had perjured himself, in order to make out a

prima facie case of perjury. Weiler v. United States, 323 U.S. 606

(1945 ). The basic corroboration it offered was the testimony of

---

31/ See, e.g., CN Ex. 58, in which FBI Director J.Edgar Hoover ordered
agents in Milwaukee to return to Thomas Grady, the typewriter salesman,
"to obtain an explanation as to how he could sell a machine which
was manufactured in 1929 to the Fansler-Martin partnership in
1927."

32/ The government's doubts about Exhibut UUU persisted through
two trials and the post-conviction proceedings. Indeed, in 1954,
well after all the proceedings had ended, the FBI obtained a portion of a typewritten letter written by Chambers. The government
subjected the letter to testing aimed at determining whether it
showed the same type characteristics as the Baltimore documents
and Hiss standards. CN Ex. 91. Obviously, the government's
success in the legal proceedings had not resolved its doubts
about the authenticity of the typewriter by means of which it
had procured Hiss' conviction. Nothing in the files of subsequent date
presents evidence which resolves the matter. The government's
present assertion is thus an attempt to settle this issue by fiat
rather than by evidence or logic.

Ramos Feehan, the government's expert document examiner, to

testify that both the Hiss standards and the Baltimore documents

were typed on the same machine. Petition, ¶ 68 [33] But, in

introducing Feehan's testimony, the government had a dilemma.

Extensive research and field work by FBI agents all over the

country had made clear that Woodstock typewriter 230,099, which

the defense would put into evidence, was not the Fansler-Hiss

machine. But Feehan's tests showed not only that the Hiss

standards and Baltimore documents had been typed on the same

typewriter, but also that Woodstock typewriter 230,099, Exhibit

UUU, was the machine on which both sets of documents had been

---

[33] There was grave doubt, even assuming, as the court and defense did,
that Ex.UUU was the Fansler-Hiss machine,as to whether Feehan's testimony
alone was sufficiently corroborative of Chambers' testimony as a
matter of law. When the government's typewriter evidence was
challenged at the first trial because no evidence of the typist
could be shown, Judge Kaufman queried:

> Is that corroboration of the transmission, delivery
> or furnishing? I am very frank to say that I am deeply
> troubled by the question in the light, and I think it is
> a very important legal question that will survive a ver-
> dict in this case, if there is an adverse verdict,of the
> rulings of the Circuit Court of Appeals and the Supreme
> Court not to dismiss indictments where there is some
> evidence, even though it is an arguable question.

Transcript, First Trial at 1414. He later reiterated that this was
"a very substantial question of law that will continue in this case
for all time". Id. at 1424.

The question did not,in fact, get to the Supreme Court. But at
least one Justice was convinced that the typewriter evidence presented, which failed to show who the typist was, offered insufficient
corroboration for Chambers' allegations. Douglas, Wm. O. Go East
Young Man (1964) at 378-79.

typed. [34/] CN Ex. 65. The government knew, from its field reports, which appeared to be conclusive, that this was impossible. [35/] If it had put into evidence the information gleaned by its agents, and Feehan's opinion that Exhibit UUU was the machine on which the Baltimore documents had been typed, a serious inconsistency would have been apparent, and Feehan's testimony would have been significantly discredited.

---

34/ The prosecutor surreptitiously gained access to Exhibit UUU before the second trial and Feehan made comparisons between the Hiss standards, Baltimore documents, and exemplars from Exhibit UUU at that time. Petition ¶ 107. Despite the claim asserted in an FBI document and repeated by respondent here that "an order was signed" permitting the government access to the typewriter without notice to the defense between the two trials (Govt. Memo, at 18, fn , but see Answer ¶ 72, denying that the prosecutor obtained an ex parte order), no such order appears anywhere in the court records of this case, although there is clear evidence that three judges refused to sign such an ex parte order, CN Ex. 64. The prosecutor's access to the typewriter may reflect an additional area of presecutorial misconduct. This issue cannot be further developed without discovery. See infra at Point.IX.

35/ In its Answer, ¶ 76, the government admits petitioner's allegation that:

> From the very moment defendant produced the type-writer which later became Exhibit UUU, the prosecution was aware of the possibility that it was not the machine which had passed from the Fansler/Martin partnership into the hands of Hiss. The FBI had the contrary testimony of Martin, Grady and others; the serial number of the defendant's machine was far higher than that of the machine the FBI had been seeking, and some of the FBI field force had warned the Director that the machine the defendant had produced might not be the genuine Fansler/Martin machine.

Petition, ¶ 13.

For Feehan's conclusion, to be probative, had also to be exclusive - it had to have eliminated the possibility that another old typewriter's typing would match the Baltimore documents and Hiss standards.[36] Otherwise, the identification would, at most, show that some typewriters typed so similarly that no specimen could definitely be attributed to a particular machine and, in consequence, the government would have failed to prove that the Baltimore documents and the Hiss standards were typed on the same machine. Thus, had Feehan's opinion that typing exemplars from Exhibit UUU matched the Baltimore documents and Hiss standards been revealed, this, coupled with the government's knowledge that Exhibit UUU could not be the Fansler-Hiss machine, would have destroyed the government's case.

---

36/ Feehan himself admitted the serious difficulty in identifying documents typed on the same machine at different times because of the tendency of type to change its characteristics over time. CN Ex. 91A. The government's claim that in the Hiss standards Feehan has "contemporaneous" documents to compare with the Baltimore documents is flatly wrong. The household papers typed by Priscilla Hiss which were located after a lengthy search were dated between 1931 and May 25, 1937, the latest being months before the first of the Baltimore documents was typed. Petition, ¶ 68. This passage of time not only made the document comparison more difficult, but also supported the Hisses' testimony that they had disposed of their typewriter before the Baltimore documents were typed. Comparison problems were even further exacerbated with respect to the samples taken from exhibit UUU in 1949.

The government solved this dilemma by suppressing all their field information,[37] adopting Ex. UUU as their own without explicitly vouching for its authenticity and restricting Feehan's testimony to eliminate all reference to his opinion regarding the typewriter. It thus served as a visible "silent witness" to convince the jury that Hiss was guilty.

Even the government admits[38] that the trial proceeded on the assumption, shared alike by defense, court, jury and the public, that the government contended that Exhibit UUU was indeed the Fansler-Hiss typewriter.[39] The government presented an FBI agent to type on it to demonstrate that it was operable, R. 3019; ... Murphy himself, in his summation, hit the typewriter keys with great dramatic flair and claimed the typewriter on the government's behalf. R. 3254. Only now do we know that

---

37/ The government seems to have become committed to a policy of suppression almost as soon as they learned of the conflict. FBI documents ordering further investigations after the defense located Exhibit UUU caution strictest confidentiality, CN Exs. 56, 58, and Murphy carefully hid from the defense the fact that he sought and had obtained access to the typewriter, supra at 69, n. 34 . Had the government disclosed its relevant information about the age of the typewriter, and Feehan's full opinion, the defense would have been able, in cross-examination, to bring out the discrepancies now known. Levin v. Clark, 408 F.2d 1209, 1215 (D.C. Cir. 1967). In any event, this failure to cross-examine was not crucial. See discussion and cases cited infra at 90-92.

38/ Answer, ¶ 55.

39/ The court acknowledges this in its charge to the jury. R. 3271.

this embracing of the defense exhibit was undertaken despite
prosecution knowledge, not shared by the defense, that it was
not what it was purported to be, and that this was a deliberate
prosecution strategy undertaken to hide relevant information and
shield the government's fragile case from being undone.  The
government engaged in wholesale suppression of all evidence which
had led it to conclude that Exhibit UUU could not be the Hiss/
Fansler typewriter, and that Feehan's opinion thus was not of
probative value, even while actively championing a piece of evidence it knew to be false in order to maintain its deception.[40/]

Only after Hiss's conviction did the defense entertain
suspicions about Exhibit UUU, incorporated in its motion for a
new trial.  Petition, ¶¶ 76-82.  At this point, the government,
fully conscious of the validity of the defense claims, CN Exs. 66,
68, Answer, ¶ 74, continued its deception by arguing that the

_____

40/  The government's claim that petitioner here seeks to re-
litigate the motion for a new trial, Govt. Memo. at 72, is
flatly wrong.  Petitioner's claim here focuses solely on governmental misconduct, completely unknown to the defense at the time
of the motion for a new trial, in suppressing relevant information from the defense, the court and the jury, thus turning the
trial into a deceitful sham and depriving petitioner of a fair trial.

Moreover, the government must be foreclosed from making its
argument that petitioner should have raised this matter earlier, relying on United States v. Aderman, 216 F.2d 564 (7th Cir. 1954),
Govt. Memo. at 74 n.   In the instant case, totally unlike in Aderman, it was the deceit of the government, continuing through and
beyond the motion for a new trial, which made it impossible for
the wrong done to petitioner to surface until the present time.

authenticity of the typewriter was irrelevant. Petition, ¶ 83.[41]

Thus the government succeeded in continuing the suppression of
material evidence, suppression in which it persisted for over 25
years until litigation under the FOIA unveiled the deception.

In an ordinary case, a prosecutor, armed with information which would catch the defense completely unaware and discredit a major element of defense evidence, would, of course do
so, not only for the strategic advantages of such a course, but
also to fulfill his obligation to present the full truth to the
jury. United States v. Zborowski, 271 F.2d 661 (2d Cir. 1959).

But this was not an ordinary case. The prosecutor's
interest in winning a conviction -- virtually a political
necessity in the highly charged atmosphere of the times --
outweighed his interest in presenting the truth. By withholding material information from the jury, the prosecutor usurped
its role and himself became the factfinder, a clear violation of
law of constitutional dimensions. As the court noted in Imbler v.
Craven, 298 F.Supp. 279, 806 (C.D. Cal. 1969), aff'd sub nom.
Imbler v. State of California, 424 F.2d 631 (9th Cir.), cert.
denied, 400 U.S. 865 (1970), "[i]t is not only affirmative misrepresentations which the prosecutor is prohibited from
employing to secure a conviction; omissions and half-
truths are equally damaging and prohibited, and their use
is no less culpable." See also Simms v. Cupp, 354 F.Supp.

---

41/ On its brief in opposition to Hiss' petition for certiorari
after his motion for a new trial had been denied, the government
again reversed itself, admitting that it had accepted Exhibit UUU
at trial as the Fansler-Hiss typewriter. Petition, ¶ 84.

698, 700 (D. Ore. 1972), ("[t]here is no distinction between false testimony and the presentation of a witness' partial testimony which, when considered in isolation, creates a distorted picture of the facts as the witness saw them.").

Thus, in Turner v. Ward, 321 F.2d 918 (10th Cir. 1963), where the prosecutor of a rape case instructed a doctor to testify in general terms that the victim had been sexually assaulted when his examination showed she was sodomized rather than raped, defendant's habeas corpus writ on due process grounds was granted because the jury was left with a false impression. [42/] The court found that the conviction was "obtained by either the knowing use of false material testimony or the intentional suppression of material testimony," id. at 920. Similarly, suppression of exculpatory ballistics tests was the basis for granting a habeas corpus writ in Barbee v. Warden, Maryland Penitentiary, 331 F. 2d 842 (4th Cir. 1964), even though the gun which was the subject of the tests was not introduced into evidence, but was merely offered for identification and shown to witnesses who testified that it was similar to the one used by defendant. The court ruled that the test results :

---

42/ The defense did not uncover this deception, despite some indication in the record that defense counsel might have had a basis to have known about it.

> became highly relevant the instant
> his revolver was produced in open court,
> formally marked for identification, and
> witnesses interrogated about it. . ..
> Once produced, it became not only appro-
> priate but imperative that any additional
> evidence concerning the gun be made avail-
> able either to substantiate or to refute
> the suggested inference.  If the pistol
> was pertinent for any purpose, so also
> was the opinion of the ballistics expert
> that it was not the weapon used. . ..

Id. at 845, fns. omitted.  The failure of the defense to
pursue this on its own was irrelevant because, as in the
instant case, "the inference strongly projected by the
state's evidence might have been destroyed by other evidence in its possession but which the [government] concealed
. . ." Id. at 846.  See also United States v. McGovern, 499
F.2d 1140, 1143 (1st Cir. 1974); infra at 90-92.

Here, as we have seen, the prosecution adopted an
exhibit as its own which it believed to be false, suppressed
evidence which would expose its falseness, and, indeed,
bolstered it by presenting the truncated testimony of an
expert whose full opinion, if revealed, would have exposed
the truth.  The prosecutor thus violated the government's
obligation to secure a fair trial for the defendant by full
disclosure of material information.

It is surely not often that a defendant in a criminal case is heard to complain that the prosecution failed to discredit defense evidence.  But in this case, the typewriter played an unusual role.  For, unimpeached, it stood as a "silent witness" to the prosecution claim that the Baltimore documents and Hiss standards were typed on the same typewriter--indeed on that very typewriter.  If, however, the prosecution had revealed the information gathered by its agents that the typewriter in evidence could not have been the Fansler-Hiss machine because of its manufacture date, it would have enabled the defense to discredit Feehan's testimony that the two sets of documents were typed on the same machine.  This would have cut the heart out of the prosecution case, both factually and legally, since Feehan's testimony provided the government with its only corroboration of Chambers' story, essential to establish the offense of perjury.

Thus, the government suppression and distortion of relevant information was deeply prejudicial to petitioner, and deprived him of a fair trial.

The government attacks the petitioner for presenting what it terms a "shaky" and "distorted" view of the FBI documents with respect to Exhibit UUU.  Govt. Memo at 70, 75.  In considering this charge, it is important to note that at the time of the Hiss trial, the government was convinced that Exhibit UUU could not be the Fansler-Hiss typewriter. Government attorneys today speculate that inconsistencies relating to the typewriter might be due to some combination of unreliable witnesses and faulty memories, Govt. Memo at 80. They thus attempt a wholesale reconstruction of the FBI investigation which took place at the time, in order to introduce now an element of uncertainty which was missing in the government officials at the time of trial.

Harry Martin, Fansler's partner in the insurance business, and Thomas Grady, the typewriter salesman, were both questioned extensively by the FBI in preparation for trial. Contrary to the government's claim now, government investigators at the time did not have "serious cause to doubt [Martin and Grady's] accuracy," Govt. Memo at 77, nor did they in fact doubt it. As the government must be aware, both Martin's and Grady's stories were in agreement that the date the insurance partnership acquired its sole Woodstock typewriter was prior to the earliest possible date that Exhibit UUU could have been manufactured and made available for sale.

The few inconsistencies in their statements, which the government now argues were sufficient to cast doubt on this basic fact, are trivial, and did not in fact create such doubts in the government investigators and prosecutors responsible for assuring a fair trial for Hiss. Thus, for instance, although Martin once did waver between 1927 and 1928 as the year in which the partnership's typewriter was purchased, compare CN Exs. 40 and 59 with CN Ex. 34A, his testimony never accommodated the possibility that the machine was purchased in 1929.[43] There is no support whatever in the FOIA records for the government's claim that Martin's accuracy on this point was doubted. Similarly, Grady consistently maintained that he sold the typewriter to the Fansler-Martin partnership before he left his position as a typewriter sales- man in December, 1927, CN Exs. 41, 42, 43, 44, a fact which the government's further investigations did not disturb.

---

[43] June, 1929, was suggested as possible date of purchase in an unsuccessful attempt by one agent just before trial to reconcile the testimony of Grady and Martin with the conflicting evidence that Exhibit UUU was a 1929 machine. Petition, ¶ 105. The government knew, however, that Ex- hibit UUU, manufactured by Woodstock in July or August, 1929, would not have been available for sale until much later. Petition, ¶ 80 n.1.

As to the government's claim that Grady was "un-reliable," Govt. Memo at 79 , the only suggestion to this effect was a statement by Martin (not by the FBI). Martin offhandedly suggested that perhaps Grady had sold them a stolen typewriter. CN 91B.[44] The FBI itself never accepted this explanation. CN 91C. Not only was Grady's reputation excellent, as the FBI found,[45] but he was later hired by the same insurance company for which Martin worked, CN Ex. 40, an unlikely occurrence if long-term company personnel such as Martin found him unreliable.

Another bit of trivia, which the government attaches, is an early FBI document requesting that inquiry be made "as to the knowledge of Thomas Grady, salesman who sold the Wood-stock to Fansler-Martin probably during nineteen twenty nine. . . Gradys present whereabouts are desired." Govt. Ex. D, p. 540, Serial #200. This document was written only four days after the FBI's search for the typewriter had begun, before Grady was located and interviewed. Almost immediately after this, it became clear to the FBI that the Fansler-Martin typewriter was purchased at an earlier date, almost undoubtedly in 1927.

---

[44] The attempted explanation is absurd - even if by dishonest means, Grady would not have been able to acquire in 1927 a typewriter not manufactured until 1929.

[45] He was let go by Woodstock solely because he did not sell enough typewriters. CN 91D at 4.

Never after this early stage did the FBI focus on a 1929
manufacture date; a mere ten days after its speculation as to
a 1929 date, in a document the government itself attaches
to its papers, the FBI asserted that "[i]n twentyseven Grady
sold a new Woodstock to Fansler-Martin partnership."  Govt.
Ex. D, p. 814, Serial #367, dated December 20, 1948.  The
government's assertion now that the FBI, at the time of trial,
believed in a 1929 manufacture date is contrary to the evidence
in the FBI files.

Another government distortion is evident in the
claims that both Martin and Grady "linked the purchase of the
Woodstock to the hiring of Anne Coyle", and that Martin indicated
that the partnership had originally had a Royal typewriter.
Govt. Memo at 77.  Both Martin and Grady quickly and convincingly
disposed of their initial confusions when reinterviewed.  Martin had initially forgotten another stenographer who preceded
Ms. Coyle at the firm.  This stenographer, Katherine Shotwell,
remembered that there was only one typewriter during her tenure,
1927-28.  Initially she thought it might have been a Royal,
CN Ex. 91E, but when interviewed by the FBI, clearly recalled
that the typewriter was a Woodstock.  CN Ex. 91F .  Martin
briefly echoed Shotwell's error about the office having a Royal
typewriter, CN Ex. 91E, but reverted to his original recollection

once Shotwell corrected herself. CN Exs. 59, 61. Grady, whose
initial recollection of Ms. Coyle in this context was uncertain,
CN Ex. 41, noted that

> he could very well have been confused
> on this matter for two reasons, the
> first being that he was acquainted
> with Martin over a period of several
> years, including the two years he him-
> self sold insurance for Northwestern
> Mutual, and does not believe he could
> recall personally the period of Ann
> Coyle's employment. . ..

CN Ex. 42. The FBI accepted both Martin's and Grady's restate-
ments of the facts. See, e.g., CN Exs. 53, 91C.

The government also deceptively asserts that Grady
"suggested" and "recollected" that the partnership had purchased two typewriters. Govt. Memo. at 79. This alleged
"suggestion" or "recollection" is drawn from CN 42 which, when
read, gives no support to the government assertion:

> GRADY was advised that an attorney
> for ALGER HISS had recovered a Woodstock
> typewriter "model 5N#230099" and that
> according to Woodstock records this
> machine was manufactured in 1929. GRADY
> stated that this typewriter could not
> have been the one he sold to FANSLER
> and MARTIN as he again pointed out that
> he sold no typewriters subsequent to
> leaving the employ of Woodstock in De-
> cember, 1927. He stated that his only

> conjecture on this point was that if
> the typewriter produced by HISS was
> the typewriter originally in the office
> of FANSLER and MARTIN it must have been
> purchased by these men from some other
> person than GRADY himself. . .

CN Ex. 42.

In raising these matters and a few other insignificant inconsistencies in the various FBI documents, the government appears to be trying to convince the court that it would have been unreasonable, based on these documents, to believe that the Fansler-Hiss typewriter and Exhibit UUU were not one and the same. As the petition shows, however, this belief was entirely reasonable and in fact was compelled by the evidence. Most important, at the time of the Hiss trial, the government - FBI agents, FBI director and prosecutors alike - did in fact believe that because of its late serial number, Exhibit UUU could not possibly be the Fansler-Hiss machine that the government was so assiduously seeking. Nevertheless, at trial the government presented expert testimony which they knew full well was, at best, open to serious doubt, and suppressed the truth.

The government maintained its deceptive posture through the motion for a new trial. Supra at 72-73. On that motion, the defense sought the testimony of Joseph Schmitt, a Woodstock engineer. An affidavit prepared for Schmitt's signature reflected his view that typewriter #230,099 must have been manufactured in mid-1929 at the earliest. Petition, ¶ 80.

FOIA documents now reveal that although Schmitt refused to sign the affidavit, he confessed to FBI agents that its content was "substantially correct." CN Ex. 70. Nevertheless, the government continued, in the motion for a new trial, to suppress this information. Although the government now admits that the Schmitt matter introduces a "new element", Govt. Memo. at 78 , it attempts to deflate the importance of the admission by claiming that the overall sense of the document in which this statement occurs actually suggests more equivocation on Schmitt's part. [46]/ The crucial judgment of accuracy must come, of course, from a reading of the full document, which shows that although the FBI agent was sent to Schmitt expressly "to give close scrutiny to this [affidavit] in an effort to determine if there are any substantial errors existing therein which are at difference with any opinions which he has previously expressed as to the time when 230099 was manufactured" CN Ex. 69, Schmitt was firm that the affidavit was "substantially correct;". He did not sign it because "he did not know what if any additional production figures might have been furnished Hiss attorney by other company employee." CN Ex. 70.

---

46/ The government accuses petitioner of "wholly ignor[ing] Schmitt's remaining statements in CN Ex. 70, to wit, that he did not sign the affidavit because, inter alia, there were no records available regarding skipped serial numbers." Govt. Memo. at 78.

Some minor quibbles with the affidavit are detailed, including the one highlighted in the government's response with respect to the exact system of skipping serial numbers.  Schmitt, however, goes on to confirm that a number in close sequence to that mentioned in the affidavit "was taken from Schmitt's records and is considered accurate.  Reliable records substantiate relatively small amount of skipping between March, 1929 and August, 1930."  Id.  Thus Schmitt's opinion of substantial accuracy must have convinced Hoover and Myles Lane that the typewriter introduced at trial was manufactured too late to be the Fansler-Martin machine,  CN Exs. 66, 68, for this is the point at which the government reversed its strategy and disavowed the importance of the typewriter to its case.  Schmitt's affirmation of the accuracy of his affidavit was of course unknown to defendants and to the court at the time of the motion for a new trial.

The effort by the government to diminish the effects of its own misconduct with respect to the typewriter thus fails upon closer examination.  The suppression of information by the government, as described above at 64-73, denied defendant a fair trial.

## POINT V

### THE GOVERNMENT'S REBUTTAL WITNESS, EDITH MURRAY, TESTIFIED FALSELY ON A MATERIAL POINT, AS THE GOVERNMENT WELL KNEW AT THE TIME OF HER TESTIMONY

As the government repeatedly has acknowledged, Edith Murray was a very important prosecution witness, the only person the government could locate during preparation for two trials who testified that she ever saw a member of the Hiss family with a member of the Chambers family.[47/] Her testimony thus provided the only corroboration of Whittaker and Esther Chambers' stories that they were close friends with the Hisses and enjoyed extensive social contacts with them, a claim that both Alger and Priscilla Hiss denied. Accordingly, the material recently discovered in government files which points to 1) extensive coaching of Murray by the government, and 2) knowing use of her perjured testimony with respect to her identification of both Priscilla and Alger Hiss demonstrates errors which were extremely detrimental to the defense. This is especially true as Murray's testimony was presented dramatically as a part of the government's rebuttal.

---

47/ The FBI's post-trial analyses repeatedly recognized Edith Murray's importance to the case. See, e.g., CN Ex. 72, Agent Ladd's memo to Hoover stating that "[t]here is no question that Edith Murray was a very important Government witness." Similar statements occur in CN Ex. 92 and CN Ex. 93, p. 6. It is only now that the government questions the value to the defense of impeaching Murray, and suggests that such impeachment would not have raised a reasonable doubt about Hiss' guilt. Govt. Memo. at 35.

In the FBI's first interview of Murray, she remembered
only a "lady from Washington" and a "slender man" whose names
she did not know, and she was uncertain whether the pictures of
Priscilla and Alger Hiss, which were shown to her, were these
persons. CN Ex. 73. The FBI identified the pictures as being
those of Priscilla and Alger Hiss, names with which she said she
was unfamiliar. Id. The government, worried that Ms. Murray would
be unable to identify Priscilla Hiss, undertook to insure that
she would do so in order "to preclude any embarrassment on the
part of the Government." CN Ex. 74. They took this "very
cooperative" and very sheltered woman to Westminster, Maryland
to meet with the Chambers, CN Ex. 76, R. 3027, and arranged to
have her travel to New York to view Alger and Priscilla Hiss.
FBI agents were ordered to meet her at the train station in New
York and to treat her with "every kindness, courtesy and consideration," CN. Ex. 77. Once Murray arrived in New York, the FBI
followed up their initial highly suggestive single-photo photographic show-up with a surreptitious and equally highly suggestive
live show-up of the Hisses arriving in court. The show-up was
even more suspect than most, [48] for Murray viewed the Hisses as
they came off the elevator in the federal courthouse, encircled
by photographers and reporters, on the first day of trial.

_____

[48]      Identifications made in this way are inherently suspect.
Stovall v. Denno, 388 U.S. 293, 302 (1967)("[t]he practice of
showing suspects singly to persons for the purpose of identification. . .has been widely condemned"); Foster v. California,
394 U.S. 440 (1969),(where, after a tentative identification in a
line-up, a one-to-one confrontation and a second lineup with new (cont.)

After this preparation, Murray was able to identify both Priscilla and Alger Hiss at trial without hesitation. In addition, she testi-fied on direct examination to a prior positive identification of the Hisses and to having known Priscilla Hiss as "Miss Priscilla."

On cross-examination, the defense strenuously attacked Murray's prior identification of the Hisses. Particularly stressed was the possibility that the FBI had provided Murray with Priscilla and Alger Hiss' names at the time they originally showed her the Hiss' photographs. We now know, from CN. Ex. 73, that this was in-deed true. But Murray repeatedly denied on cross-examination that the FBI had told her the Hiss' names and the defense was unable to shake her testimony. R. 3032, 3033, 3036-37, 3053, 3056.

Murphy was aware of the false nature of Murray's testi-mony, and stood idly by. A copy of Edith Murray's statement made at her first interview with FBI agents, CN Ex. 73, in which she clearly states that the agents showed her pictures of Priscilla and Alger Hiss and identified them by name, appears in his file.[49]

---

48/ (cont.)
composition except for petitioner, were arranged, "[t]he suggestive elements in this identification procedure made it all but inevitable that David would identify petitioner. . ." Id. at 443.) Even the government admits the unreliability of the identification. Govt. Response to Petition for coram nobis, March 30, 1979 (hereinafter "Answer") ¶ 80.

49/ Once again, the government appears to be ignorant of the con-tents of its own files, stating that there is "no reason to conclude that Murphy was aware of [Edith Murray's prior FBI statement]." Govt. Memo. at 41, n. 2. But petitioner received from the United States Attorney a copy of this document with a letter saying that it came from the prosecutor's files. CN Exs. 94, 95.

Even if Murphy had not known about the statement, "the prose-cution is charged with the knowledge of its agents, including the police," Imbler v. Craven, 298 F.Supp. 795, 800, 806 (C.D. Cal. 1969), aff'd sub nom. Imbler v. State of California, 424 F.2d 631 (9th Cir.), cert. denied, 400 U.S. 865 (1970); see also Giglio v. United States, 405 U.S. 150 (1972); Barbee v. Warden, Maryland Penitentiary, 331 F.2d 842 (4th Cir. 1964).

When a prosecutor knowingly permits false testimony to reach
the jury, whether by actively suborning perjury, or by remaining
mute and letting it stand uncorrected, he has denied the defendant due process of law. Mooney v. Holohan, 294 U.S. 103 (1935);
Pyle v. State of Kansas, 317 U.S. 213 (1942); White v. Ragen,
324 U.S. 760 (1945); Alcorta v. Texas, 355 U.S. 28 (1957);
Napue v. Illinois, 360 U.S. 264 (1959); United States v. Kahn,
472 F.2d 272 (2d. Cir.), cert. denied, 411 U.S. 982 (1973);
Application of Kapatos, 208 F.Supp. 883, 887 (S.D.N.Y. 1962); United
States ex rel. Montgomery v. Ragen, 86 F.Supp. 382 (N.D. Ill. 1949).
A conviction so obtained must be reversed if there is "any
reasonable likelihood that the false testimony could have affected
the judgment of the jury," Annunziato v. Manson, 566 F.2d 410, 414
(2d Cir. 1977), quoting United States v. Agurs, 427 U.S. 96 (1976)
at 103. In this case, that standard is met.

Even if the falseness of Murray's answer on direct
examination did not immediately strike the prosecutor, repeated
questioning by the defense on cross-examination as to whether
the FBI identified the people in the photos by name could not
but have flagged for him the importance of this issue to the
defense. United States v. Miller, 411 F.2d 825, 831-32 (2d Cir.
1969). In Miller, the Second Circuit Court of Appeals found prosecutorial misconduct where repeated questioning by the defense
on cross-examination on a subject about which the witness had
testified falsely failed to alert the prosecutor to correct the
false testimony. The Court found:

> After full allowance for the problems confron-
> ting counsel in the stress of a long and heated
> trial . . .the prodding furnished by these episodes
> must be taken to have served the "valuable office"
> of "flagging". . .thus placing upon [the prosecutor]
> a duty of disclosure he did not discharge. Even if he
> did not recall the hypnosis or remember or locate his
> memorandum of it, he should have. . .

Id. at 831-32.

Edith Murray's identification of the Hisses had enormous import at the trial, and, indeed, her ability to make this
identification was the sole reason for her appearance at the trial.
Her corroboration of Chambers on one detail of his story provided
support for his general credibility, around which the entire case
revolved.[50] Thus the prosecutorial misconduct in failing to correct
her testimony, on a matter directly relevant to the suggestiveness
of her identification, is clearly material.

The error was prejudicial to the defense. The "bombshell"
nature of this witness, who appeared on the very last day of trial,[51]

_____

[50] Prosecutorial misconduct with respect to use of perjured
testimony or suppression of evidence is no more tolerated by the
courts when it concerns an issue of credibility than an issue more
directly affecting guilt or innocence. Napue v. Illinois, 360
U.S. 264 (1959); United States ex rel. Washington v. Vincent,
525 F.2d 262 (2d Cir. 1975), cert. den., 424 U.S. 934 (1976).

[51] The government acknowledges that Murray was a "bombshell
witness," Answer, ¶80. The defense, surprised by her unexpected
appearance, moved to strike her testimony on the ground that it
should have been part of the prosecution's direct case. The
trial court agreed that the testimony "might more properly have
been offered in the direct case," but denied the motion to strike.
R. 3177-78.

the central role of her identification of the Hisses to the credibility of her overall testimony, and the importance of her corroboration in view of the credibility of Chambers made Murray's
ability to identify Priscilla and Alger Hiss crucial to the
government, as it repeatedly recognized, both while preparing
her for trial and in post-verdict evaluations of the trial.[52]
Further, her testimony that she remembered being introduced to
Mrs. Hiss and calling her "Miss Priscilla," R. 3026-27, was
particularly devastating to the defense, since it suggested a
positiveness of recall and a familiarity with the defendant's
wife which we now know were totally lacking.  Had the defense
been able to get an honest answer to its repeatedly asked question
whether the FBI told Murray the Hisses' names while showing her
their pictures, it well may have been able to successfully impeach
her identification and neutralize her testimony.  Instead, her
reiteration of the falsehood that she had not been told their
names, uncorrected by the prosecutor, strengthened her identification.  Murray's unimpeached testimony provided the second
jury with a concrete basis to believe Chambers, and contributed
significantly to their verdict.

The government's argument that the defense counsel
should have requested Murray's prior statement and attempted to

---

52/        See footnote 47, supra at 85.

"cure" the prosecution's error, has no bearing on the misconduct of the prosecutor and on the necessity for an appropriate remedy from this Court.

In Simms v. Cupp, 354 F.Supp. 698 (D. Ore. 1972), the defense's failure to cure prosecutorial error did not preclude relief. In that case, where identification of the defendant's alleged accomplice in an earlier crime was a crucial issue at trial, the victim testified that it was perpetrated by a Negro boy. She did not testify further as to the details of his appearance, which, as the government knew, were inconsistent with the description of defendant's accomplice and thus would have been exculpatory. Defense counsel, surprised by her testimony, did not cross-examine this witness on the details of her assailant's appearance, as he was of course free to do. Again, the defense's failure to cure the error was held not to prevent relief from prosecutorial misconduct in permitting a witness' technically true but partial and misleading testimony to stand uncorrected. See also Imbler v. Craven, 298 F.Supp. 795, (C.D. Col. 1969), aff'd sub nom Imbler v. State of California, 424 F.2d 631 (9th Cir.), cert. denied, 400 U.S. 865 (1970); Grant v. Alldredge, 498 F.2d 376, 382 (2d Cir. 1974). The same should be true here, and the failure of Hiss' trial counsel to request a prior statement of a totally unexpected witness, on the last day of a lengthy and grueling trial, cannot foreclose relief for the prosecutor's knowing use of perjured testimony by this witness. The failure of the government to correct Murray's false testimony on the material issue of her identification of the Hisses which, had it been corrected, could have affected the judgment of the jury, United States v. Agurs, supra, 427 U.S. 96, requires reversal of the conviction.

POINT VI

THE PROSECUTION'S CONDUCT WITH
RESPECT TO GEORGE NORMAN ROULHAC
DEPRIVED PETITIONER OF A FAIR TRIAL

Murphy, in a letter to the United States Marshal requesting payment for Roulhac for his services to the prosecution, asserted that he met with Roulhac daily from November 1 to November 30, and would do so again from December 12 until the date Roulhac testified.  CN Ex. 82.[53]

---

[53] The letter was dated December 13, 1949; Roulhac testified on January 16, 1950.  In the letter, Murphy wrote, in pertinent part:

Sergeant Roulhac reported to me at my office on November 1, 1949, pursuant to written orders from his Commanding Officer.  I, together with other Agents, saw the Sergeant daily from that time on to and including the 39th [sic] of November [illegible] for the purpose of interrogating him and learning certain facts relative to an alleged defense in this case with which he is extremely familiar.

On November 30th, I told Sergeant Roulhac to report back to Mitchel Field and to await my 'phone call.

Pursuant to the 'phone call, he has reported to me since December 12th and it is my plan to keep him in the Court House each day until his testimony is actually needed.

Although he is physically here and not testifying, he is serving a very useful purpose in connection with the Government's case, which I cannot disclose in this memorandum because of its secrecy.

Yet at trial, Roulhac testified that he only visited the
United States Attorney's office "three or four times". R. 2968. A
comparison of the letter with Roulhac's trial testimony
showed unmistakably that perjury had occurred and petitioner
so alleged.  But the government now contends, in substance,
that it was the prosecutor who was lying, and that in writing
the letter he was defrauding the United States government
in order to give undeserved compensation to a witness in return for favorable testimony.  In either case, Hiss was deprived of a fair trial.

If Murphy's letter to the United States Marshal is
truthful, his awareness of Roulhac's perjury cannot be disputed, for Murphy wrote CN Ex. 82 just four weeks before
Roulhac's testimony, and Roulhac's testimony indubitably was
false.  A prosecutor's knowing use of false testimony is an
egregious error in derogation of his duty, and has been repeatedly condemned by the courts and resulted in reversals.
See  cases cited with regard to Edith Murray's testimony,
supra, Point V.

On the other hand, if Murphy lied about the frequency of Roulhac's services, and requested compensation for
services not performed, the government abrogated its obligation to the defense to reveal exculpatory information.  For
payment to a witness is exculpatory information which must be

disclosed. <u>United States</u> v. <u>Partin</u>, 552 F.2d 621, 645 (5th Cir. 1977); <u>United States</u> v <u>Quinn</u>, 543 F.2d 640 (8th Cir. 1976); <u>Sanders</u> v. <u>United States</u>, 541 F.2d 190 (8th Cir. 1976), <u>cert.</u> <u>denied</u>, 429 U.S. 1066 (1977); <u>United States</u> v. <u>Librach</u>, 520 F.2d 550, 553-54 (8th Cir. 1975).

In <u>Librach</u>, where the prosecutor failed to reveal that a government witness had been placed in protective custody and provided with compensation, the court termed it "an egregious case of prosecutorial suppression of evidence that was both favorable and material to the defense." 520 F.2d at 553. Like a promise not to prosecute or an agreement to recommend a reduced sentence in return for testimony, <u>Napue</u> v. <u>Illinois</u>, 360 U.S. 254 (1959), <u>Giglio</u> v. <u>United States</u>, 405 U.S. 150 (1972), monetary compensation, because it offers a motive for false testimony, is exculpatory and must be disclosed to the defense for use in discrediting the witness. This is all the more true when the payment is not for services actually rendered.

Although Murphy's letter alone does not reveal whether actual payment was made, it meets petitioner's burden of proving a <u>prima facie</u> case of payment by the prosecutor, <u>United States</u> v. <u>Keogh</u>, 440 F.2d 731, 741 (2d Cir. 1971). And the government's own argument in opposition to the petition proves that the payment could only have been in exchange for Roulhac's testimony, for they claim his actual services occupied only three or four days.[54]/

    The change in Roulhac's testimony over the period of his contact with the FBI and prosecution reveals further perjury which was committed by this witness. Roulhac was known to the prosecution during the first trial, and could have been made available to testify at that time.[55]/ But since on his initial interview Roulhac knew nothing of value to the prosecution, he was not called to trial. Only after the first jury could not agree on a verdict did the government decide that it was worthwhile to bring Roulhac to New York, arrange compensation for him, and work on his testimony.

---

[54]/ Moreover, as CN Ex. 82 itself makes clear, Roulhac was in active service in the army and assigned to the prosecution during the period in question, so the prosecutor's efforts were directed towards getting him __double__ compensation for the days in question, and not a "subsistence" payment as the letter claims.

[55]/ When he testified at the second trial, Roulhac lied about the date he was first contacted by the FBI, which made it appear that he had not come to the government's attention until after the first trial was over. He testified that his first contact with the FBI was in August, 1949, R. 2968, but he was in fact interviewed on or before June 30, 1949, while the first trial was still in progress, CN Ex. 79. The first trial did not end until July 8, and Murphy made no effort to request a continuance, if one was needed, to bring Roulhac from Alaska. Rather than correct this false testimony, Murphy bolstered it on redirect examination by having Roulhac explain that he was in Alaska while the first trial was in progress. R. 2970-71.

At his first interview, Roulhac was "very vague as to dates and events." CN Ex. 79. He said he saw a small black portable typewriter in a case at the Catlett's at some point, either before or after they moved. He mentioned that he lived away from the Catlett's for about a year when he was first married, and saw the typewriter on his return. CN Ex. 79. After being brought to New York by the FBI, Roulhac's testimony was transformed. All references which did not support the prosecution theory were expunged. The typewriter became a large office-model Woodstock without a case; his marriage and year's absence disappeared, and thus the fact that he first saw the typewriter after returning from a long absence. The earlier residence where he might also have seen the typewriter was not mentioned. CN Ex. 81. By the time of trial, the remaining inconsistencies were gone and Roulhac testified he had been living at the Catlett's continuously over a several month period when he first saw the typewriter. R. 2967. This, of course, directly contradicted his first statement, CN Ex. 79.

The government's misconduct materially affected the defense under either theory of wrongdoing. If Roulhac perjured himself about the number of times he met with the government, his credibility on all aspects of his testimony is called into question. If he was promised and/or received

compensation, Roulhac's bias is clear and his entire testimony thus equally suspect. In either case, his testimony in chief was false. But for the prosecutorial misconduct, the defense would have been able to effectively discredit Roulhac.

Hiss was prejudiced by the defense's inability to shake Roulhac's testimony. Although it was short, Roulhac's testimony was important: only through Roulhac could the prosecution overcome the defense claim that the Hisses had disposed of their typewriter before the time when the Baltimore documents must have been typed. Like Edith Murray, [56] Roulhac was one of the new prosecution witnesses at the second trial, and, like Edith Murray, his false testimony caused the jury to convict Alger Hiss.

_____

56 / Supra, Point V.

## POINT VII

THE PROSECUTOR IMPROPERLY ARGUED BEFORE
THE JURY THAT IT COULD DRAW CONCLUSIONS
AS TO THE TYPIST OF THE BALTIMORE DOCU-
MENTS AND THE HISS STANDARDS, ALTHOUGH
ITS OWN EXPERTS, UNKNOWN TO PETITIONER,
HAD ADVISED THAT SUCH CONCLUSIONS COULD
NOT BE DRAWN.

The government asserts that the prosecutor acted

properly when he deliberately sought to mislead the jury by

making an argument which his own experts could not support

and about which evidence had not been introduced. Govt.

Memo. at 86-87. [58]  In taking such a position, the govern-

ment now carries on the tradition of the original prosecutor

in this case, who was heedless of the admonition of Berger

v. United States, 295 U.S. 78, 88 (1935) that as a prosecutor,

he bore a duty to the state "to refrain from improper methods

calculated to produce a wrongful conviction ..."

_____

[58] The government also claims that according to CN Ex. 83
(incorrectly referred to in the Petition as CN Ex. 82), the
government expert did not compare precisely the same documents that Murphy referred to in summation. Govt. Memo.
at 86. CN Ex. 83 concludes with a request from Murphy that
common typing errors from all relevant documents be collated
for "whatever use [he] may see fit ..." Other FBI documents,
CN Ex. 96, show that the expert had reviewed errors in all
Hiss standards and Baltimore documents, but could not conclude
from them who was the typist.

Newly discovered evidence reveals that at the close of the first trial, a juror informed Murphy that jurors favoring conviction had noticed common typing errors in the Hiss standards and the Baltimore documents, and had found them persuasive of the claim that Priscilla Hiss had typed the government documents,[59] and thus persuasive of Alger Hiss' guilt. CN Ex. 83. Ramos Feehan, the government's document expert, had previously been asked to examine the common errors to see if a conclusion could be drawn as to who was the typist. Feehan carried out the requested examination and determined that no such conclusion could be drawn. CN Exs. 83, 96. Murphy then consciously determined, since no evidence would identify the typist of the Baltimore documents, to poison the jury at the second trial by introducing in his summation argument, without evidentiary support, the common typing errors, inviting the jury to infer that

---

[59] Priscilla Hiss typed three of the Hiss standards, R. 700, 707, 742, and the defense provided the government with two additional documents typed by Mrs. Hiss which the government did not enter into evidence. CN Ex. 97.

Priscilla Hiss was the typist.   CN Ex. 83. [60]

Murphy did make this calculated and grossly improper
argument, R. 3258, and the jury was, indeed, responsive to it.
After planting his invidious inference, Murphy suggested that
the jurors compare the errors in the documents for themselves.
After several hours of deliberation, the jurors did request to
see the typewritten documents in evidence -- the Baltimore
documents, the Hiss standards, and some FBI sample typing.
When they did not receive the requested documents within the
half-hour, the jurors requested them again. R. 3277, 3278,
3280, 3282-83.   It can be assumed that they wanted to examine
the documents to draw the very unsupportable conclusion to

---

[60] After making this resolve, Murphy was confronted with a
defense discovery request for documents typed by Chambers in order
to make the same determination as to the identity of the typist
of the Baltimore documents. Murphy opposed this motion, arguing
that it was absurd to think that a typist's identity could be
determined in this way. Murphy's affidavit stated: "It can hardly
be claimed that an expert could tell what individual typed a
certain instrument by having a specimen of his typing since the
impressions are made by a mechanical means..."  Affidavit of
Thomas Murphy opposing defense discovery motion, November, 1949.
CN Ex. 98.  Even while swearing that such an inference was
insupportable, Murphy had already determined to use that very
false inference in his summation argument.

which the prosecutor had cleverly led them.

By drawing the jury's attention to the common typing errors in the documents before it, and thereby implying that Priscilla Hiss typed the Baltimore documents, the prosecutor plainly violated the rule that a conviction may not be obtained by knowing use of false evidence, Miller v. Pate, 386 U.S. 1 (1967), nor by inferences not reasonably deducible from the evidence, see Eastman v. United States, 153 F.2d 80 (8th Cir.), cert. denied, 328 U.S. 852 (1946). The prosecutor knew that the true typist of the Baltimore documents could not be shown, that the government's own expert had said so, and that the inference he asked the jury to draw was thus not a reasonable one. Nevertheless, he stood up at summation and asked the jury to draw the damning inference which he knew was unsound. The prosecutor, by arguing to the jury an inference he knew to be unfounded, engaged in conduct tantamount to the knowing introduction of false testimony, conduct which has repeatedly been deplored. Mooney v. Holohan, 294 U.S. 103 (1935); Pyle v. Kansas, 317 U.S. 213 (1942); Alcorta v. Texas, 355

U.S. 28 (1957); <u>Napue</u> v. <u>Illinois</u>, 360 U.S. 264 (1959). [61]

The rule against knowing use of false testimony applies with particular force where, as here, false expert testimony is presented or false inferences drawn from evidence which ought to be the subject of expert testimony. Thus, in <u>King</u> v. <u>United States</u>, 372 F.2d 383 (D.C. Cir. 1966, amended 1967), the prosecutor did not present expert evidence of the defendant's sanity, but, in his summation, offered his opinion concerning the reliability of the defense expert and his methods. The Court held that the doctrine prohibiting a prosecutor from importing his own testimony into a criminal trial "has full vitality not only where the prosecutor is asserting a fact within his individual cognizance, but also where, as here, the prosecutor is asserting a

---

[61] The government relies on cases where prosecutorial comment on "obvious physical features" of an exhibit was proper. Govt. Memo. at 88. These are not applicable to the instant case, where the prosecutor knew that the common feature of the documents to which he referred did not support the inference he made, and the cited cases thus do not advance the government's position.

belief or opinion that is properly the subject of expert testimony. The prosecutor is not free to offer his opinion in lieu of calling an expert witness." Id. at 394. In King, as in the instant case, the prosecutor erroneously put forth arguments which required the support of expert testimony. In this case, however, the misconduct was far worse, for the prosecutor knew full well that his argument was fallacious.

It made no difference in King, nor does it here, that the prosecutor's transgression was framed with subtlety. In King, for example, the prosecutor refrained from asserting his own belief or assurance to the jury. The court recognized, however, that it is no less misconduct for a prosecutor to put his assertion of fact "in the form of an assumption of a question, unless...proffer[ing] direct testimony of that fact." Id., footnote omitted. See also United States v. Brawner, 471 F.2d 969 (D.C. Cir. 1972).

Another instructive case is <u>United States</u> v. <u>Carter</u>,
522 F.2d 666 (D.C. Cir. 1975), which, although it did not
involve knowing prosecutorial misconduct such as we have here,
also illustrates the impropriety of leading a jury to draw
inferences which expert testimony would not support.  In
<u>Carter</u>, the jury was asked to compare a doodle which was
found at the scene of the crime with doodles drawn by the
defendant during the trial.  The FBI agent who introduced the
defendant's doodles testified that there had been insufficient
time to obtain expert comparison of the doodles, but conceded
on cross-examination, that "older, more experienced" FBI
agents had told him "that there were not enough definitive
markings or points of identity to effect a valid comparison..."
522 F.2d at 684.  Nevertheless, defendant's doodles were
admitted into evidence, on the theory that they were probative facts based on which the jurors might find similarities
and draw inferences.  The Court of Appeals reversed defendant's
conviction, holding that:

The government's proposition assumes
that the evidence was probative and
that the lay jury was capable of making
the necessary comparative analysis, to
determine whether the sketches in question were produced by the same individual.
However, in this instance, where the
government's own witness cast doubt on
the possibilities for reliable expert
analysis, we are of the belief that the
exhibits, as offered, were not of probative value; hence, they should not have
been received in evidence for the jury's
consideration.

Id. at 685, footnote omitted. Similarly in this case, the

prosecutor's argument, which he knew to lack foundation,

should not have been put before the jury.

The prosecutor not only should have refrained from

drawing unsupported inferences from the evidence; but he also

owed the defense an affirmative duty to disclose his expert's

opinion that no conclusion as to the typist could be drawn from

the documents in evidence. [62] In Ashley v. State of Texas, 319

---

[62] Because the prosecutor had the government expert present
only a truncated version of his information with respect to the
typewriter and typewritten documents in evidence, supra at Point IV,
the defense forewent cross-examination. Full disclosure by
the prosecution would undoubtedly have presented many oppor-
tunities for cross-examination.

F.2d 80 (5th Cir. 1963), the prosecutor failed to inform the

defense of the opinion of a psychiatrist who examined the

two defendants in a murder case and concluded that they

were insane.[63] The state argued that their failure merely

to disclose an opinion was not error. The Court found

that "[t]he vice of this argument is that it is not the

nature or the weight to be accorded to an opinion, but the

fact that such an opinion had been formed by such an

obviously objective witness as one engaged by the prosecu-

tion to make the examination," id. at 85, (emphasis in the

original), and granted defendants' petition for habeas

corpus. Similarly, in United States v. Hart, 344 F.Supp.

522 (E.D.N.Y. 1971), where a government witness had

taken a lie detector test at the prosecution's request,

and failed it, the Court ruled that "the burden should

be on the government to convince a jury that this test

was of no significance," id. at 523. And in United

States v. Poole, 379 F.2d 645 (7th Cir. 1967), the

_____

[63] The defense was informed of the opinion of another
psychiatrist that defendants were sane. No insanity
defense was proferred.

failure of the government to disclose a doctor's report

that examination of the kidnap victim was negative for

evidence of sexual intercourse, although she testified

that she had been raped, 64/ denied defendant a fair trial.

See also Smith v. United States, 312 F.2d 867 (D.C. Cir.

1962). In such cases as these, where the government

possesses negative exculpatory evidence, it has a clear

duty to divulge that evidence to the defense.

Murphy's misconduct in these respects was not

merely inadvertent or negligent. Despite his expert

witness' opinion that there was no evidence from which

he could identify the typist, Murphy made a calculated decision,

of which he informed FBI agents, to withhold all expert

testimony on this matter and, at summation, to lead the

jury wrongly to infer that the typist was Priscilla Hiss.

CN Ex. 83. His cold calculation is further reflected in

his opposition to the defense discovery request for access

to documents in order to try to make a similar determination

as to Chambers' typing. Supra, at 102 n.60. The prosecutorial

---

64/ Rape was not an element of the crime charged in Poole.

misconduct demonstrated here was thus not "improper argument springing from the heat and enthusiasm of advocacy," Pierce v. United States, 86 F.2d 949, 953 (6th Cir. 1936), but, as in Pierce, was "a studied effort" to improperly introduce prejudicial and unsupported evidence. "Indulgence was designed rather than inadvertent, and an improper purpose its only explanation. That it was intended to prejudice the jury is sufficient ground for a conclusion that in fact it did so." Id. at 953.

The evidence of prejudice is clear in this case. The identity of the typist of the Baltimore documents was important in the case, 65/ for, if known, it would have clearly established guilt or innocence. Knowing there was no evidence to establish that Priscilla Hiss was the typist, Murphy consciously undertook to introduce this fatally prejudicial inference at the very end of his summation argument, 66/

_____

65/ The identity of the typist was seen as vital to the prosecution, for the judge at the first trial had suggested that without it the prosecution might be lacking the corroborative evidence necessary to sustain a conviction for perjury. Supra, n. 33 at 68.

66/ The reference occurs within five pages of the end of a 49-page long summation argument. R. 3258.

"these [final few] minutes which probably have the greatest influence on the jury," <u>United States</u> v. <u>De Loach</u>, 504 F.2d 185, 191 (D.C. Cir. 1974). Thus, like <u>United States</u> v. <u>Carter</u>, <u>supra</u>, where the court criticized the prosecution for introducing the defendant's doodles after the close of the defense case, depriving them of an opportunity for effective rebuttal, the timing of the error here added to its prejudicial effect. The <u>Carter</u> jury was, at least, apprised of the possibility that expert testimony would not support the prosecution's theory. The Hiss jury was deprived of such information. Further, by mentioning the similarities of the typing errors in the two sets of documents himself during the summation argument rather than presenting evidence on this topic, the prosecutor denied Hiss any opportunity at all for cross-examination or rebuttal evidence, <u>Taliaferro</u> v. <u>United States</u>, 47 F.2d 699 (9th Cir. 1931), and invested the comparison with the authority of his office. <u>United States</u> v. <u>Spangelet</u>, 258 F.2d 338 (2d Cir. 1958); <u>Hall</u> v. <u>United States</u>, 419 F.2d 58 2, 583-84 (5th Cir. 1969). ("The power and force of the government tend to impart an implicit stamp of believability to what the prosecutor says.") [67/] Finally, we know from the fact that the jurors twice requested the documents, that they did indeed make the comparison that the prosecutor wanted them to make, and drew the unsupported and incorrect inference therefrom. United States v. Artus, 591 F.2d 526 (9th Cir. 1979); Smith v. United States, 312 F.2d 867 (D.C. Cir. 1962).

For Alger Hiss, Prosecutor Murphy's misconduct meant a four-year prison sentence and a thirty-year effort to clear his name. No more prejudice than this need be shown.

---

67/ The government makes the extraordinarily self-serving claim that only "consistent and extensive misconduct on summation" should cause reversal. Govt. Memo. at 88. Besides appearing to condone single acts of prosecutorial misconduct, which the courts have repeatedly refused to do, see, e.g., United States v. Spangelet, 258 F.2d 338, 342-43, (2d Cir. 1958), Smith v. United States, 312 F.2d 867, 869 (D.C. Cir. 1962), the government misunderstands the purpose of collateral proceedings such as coram nobis: to insure that convictions obtained by unconstitutional means be undone. United States v. Morgan, 346 U.S. 502 (1954). The proper focus for the court must be not the frequency with which the misconduct occurs but the prejudice it caused, prejudice which, in this case, was grave.

POINT VIII.

**BECAUSE OF UNLAWFUL SURVEILLANCE, PETITIONER'S
CONVICTION SHOULD BE VACATED; ALTERNATIVELY,
DISCOVERY AND A HEARING SHOULD BE ORDERED.**

The nature and extent of surveillance of Hiss, his
family and associates was not known at the time of trial by
the defense.  Even now, with the release of some of the government documents concerning FBI investigative techniques regarding
Hiss, the full extent of surveillance -- wiretapping, mail openings, mail covers, physical surveillance, and other intrusive
techniques -- is still not clear.  Nevertheless, it is apparent
that information gathered through the exploitation of unlawful
wiretaps and other illegal surveillance was used at trial and
consequently the conviction must be reversed.  Alternatively,
further discovery and a hearing is essential to a fair determination regarding these issues.

FBI surveillance of Hiss began in earnest in 1941 with
the institution of a mail cover on his incoming correspondence
at his home in connection with an FBI investigation of possible
Hatch Act violations.  CN Ex. 98A.  Another mail cover was placed

on the Hiss mail in 1945, and at the same time the FBI obtained toll call records from the Hiss residence Telephone for the years 1943 and 1944 as well. CN Ex. 99. In September, 1945, the FBI intercepted telegrams to Hiss as well. CN Ex. 100.

In late November, 1945, FBI surveillance of the Hiss residence in Washington, D.C., escalated. For the third time, a mail cover was instituted beginning on November 28, 1945, which was continued at least until 1946. CN Ex. 101 at p. 70; CN Ex. 102. Continuous physical surveillance of Hiss was begun as well. CN Ex. 101 at p. 72. Although this twenty-four-hour surveillance was discontinued on December 14, 1945, physical surveillance was conducted frequently at various times until September, 1947. [68/] CN Ex. 102; CN Ex. 103.

The most intrusive invasion of petitioner's rights

_____

68/ Also before 1947, a letter from Priscilla Hiss addressed to her son, Timothy Hobson, was intercepted and its contents read. CN Ex. 100A at p. 167. In approximately March, 1947, a letter from a Michael Greenberg addressed to petitioner regarding an application for employment with the United Nations was also intercepted, in a manner not revealed by the documents. CN Ex. 100B

occurred from December 13, 1945 until the Hisses moved from
Washington, D.C. to New York City on September 13, 1947. A
"technical surveillance," -- a wiretap -- was placed on the Hiss
telephone at their residence on P Street in Washington, D.C.
The logs of this surveillance constitute twenty-nine volumes
of FBI serials and are roughly 2,500 pages in length, in which
an enormous amount of information concerning the Hisses' personal lives, relationships with friends and associates, and
habits is recorded.

The wiretap was installed following FBI Director Hoover's
application to the Attorney General for authorization, [69] although
no written authorization appears in the documents released to
Hiss. The purpose of the application was to gather information
regarding Hiss' alleged contacts with Soviet espionage agents and
communists in government service, general allegations which had
been made by Elizabeth Bentley and Chambers.

As one would expect, the interception of every telephone

_____

[69]    Hoover's initial request was answered by a note requesting information on Hiss. CN Ex. 104 . Additional information
was furnished by letter dated November 30, 1945. CN Ex. 105 .

call made to or from the Hiss telephone gave the FBI a wealth

of information which could well have formed the source for much

of the testimony of the "intimate knowledge" details of the Hiss

family's life the government asserts as corroborating Chambers'

allegations. Govt. Memo. at 8. For instance, the FBI conducted

pre-trial interviews with Hiss' associates and friends who had

been identified by the Washington wiretap. CN Ex. 106    It

attempted to exploit its wiretap knowledge when agents contacted

the Carnegie Endowment in an effort to gather Hiss' "personal

material":

> Information was received from the Washington
> Field Office that Alger Hiss had two file
> drawers of personal material and three
> shelves of books sent from Carnegie Endowment
> in Washington, D.C., to the Carnegie Endowment
> in New York City. CN Ex. 107 at p. 73.

The source of the Washington Field Office's

"information" was the wiretap. CN Ex. 108    Although this

particular attempt to use wiretap information to develop evidence

for use at trial was unsuccessful, see CN Ex. 107, it

demonstrates that FBI agents were free to refer to and did

utilize wiretap information in the course of their investigation.

At the time of Hiss' trial, the interception of any
wire conversation and the use of the intercepted conversation or
its fruits, direct or indirect, in a criminal proceeding was for-
bidden by law. <u>Nardone v. United States [I]</u>, 302 U.S. 379 (1937);
<u>Nardone v. United States [II]</u>, 308 U.S. 338 (1939); Communications
Act of 1934, 47 U.S.C. §605 (1934).  Once unlawful wiretapping
is shown to have occurred, the burden is upon "the prosecution
to prove that the information so gained has not 'led,' directly
or indirectly, to the discovery of any of the evidence which
it introduces."  <u>United States v. Coplon</u>, 185 F.2d 629, 636 (2d
Cir. 1950), <u>cert</u>. <u>den</u>., 342 U.S. 920 (1952); <u>Alderman v. United
States</u>, 394 U.S. 165 (1969).  The prosecution never was put to
its task because it failed to disclose the fact of the wiretapping.

Even as to the Washington wiretap, the files released
to Hiss are incomplete.  Although it apparently was FBI practice
for the field office operating a wiretap to submit to FBI Head-
quarters periodic "justifications" for continuing electronic
surveillance, only one such justification was released.  Set
out on an FBI form, "FD-143", dated August 12, 1947, the Special
Agent in Charge (SAC) of Washington Field Office concluded that

"[i]n the past this [Hiss] surveillance has furnished valuable information." The SAC noted that "[d]uring the major portion of the past 60 days, subject and his family have been away from Washington," and the FBI's Assistant Director recommended:

> It is recommended that this technical surveillance be continued for an additional 60 days inasmuch as the Gregory Case is being presented to a Federal Grand Jury in New York City.

CN Ex. 109..

No other periodic reports were released although it is evident that they were prepared every sixty days. [70] Furthermore, there are extensive gaps in the surveillance logs released to Hiss which do not correlate with the Hisses' absences from Washington. Information obtained from the wiretap is reported

---

[70]    If this August 12, 1947 was the only report summarizing results and seeking further authorization, then the initial authorization was continued for almost 1-1/2 years without review. Indeed, it does not appear that these reports were sent to the Attorney General for any review at all, creating a situation where by virtue of an Attorney General approval of a wiretap, the FBI could claim authority to wiretap indefinitely. Thus, even if the Court accepts the government's argument that Attorney General authorization is sufficient to legitimate warrantless electronic surveillance in some cases, grave constitutional issues would be raised by the procedure that was followed here. See infra at pp. 122-3.

in summary memoranda reflecting conversations on days for which there are no log entries. CN Ex. 110.————————————— Since the released reports reflect no reluctance on the part of the FBI to utilize wiretap information to develop further leads and evidence for use in the criminal case, at a minimum further discovery regarding electronic surveillance is necessary.

The government dismissed petitioner's wiretap surveillance claim by asserting, without discussion, that national security surveillance where a foreign power is involved is lawful. Government's Memorandum in Opposition, dated March 21, 1980 at p. 20. The issue is far from settled, nor is it as simple as the government's one sentence response suggests. Whether warrantless surveillance with respect to activities of foreign powers or their agents is constitutional has not been passed on by the Supreme Court. <u>United States v. United States District Court</u>, 407 U.S. 297, 321-22 (1972). At the time of the Hiss trial, however, the Southern District for New York, (Goddard , J.) concluded that although wiretaps in another case had been installed pursuant to written authorization of the Attorney General, an authorization which if existing regarding

Hiss has not been disclosed to petitioner here:

> Such authorization did not clothe with
> legality the unlawful activities of the
> wire tappers nor detract at all from the
> interdiction of the Supreme Court on evidence
> secured by this type of investigation.

United States v. Coplon, 88 F.Supp. 921 (S.D.N.Y. 1950), aff'd.,

185 F.2d 629 (2d Cir. 1950), cert. den., 342 U.S. 920 (1952). [71]/

In Zweibon v. Mitchell, 516 F.2d 594 (D.C. Cir. 1975)

(en banc), cert. den., 425 U.S. 944 (1976), and Halperin v.

Kissinger, 606 F.2d 1192 (D.C. Cir. 1979), cert. granted, ____

U.S. ____, 48 U.S.L.W. 3750 (May 20, 1980), the Court of Appeals

for the District of Columbia discussed in detail the legality

of warrantless electronic surveillance which had been authorized,

at least when the surveillance initially was installed, by the

Attorney General. [72]/ After careful analysis, the court rejected in

---

[71]/ The Second Circuit did not reach precisely this issue on
the appeal, 185 F.2d at 640, but noted that it adhered to the
principle that "when the Government chose to prosecute an individual
for crime, it was not free to deny him the right to meet the
case against him by introducing relevant documents otherwise
privileged. . . .[T]he prosecution must decide whether the public
prejudice of allowing the crime to go unpunished was greater than
the disclosure of such 'state secrets' as might be relevant to
the defence." 185 F.2d at 638.

[72]/ The court found it "curious" that the Attorney General had
been delegated authority to approve warrantless wiretapping rather than
the Secretary of State in light of the government's assertion that
delicate and complex foreign policy matters were involved in the
decision to tap. Zweibon at 614.

Zweibon the assertion of presidential power to conduct warrantless wiretapping on a domestic target who was not acting in collaboration with a foreign power. Zweibon at 614. The court's opinion hinted that even when purported "agents" of a foreign power were the targets of the electronic surveillance, the same considerations which compelled the court to its holding would govern as well. Id. at 635-36, 639-41. Indeed, in a cogent, well-reasoned analysis, the Zweibon court reviewed the cases cited by the government in its brief in this case [73] and commented:

> Our reading of these opinions indicates that they simply overlooked the substantial body of case law, including Keith, which rejects the contention that the warrant requirement may be abrogated merely because the Government has a legitimate need to engage in certain activity. Instead of following the proper analysis of determining whether a warrant would frustrate the legitimate need of the Executive to acquire foreign intelligence information, these courts treated the need itself as determinative of the legality of warrantless surveillance. We find this methodology simply inconsistent with the spirit and holding of Keith and prior cases particularly given the substantial First and Fourth Amendment interests that may be infringed by unsupervised surveillance.

---

[73] Govt.'s March 21 brief at pp. 20-21. The court, of course, did not review the decision in United States v. Humphrey, 456 F.Supp. 51 (E.D. Va. 1978) since it had not been decided, but the analysis rejecting the holding is equally valid.

Zweibon, 516 F.2d at 640-41 [footnotes deleted; emphasis in original].

In _Halperin_, the court held as well that the "Fourth Amendment's reasonableness standard" governs even surveillance "genuinely based on national security concerns." _Halperin_, 606 F.2d at 1206. Remanding the case to the district court for further fact-finding necessary to a determination of for how long that standard was violated,[74] the court explained:

> The duration or conduct of the surveillance might well be deemed to have been unreasonable in view of the likely product of the wiretap, especially after the initial period.

_Id._ at 1206. The court in _Halperin_ teaches that even if no warrant is necessary to the institution of a wiretap, the surveillance still is subject to judicial review of its reasonableness. _Id._ at 1202.

_Halperin_ in particular demonstrates the need for further discovery in this case in order to determine the basis and extent of the surveillance insofar as to those facts the court may

---

74/     The court did agree with the finding of the district court "that at some point during the surveillance" the wiretap had developed into an unreasonable and unconstitutional dragnet. _Id._ at 1205-06.

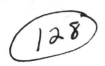

conclude have not been revealed fully. Whether a wiretap in fact was instituted for legitimate national security reasons is a decision the courts must make, and even if a "national surveillance" tap initially, it may become unreasonable./ later. Id. at 1204-06; see Smith v. Nixon, 606 F.2d 1183, 1188-89 (D.C. Cir. 1979). Here, the Washington wiretap was in use for almost two years. It is not apparent whether the asserted basis for its institution is accurate or merely a subterfuge; whether it was reviewed periodically by the Attorney General; or whether, in light of the information gathered and its duration, the wiretap was "reasonable" for the entire two years.

Nevertheless, based on the documents which were released, there is no question that this warrantless tap, if not unlawful because it was warrantless, was unreasonable and hence illegal. Hiss was not accused of current espionage activity when the tap was installed. It was of unlimited duration and apparently never reviewed periodically by the Attorney General. No "minimization" of interception occurred whatsoever - everything was recorded, from the Hisses' dinner plans to conversation with journalists. 75/

---

75/    In the August 12, 1947 document, the FBI describes as an example of "specific valuable information" obtained from the tap a May 31, 1947 conversation between the journalist Walter Lippmann and Hiss. Although "valuable," the FBI conceded that the conversation was "not important from an investigative standpoint." It is clear the wiretap was the equivalent of a general search having nothing to do with an espionage investigation. See CN Ex. 109.

Thus, the wiretap was unlawful even if a warrant was unnecessary.

If the court does not conclude on the basis of the information before it that the tap was unlawful, at a minimum a hearing and discovery is necessary. Even in <u>United States</u> v. <u>Butenko</u>, 494 F.2d 593 (3d Cir. 1974), <u>cert</u>. <u>den</u>., 419 U.S. 881 (1974), <u>affirming</u> 342 F.Supp. 928 (D.N.J. 1972), <u>on remand from</u> 394 U.S. 165 (1969), which involved an actual espionage case, a full, detailed hearing was held as to whether "there was electronic surveillance which violated [defendants'] rights" and the possible use to which unlawfully overheard conversations were put. <u>Id</u>., 394 U.S. at 186.

The Washington wiretap was operated until the very day Hiss and his family moved to New York City, on September 13, 1947. The documents released to Hiss from the New York field office are silent as to explicitly whether this surveillance, which according to the FBI was furnishing valuable information unobtainable "from other sources [or] by other means," CN Ex. 109, was reinstalled in New York City. Whether the appropriate records were purposely destroyed and and when is not known. 76/ However, there are strong reasons

_____

76/  In <u>United States</u> v. <u>Coplon</u>, <u>supra</u>, 185 F.2d at 637, the court noted that the New York field office destroyed wiretap documents as a matter of course <u>and</u> in anticipation of litigation.

to believe the surveillance continued after September, 1947.

First, it must be noted that the absence of explicit wiretap records from the New York office is not determinative of the question of whether Hiss' conversations were intercepted. In United States v. Coplon, supra, the FBI was compelled to disclose wiretap records documenting its electronic surveillance of Coplon who, like Hiss, was alleged to have been assisting Soviet agents. While the Washington FBI office produced logs and other detailed records of its wiretapping, as has happened in this case, the New York records had been destroyed for the most part by the FBI. Only by chance did some summaries exist, for it was the New York office's practice to destroy records of wiretapping. Id. at 637.

The disclosures of extensive wiretapping in Coplon caused widespread public outcry. See, e.g., New York Times of June 1, 4, and 9, 1949. The FBI responded in a curious fashion: electronic surveillance records were to be kept in special "secure" files and no longer filed with the regular "main" file in a subject. Maintained as "subfiles" and "charged out" from the main file, the records of wiretaps were effectively isolated from the rest of a file. References to the source of information were disguised to prevent wide-spread knowledge even with the Bureau of wiretapping. It appears that these types of "charge-outs" and subfiles were kept in New York regarding the Hiss case. See, Deposition of Special Agent Martin Wood, taken in Hiss v. Department of Justice, 76 Civ. 4672 (S.D.N.Y.), on May 19, 1980, at pp. 108, 111-116.

Subfiles "A" through "D" of the Hiss-Chambers Perjury file # 65-14920, of the New York field office, were destroyed at some unknown time. The New York office's Assistant Director's "personal" file on the case, Subfile 65-14920-EJC, apparently was destroyed as well. So, too, the Alger Hiss "main file," 101-141, and Whittaker Chambers main file, 65-6766, were destroyed. See Defendant Federal Bureau of Investigation Answers and Objections to Plaintiffs' Interrogatories (Second Set) in Hiss v. Department of Justice, supra, dated July 20, 1979, at pp. 7-8. Petitioner believes that in these destroyed files the missing wiretap records may have been filed. The need for discovery to resolve the matter is apparent. 77/

77/ Although the files allegedly have been destroyed, through discovery, agents involved in the case and other FBI personnel could be deposed. Moreover, there are files concerning destroyed surveillance records called "Destruction of Files" files which the FBI has refused to produce in the FOIA case which might shed light on the matter.

Despite this absence of explicit New York wiretap
records, there is no reason to expect that the FBI's electronic surveillance of Hiss ended abruptly when he moved from
Washington.  The "Gregory case" grand jury presentation,
which was the basis upon which the Assistant Director recommended continuance of the tap in August, 1947, was continuing;
Hiss in fact appeared before the grand jury in March, 1948.
R. 206.

The investigation of Hiss intensified after his
move to New York.  Other key figures in Chambers' allegations
were subjected to wiretaps and warrantless entries: two unidentified persons were tapped, CN Ex.111; another's residence entered and documents photographed, CN Ex.112.  The Hiss
1936-7 summer residence, the landlord of which was a defense
witness at the first trial, was subjected to a mail cover and
toll call checks in September, 1949, CN Ex.113.  Hence, it is
not likely that the FBI would fail to have used the technique
which gathered information which otherwise could not be obtained, a wiretap.  See CN Ex. 109.

Several entries in released documents also suggest
wiretapping of Hiss.  In a report dated October 29, 1949, the
source of information is described as "gathered from monitory

telephone contacts of Alger Hiss." CN Ex. 114. A

March 9, 1948 memorandum notes that "confidential informant

[deleted] who is in a position to report upon Collins' activ-

ities, advised that Collins is in frequent contact with Alger

Hiss." CN Ex. 115.          The "confidential informant" may

well have been a wiretap.[78/]    And, Special Agent Wood testi-

field that an October 8, 1948 memorandum, CN Ex. 116, "appears to" reflect

a technical surveillance of a toll call to Alger Hiss.

Deposition of Wood, supra at 108-9.

---

78/ Other records released pursuant to Hiss' FOIA request
contain references, the sources of which, because of deletions, cannot be determined. Also, the FBI deliberately
adopted a style of reporting in order to disguise the source
and method of collection of information. See, Deposition of
Agent Wood, supra.

In addition to the documents suggesting post-September, 1947 wiretaps, there is substantial evidence suggesting other intrusive techniques were employed in the investigation leading up to and during the Hiss prosecution, both by the FBI and by the prosecutors themselves.

As described before, "mail covers" on Hiss' correspondence were instituted through 1947. Between May and October, 1950, "mail tracings", which the FBI has described as "return addressed information found on first-class mail envelopes" were made in connection with the Hiss prosecution. See, FBI Answers and Objections to Plaintiffs' Interrogatories, Third Set at 12-12a, Hiss v. Department of Justice, supra.

Since there has been no discovery in this matter, it is impossible to determine the nature and parameters of the mail covers and mail tracings revealed by the documents. While in general mail covers have been found to be constitutional, United States v. Choate, 576 F.2d 165, (9th Cir.), cert denied, 439 U.S. 953 (1978 ), the Hiss covers and tracings may have been in violation of the applicable postal regulations and hence illegal. Id. at 171. Moreover, if the mail covers had resulted in the delay of mail delivery, there would have been an invasion of Hiss' "expectation of privacy," Katz v. United States, 389 U.S. 347 (1967), for it is not reasonable to expect that information appearing on

an envelope would be seized and delayed in delivery.  See
Lustiger v. United States, 386 F.2d 132, (9th Cir. 1967), cert.
denied 390 U.S. 957 (1968); United States v. Choate, supra,
Hufstedler, J., dissenting at 183 et seq.

The warrantless interception of the content of mail
sent to or from Hiss or his attorneys was and still is unlawful.
United States v. Van Leeuwen, 397 U.S. 249 (1970); Ex Parte
Jackson, 96 U.S. 877 (1878).  That Hiss was subject to such
interceptions appears to be the case.  In 1950, a letter addressed to Hiss was given prosecutor Murphy by the Post Office.
Although it is not explained how the Post Office obtained the
letter, the documents reflect that the prosecutors and the FBI
decided not to inform the Justice Department about the letter.
The FBI also was concerned that FBI reports of an investigation
conducted to learn the identity of the writer might arouse
suspicion at the Justice Department as to the origin of the letter.
These highly questionable concerns and procedures suggest that
the letter was intercepted unlawfully and that fact was deliberately hidden from even the prosecutors' superiors.  CN Ex.
117.

Also appearing in the files is a one-page letter,
dated August 6, 1950, the author of which was not revealed to

Hiss in the released documents, which was addressed to "Alger Hiss, 22 East 8th Street, New York, New York." Again, how this letter came into the possession of the FBI has not been revealed by the government. CN Ex. 118.

Letters were not the only documents intercepted. The FBI intercepted a telegram from David Sherman to the Hiss attorneys. How this domestic communication was obtained again is not evidenced from the documents. CN Ex. 119.

Post-trial, while Hiss' attorneys were preparing their motion for a new trial, correspondence to them regarding the case also was intercepted. Two letters from Paul Willert, dated in December, 1951, one of which was addressed to Hiss' lawyer, Cross, were sent from Washington to the New York field office. CN Ex. 120. Although the letter was not sent to Hiss, there nevertheless is a violation of Hiss' fundamental right to the assistance of counsel.

Given the current state of the record with regard to these interceptions, petitioner concedes that further discovery and a hearing may be necessary to resolve whether there has been a violation sufficient to warrant reversal of the conviction. However, petitioner's assertions that he was subject to unlawful surveillance are sound and hence the required discovery should go forward. See Point IX, infra.

POINT IX

PETITIONER IS ENTITLED TO
DISCOVERY AND AN EVIDENTIARY
HEARING IF THE COURT DOES
NOT GRANT THE PETITION ON
THE PAPERS.

The allegations in the instant petition go to the heart of Hiss' right to a fair trial, and if proven true, create severe doubt as to his guilt. Granting of this writ would not "thwart justice" as the government contends, Govt. Memo at 301, but is demanded by justice. Alternatively, if this court does not grant the petition on the record before it, petitioner has met the "rather low" threshold showing necessary to entitle him to an evidentiary hearing, and such a hearing should be ordered. United States v. Keogh, 391 F.2d 138, 142 (2d Cir. 1968).

The general rule regarding hearings on coram nobis petitions is that "[o]nly where the files and records show con-clusively that a petitioner is entitled to no relief can a hear-ing be denied." Waller v. United States, 432 F.2d 560, 561 (5th Cir. 1970), United States v. Liska, 409 F.Supp. 1405, 1406 (E.D. Wisc. 1976). 79/

---

79/ Further guidance on this issue can be obtained by referring
(Fn. Cont'd)

In <u>Lujan</u> v. <u>United States</u>, the Fifth Circuit Court of Appeals warned that although evidentiary hearings in <u>coram nobis</u> proceedings, as in other post-conviction motions, are not to be automatically granted,

> [h]earings to consider attacks on the constitutionality of a criminal conviction are not to be nonchalantly denied. On the contrary, courts have a solemn duty to ferret the allegations for symptoms of constitutional infirmities. The petition and documents before us convince us that Lujan's claims are neither fatuous nor groundless. It is only where the files and records show that a petitioner is entitled to no relief that a hearing can be denied.

424 F.2d 1053, 1055 (5th Cir. 1970), <u>cert. denied after remand</u>, 400 U.S. 997 (1971).

Thus, it is well established that a hearing on a

---

<u>79/</u> (Fn. Cont'd)

to proceedings brought pursuant to 18 U.S.C. §2255. The same standards are used in determining the necessity of a hearing in both <u>coram nobis</u> and §2255 proceedings. <u>Owensby</u> v. <u>United States</u>, 353, F.2d 412, 417 (10th Cir.), <u>cert. denied</u>, 383 U.S. 962 (1965). 28 U.S.C. §2255 requires a prompt hearing unless the record conclusively shows no relief is warranted. <u>See, e.g.</u>, <u>Sanders</u> v. <u>United States</u>, 373 U.S. 1, pp. 20-23 (1963); <u>Fontaine</u> v. <u>United States</u>, 411 U.S. 213, 215 (1973); <u>United States</u> v. <u>Miranda</u>, 437 F.2d 1255, 1257 (2d Cir. 1971), <u>cert. denied</u>, 409 U.S. 874 (1972); <u>Kyle</u> v. <u>United States</u>, 297 F.2d 507, 511 (2d Cir. 1961), <u>cert. denied after remand</u>, 377 U.S. 909; <u>United States</u> v. <u>Rutkin</u>, 212 F.2d 641, 644 (3rd Cir. 1954).

coram nobis petition is required when, as in the instant case,
the petition alleges facts supporting a claim of deprivation of
a constitutional right, is accompanied by supporting affidavits
and documentary proof, and issue has been joined as to some
material fact. United States v. Tribote, 297 F.2d 598, 600
(2d Cir. 1961); Lujan v. United States, supra, 424 F.2d 1053,
1055. See, United States v. Keogh, 391 F.2d 138, 149 (2d Cir.
1968); Morgan v. United States, 396 F.2d 110, 115 (2d Cir. 1968);
United States v. Forlano, 319 F.2d 617 (2d Cir. 1965); United
States v. Platner, 330 F.2d 271, 273 (2d Cir. 1964); United
States v. Capsopa, 260 F.2d 566, 568 (2d Cir. 1958) (all remanding coram nobis petitions with directions to hold evidentiary
hearings). See also, Taylor v. United States, 487 F.2d 307, 308
(2d Cir. 1973); Reagor v. United States, 488 F.2d 515 (5th Cir.
1973); Lindhorst v. United States, 585 F.2d 361 (8th Cir. 1978)
(all remanding motions under 28 U.S.C. §2255 with directions to
hold evidentiary hearings).

The Second Circuit has noted that strong policy considerations favor granting an evidentiary hearing on such petitions:

There is an understandable tendency to try to

avoid hearings in <u>coram</u> <u>nobis</u> proceedings
where it appears that there is little merit
in the petition, and that a hearing might
well be of no avail to the petitioner.
With the crowded dockets and delay caused
by a heavy judicial workload, a diligent
judge, out of concern for our goal of
speedy justice, may well overlook the fact
that a particular application alleges
sufficient particulars to require a hearing.
Our concern for efficiency must not out-
weigh our concern for individuals' rights.
We cannot refuse a hearing because hearings
generally show that there is no real basis
for relief, or even because it is improbable
that a prisoner can prove his case. Once
we embark upon shortcuts by creating a
category of the 'obviously guilty' whose
rights are denied, we run the risk that the
circle of the unprotected will grow.

<u>United States</u> v. <u>Tribote</u>, 297 F.2d 598, 603 (2d Cir. 1961)

(Kaufman J. reversing district court and remanding <u>coram</u> <u>nobis</u>

petition with instructions to hold evidentiary hearing. 80/

---

80/ Tribote's petition alleged that he had been denied assistance
of counsel at sentencing. The government contended that, although
the record was silent as to the presence of counsel when sentence
was imposed, waiver of the right to counsel could be inferred from
surrounding events, <u>e.g.</u>, counsel was present, according to the
record, when petitioner entered his plea of guilty and at a collo-
quy prior to sentencing, and petitioner was familiar with state
criminal proceedings. The Court of Appeals found that, assuming
petitioner's allegations to be true, he had established a <u>prima
facie</u> case, that the inference of waiver urged by the government

(Fn. Cont'd)

See also, United States v. Capsopa, 260 F.2d 566

(2d Cir. 1958) (Moore, J.):

> In final analysis, both appellant and the
> government should be better satisfied after
> a hearing.  If he fails, appellant will at
> least know that the courts have endeavored
> to give him the protection which the consti-
> tution affords.  The government, in turn,
> should be desirous of knowing that appel-
> lant's potential life imprisonment is founded
> upon a solid basis of fact.  If not so based,
> it should be the first to urge that the con-
> viction be modified accordingly.

Id.at 568. 81/

---

80/ (Fn. Cont'd)

was not inescapable, that the files and records of the case did not
conclusively show petitioner was entitled to no relief and therefore controverted issues of fact were presented which required a
hearing.  Id. at 602-603.

81/ The coram nobis petitioner in Capsopa alleged that he had
pleaded guilty to a narcotics violation without assistance of counsel.  The government filed the affidavit of an attorney who alleged
that he had represented petitioner at the criminal proceeding.  The
petitioner requested an evidentiary hearing in order to cross-
examine the trial attorney.  260 F.2d at 568.  The Court of Appeals
reversed the district court and remanded with instructions to hold
a hearing.

The leading Second Circuit decision discussing coram nobis proceedings, United States v. Keogh, supra, warrants some discussion here. Keogh bears some resemblance to this case; it involved an FBI document that was arguably exculpatory and was discovered by the petitioner after his sentence had been served.

Keogh, a former New York State judge, had been convicted of conspiracy to obstruct justice, specifically, of having accepted bribes to "fix" cases. The bribe money was allegedly relayed to Keogh through his personal physician and friend, Erdman. Erdman (also under indictment) and the instigator of the bribe, Moore, were the chief prosecution witnesses at the trial.

At Keogh's post-conviction disbarment proceeding, his attorney came into possession of an FBI report showing that there had been deposits into Erdman's bank account, approximately totaling the amount of the bribes, which could not be accounted for by Erdman's accountant. Keogh moved for coram nobis relief, based on this newly discovered evidence, which he argued was exculpatory since it showed that Erdman may very well have never given the money to Keogh, and should have been disclosed by the prosecution. The petition was dismissed without a hearing. 271 F.Supp. 1002 (S.D.N.Y. 1967, Weinfeld, J.)

On appeal, in a decision written by Judge Friendly, the matter was reversed in part and remanded for a hearing. 391 F.2d 138 (2d Cir. 1968). The court noted that the threshold showing necessary to entitle a _coram nobis_ petitioner to an evidentiary hearing is "rather low". _Id._ at 142. Because Keogh's allegations concerning the FBI report met this threshold, a hearing was ordered to determine the source of the deposits to Erdman's account and the prosecution's motivation, if any, for withholding the FBI report at trial, as well as to pursue "other lines of inquiry...." _Id._ at 149. [82]

The later history of Keogh's unsuccessful attempt to be vindicated is also instructive. After Judge Weinfeld once again dismissed the petition, 289 F.Supp. 265 (S.D.N.Y. 1969), and the Second Circuit affirmed the dismissal with leave to file a new petition based on new evidence discovered during the origi-

---

[82] The hearing on remand lasted 7 days, during which 19 witnesses were called (including Erdman and his wife, bank officers, and Department of Justice officials) and scores of exhibits were received in evidence (including bank records and at least one additional FBI report). 289 F.Supp. at 265-66.

nal _coram_ _nobis_ proceedings, 417 F.2d 885 (2d Cir. 1969), a second petition was filed. Now the government indicated that
"extensive preliminary investigation and a full evidentiary hearing" would be necessary on the second petition, but Keogh's
attorney urged the Court to decide the matter on the papers.
The Court did so and denied the petition. The Second Circuit
once again affirmed, 440 F.2d 737 (2d Cir.), _cert._ _denied_, 404
U.S. 941 (1971). The Court expressed "some regret that an evidentiary hearing was not held" and noted that "the further proceedings took a course quite different from what we had en-
visioned. Although we had not directed an evidentiary hearing
in so many words, our opinion rather clearly contemplated one."
_Id_. at 739, 740.

In the instant case, as in _Keogh_ and _Lujan_, the _coram_
_nobis_ petition sets forth specific documented allegations, which,
if true, might well entitle petitioner to relief. Clearly, petitioner's claims are neither "fatuous", nor "groundless." Thus,
the "courts have a solemn duty to ferret the allegations for
symptoms of constitutional infirmity." _Lujan_, _supra_, 424 F.2d
at 1055.

Although the Court in _Lujan_ was discussing the limits

of discretion in granting an evidentiary hearing on a *coram nobis* proceeding, the same limits are applicable to the issue of discovery. When the right to a hearing is fairly well made out, there is a duty to grant the petitioner access to needed information as a component of the Court's duty to grant a full hearing. Since the integrity of the judicial system is one of the policy considerations underlying *coram nobis*, the Court must aid petitioner in carrying the burden of proving his allegations of fundamental error by permitting discovery of facts, many of which may lie peculiarly within the province of the prosecution and its investigatory arm.

Few cases have been decided specifically on the issue of discovery in *coram nobis* proceedings, but decisions discussing *habeas corpus* applications and motions to vacate sentence, 28 U.S.C. §2255, are instructive. In *Harris* v. *Nelson*, 394 U.S. 286 (1969), the United States Supreme Court held that:

> [W]here specific allegations before the
> court show reason to believe that the
> petitioner may, if the facts are fully
> developed, be able to demonstrate that
> he is...entitled to relief, it is the
> duty of the court to provide the neces-
> sary facilities and procedures for an
> adequate inquiry.

*Id.* at 300.

Although <u>habeas</u> proceedings are technically civil, the
Court indicated that the Rules of Civil Procedure are not
directly applicable to them. However, pursuant to the All Writs
Act, 28 U.S.C. §1651,[83] courts can fashion discovery procedures
when needed for an "adequate inquiry" by analogy to the civil
or criminal rules or otherwise in accordance with the "usages
and principles of law." <u>Id</u>. at 300. More than a power, fashion-
ing discovery procedures is a duty when petitioner has alleged
facts which, if established, may entitle him to relief. <u>Id</u>.

The principles enunciated in <u>Harris</u> have also been
applied to discovery in proceedings brought pursuant to 28 U.S.C.
§2255:

> A party may invoke the processes of dis-
> covery available under the Federal Rules
> of Criminal Procedure or the Federal
> Rules of Civil Procedure or elsewhere in
> the usages and principles of law if, and
> to the extent that, the judge in the ex-
> ercise of his discretion and for good
> cause shown grants leave to do so, but
> not otherwise.

Rule 6(a), Rules Governing §2255 Proceedings, 28 U.S.C.A. Foll.

---

[83] The Supreme Court has also held that the jurisdictional
authority for <u>coram</u> <u>nobis</u> actions derives from this same statute.
<u>United States</u> v. <u>Morgan</u>, 346 U.S. 502 (1954).

§2255 (Supp. 1979). In accord with this rule, the practice in the Second Circuit has been to allow discovery as an aid to the preparation of a hearing in <u>coram</u> <u>nobis</u> proceedings. Discovery was ordered in connection with the hearing on remand in <u>United States</u> v. <u>Keogh</u>, <u>supra</u>, 417 F.2d 885 at 888-89. <u>See</u>, docket sheet, CN Ex.121 at 9, 10.

As for the scope of discovery allowed, the Keogh proceedings show that it should be broad.[84]

On appeal from denial of the first <u>Keogh</u> petition, the Court of Appeals found that the proceedings below, which had been limited in scope by the district court, had not developed a sufficient evidentiary record. Accordingly, the Court agreed to "leave open for exploration at a new proceeding the issue whether the evidence developed by the Government...or to which petitioner would have been led by disclosure of the February 26, 1976 report constitutes a sufficient basis for issuance of the writ...." 417 F.2d at 889-90. Keogh based his second <u>coram</u>

---

[84] Assessment of the particular discovery needs of petitioner in this action must await the determination of his right to discovery.

nobis petition, in part, on an additional FBI report which had been discovered in the first _coram nobis_ proceeding. _United States_ v. _Keogh_, 316 F.Supp. 921 (S.D.N.Y. 1970). The docket sheet, CN Ex.121, page 12, reflects that petitioner was granted additional discovery in conjunction with this second proceeding.

Although the cases do not clearly indicate whether [85]
_coram nobis_ is civil in nature or criminal, the Supreme Court,

---

[85] When the Supreme Court affirmed the viability of the proceeding in _United States_ v. _Morgan_, 346 U.S. 502 (1954), it stated in a footnote that _coram nobis_ "is a step in the criminal case and not, like _habeas corpus_, where relief is sought in a separate case and record, the beginning of a separate civil proceeding." 346 U.S. 502 at 505, fn. 4. However, the same footnote went on to characterize _coram nobis_ as "of the same general character as one under 28 U.S.C. §2255," which is a civil proceeding. _Id._ _Morgan_ thus preserves the question whether _coram nobis_ proceedings are civil or criminal. The answer probably is that _coram nobis_ is a hybrid action, neither strictly civil nor strictly criminal. _United States_ v. _Tyler_, 413 F.Supp. 1403, 1404-05 (M.D. Fla. 1976).

When it comes to procedures, however, the writ of error _coram nobis_ is generally regarded by both federal and state courts as essentially civil in nature. _See_, _United States_ v. _Keogh_, 391 F.2d at 140; _Neely_ v. _United States_, 546 F.2d 1059, 1066 (3rd Cir. 1976); _Bruno_ v. _United States_, 180 F.2d 393, 395 (D.C. Cir. 1950); _United States_ v. _Tyler_, 413 F.Supp. 1403, 1404-05; _Ex parte Wilson_, 275 Ala. 439, 155 So.2d 611, 612 (1963); _Ex parte Allison_, 42 Ala. 507, 169 So.2d 436 (1964); _People_ v. _Kemnetz_, 296 Ill. App. 119, 15 N.E.2d 883 (1938); _State ex rel Emmert_ v. _Gentry_, 223 Ind. 535, 62 N.E.2d 860, 861 (1945); _State_ v. _Miller_, 161 Kan.

(Fn. Cont'd)

in <u>Harris</u>, suggests that the denomination of an action as "civil"
or "criminal" is not determinative of the procedure to use in
discovery, and authorizes the courts to use their discretion to
decide and use such procedures of inquiry as are appropriate.
Furthermore, the policy reasons favoring limited discovery in
criminal cases are notably absent in <u>coram</u> <u>nobis</u> proceedings.
The policy reasons for the criminal law's peculiarly narrow

---

<u>85</u>/ (Fn. Cont'd)

210, 166 F.2d 680, 683 (1946), <u>cert</u>. <u>denied</u>, 329 U.S. 749; <u>Com-</u>
<u>monwealth</u> v. <u>Sirles</u>, 267 S.W.2d 66 (Ky. 1953); <u>Duncan</u> v. <u>Robbins</u>,
159 Me. 339, 193 A.2d 362, 364 (Me. 1963); <u>State</u> v. <u>Smith</u>, 324
S.W.2d 707 (Mo. 1959); <u>Hawk</u> v. <u>State</u>, 151 Neb. 717, 39 N.W.2d
561, 565 (Neb. 1949), <u>cert</u>. <u>denied</u>, 339 U.S. 923; <u>Dobie</u> v. <u>Com-</u>
<u>monwealth</u>, 198 Va. 762, 96 S.E.2d 747, 752 (Va. 1957).

The court in <u>Neely</u> v. <u>United States</u>, <u>supra</u>, noted that a
<u>coram</u> <u>nobis</u> proceeding "bears no resemblance to a criminal pro-
ceeding. The government is the defendant, not the initiating
party; the rights asserted are private, not public. An examination of the Federal Rules of Criminal Procedure reveals how irrelevant they are to this action. We find this case most analo-
gous to a proceeding under 28 U.S.C. §2255 which, though it may
seek relief from a prior criminal judgment, is authoritatively
recognized as civil in nature." 546 F.2d at 1066.

In the final analysis, since <u>coram</u> <u>nobis</u> is neither strictly criminal nor strictly civil, courts probably have discretion
to apply either the civil or the criminal rules of procedure, as
is the rule in motions to vacate sentence, 28 U.S.C. §2255, and
in <u>habeas</u> <u>corpus</u> proceedings.

discovery include: (1) defendant's knowledge of the essentials of the prosecution's case would result in perjury and manufactured evidence, (2) heretofore confidential witnesses would be subject to intimidation, and (3) defendant's insulation from reciprocal discovery because of the Fifth Amendment protection would give defendant an undesirable advantage. Note, "Developments in the Law-Discovery", 74 Harv. L. Rev. 940, 1052 (1961). See also, Carter, J. "Pretrial Suggestions for Section 2255 Cases", 32 F.R.D. 391, 396 (1963), where the author, a federal judge, notes:

> Since the cases under §2255 have made vulnerable every past criminal judgment...where the court is required to grant a hearing, this hearing should be as broad in scope as possible.

In the final analysis, the nature of the instant case is probably the strongest argument for granting discovery and an evidentiary hearing:  petitioner has made well-documented allegations that fundamental constitutional errors were committed in order to obtain his conviction. Although three decades have passed since the trial, the controversy surrounding petitioner's conviction has never left the public eye. Thus, it is not only petitioner's "good name" which is sought to be redressed in this proceeding, but that of the convicting court as well. The interests of petitioner and of the court in a full hearing of the

issues are allied.

POINT X

THE TOTAL EFFECT OF THE CONSTITUTIONAL
VIOLATIONS PREVENTED PETITIONER FROM
OBTAINING A FAIR AND IMPARTIAL TRIAL.

Each of the errors discussed in Points I - IX above constitutes a sufficient basis for the granting of the writ prayed for.  Each, standing alone, denied petitioner the fair trial to which he was entitled under the Constitution.

But this Court will understand that we have not merely several separate and distinct violations; all of these errors occurred in a single close case, in an overheated public atmosphere, and their cumulative effect must be considered by the Court.  United States v. Semensohn, 421 F.2d 1206 (2d Cir. 1970); United States v. Guglielmini, 384 F.2d 602 (2d Cir. 1967), cert. den., 400 U.S. 820 (1970); United States v. Bledsoe, 531 F.2d 888 (8th Cir. 1976).  Moreover, the significance of these newly discovered errors should be viewed as themselves cumulative to the errors known to the appellate court at the time of the appeal from Hiss' trial.  Viewing the constitutional violations in sum, then, there is no doubt that petitioner was severely prejudiced and prevented from obtaining a fair trial.

## CONCLUSION

The petition for a writ of error _coram_ _nobis_ should be granted, and the verdict of guilty entered against petitioner should be vacated.

In the alternative, an evidentiary hearing should be directed on petitioner's application for a writ and appropriate discovery permitted in aid of such a hearing.

Respectfully submitted,

RABINOWITZ, BOUDIN, STANDARD,
    KRINSKY & LIEBERMAN
30 East 42nd Street
New York, N. Y. 10017
(212) 697-8640

Attorneys for Petitioner

Of Counsel:

Victor Rabinowitz
Gordon J. Johnson
Ellen J. Winner
James M. Pruitt (Applicant for Admission to
           the New York Bar)
Susan Davis (Third Year Law Student)

Dated:  July 8, 1980

       New York, N. Y.

*APPENDIX*

A.  The Rugs

       The second point raised by the government is that of
the rugs.  This matter was never really settled at trial as
the prosecution and the defense offered conflicting testimony.
Examination of the material submitted since the trial as
a result of the FOIA proceeding, including statements by
Chambers that should have been given to Hiss at trial, have
demonstrated that Chambers' story underwent considerable
revision from the time he first mentioned the rugs to the
time he testified, and that, buried away in FBI files and
grand jury testimony, there was still further evidence to cast
doubt upon the government's story.

       Hiss was the first person to mention the rugs.  He
told the HUAC in August, 1948 that Chambers had showed up
at his door one day with a rug he claimed to have received
from a wealthy patron.  Hiss said he accepted it as "payment
on account" for monies owed to him by Chambers.  Report of
Proceedings, House Committee on Unamerican Activities, Vol.
6, page 282.

       Chambers contended at the trial that the rug was a
gift to Hiss from the Communist Party.  He testified that four
rugs were purchased in December, 1936 as gifts for his associates

in the Party, R. 254, 263, namely, Wadleigh, Silverman, White and Hiss. He stated that Hiss received his rug behind a restaurant located on the outskirts of Washington and that Silverman had driven Chambers to the restaurant with the rug in his car to help make the delivery. R. 255. In support of Chambers' testimony, the government placed in evidence a sales slip and delivery receipt and a cancelled check, all allegedly indicating that the rugs were purchased by Chambers' friend, Meyer Schapiro, at a cost of $200 each, R. 719, 725. _/

Chambers had first mentioned the rugs to the Bureau on December 8, 1948. His story then was quite different. In a signed statement he said that three rugs were purchased after he had made inquiries of a rug dealer in New York and that the rugs were sent directly from the dealer to Silverman's house. CN Ex. 122. Chambers said that the rugs were for Silverman, White and Hiss. There was no reference to Meyer Schapiro nor to Wadleigh in connection with the transaction.

This statement was one of those called for by the defense at the first trial. The court directed <u>in camera</u>

---

_/ The cost, as originally set forth in the statement, was $600 for each rug; this figure was crossed out and $200 substituted.

inspection and advised counsel that there was nothing inconsistent between Chambers' testimony and the statement. This incident is an excellent example of the importance of the rule in the Jencks case (Jencks v. United States, 363 U.S. 656 (1957)) and of the decision in United States v. Alderman, 394 U.S. 165 (1969); in both, the Court pointed out that a trial judge, reading a document in camera, is in no position to determine its significance. In this case, the significance of the document is clear since it was inconsistent with Chambers' testimony -- had it been produced, Chambers' trial testimony would not have seemed so convincing.

A few days after Chambers' 1948 interview with the FBI, Wadleigh informed the FBI that in 1937 or 1938 he had received a rug from Chambers as a New Year's gift, CN Ex. 123, and, a few days later, he signed a statement saying that he received the gift in 1936-37, that it was worth about $200 or $300, and was given to him by "the authorities in Moscow." CN Ex. 123A.

Two weeks later, Chambers' story began to change to accommodate itself to Wadleigh's testimony. The "three rugs" now became "four costly rugs," and Wadleigh was added to the list of recipients. CN Ex. 124. In February, 1949, Chambers' story had been still further developed./ The cost of the rugs had changed from $200 for each of three rugs, to $1,000 for all four. Moreover, Dr. Schapiro made his first appearance in the story as the purchaser of the rugs and the one who accepted delivery in New York and who forwarded the rugs to Silverman in Washington (CN Ex. 125.

Thus, by the time Chambers testified at the trial, his original recollection had been changed as to the number of rugs purchased, their price, the recipients, the manner of their purchase and the manner of their delivery.

Other information received as a result of the FOIA proceedings shed additional light on the matter. The FBI, on a number of occasions, interviewed Florence Thompkins, a former maid of Silverman. She originally recalled the delivery of only three rugs, one of which was to go to White. CN Ex. 126. In a later interview, she changed her testimony to name Hiss as the intended recipient of the third rug. Id. In still a third statement, two weeks before the first trial, she repeated her recollection that there were only three rugs, but could not recall a conversation to indicate that Hiss was to get the third rug. CN Ex. 127.

An FBI document supplied to petitioner summarizes Silverman's grand jury testimony on December 15th, the date of the indictment. His description of his relations with Chambers was surprisingly similar to that of Hiss. Like Hiss, he said he met Chambers in the thirties when Chambers came to his office claiming to be a free-lance writer. Like Hiss, he recalled meeting Chambers several times for lunch when Chambers borrowed small sums of money from him. He also said that Chambers "paid off" this debt with two rugs. CN Ex. 128.

Silverman further testified that actually four rugs were delivered to his house. He gave one of them to Harry Dexter White, an old friend; retained one; and returned the other two to Chambers at a later date. He never delivered any rug to Hiss. Id.

Defense files show efforts to secure the testimony of Silverman, but they were unsuccessful. Bernard Jaffee, Silverman's lawyer, would not permit Hiss' lawyers to interview Silverman. He said that Silverman's emotional condition by that time had so deteriorated that he would not make a satisfactory witness. CN Ex. 129.

We have here no overwhelming evidence of the guilt of Hiss, but rather much evidence of the unreliability of Chambers' trial testimony. There is unclarity as to whether there were three rugs or four, and a conflict of testimony as to the reason for delivery of the rugs. The method of both purchase and delivery of the rugs is likewise uncertain, as is their value.

B.  The $400 Loan

One of the elements of circumstantial evidence

upon which the government relied to establish the second

count of the indictment, namely, that Hiss and Chambers

had met after January 1, 1937, was a transaction alleged

to have occurred in November of that year.  Chambers testi-

fied that, in preparation for his break with the Party, he

had wanted to buy a car in the latter part of 1937 and needed

$400 for that purpose.  He asked Hiss for a loan and Hiss

agreed.  R. 263-64, 547-8, 626-27.  The trial testimony

shows that Chambers did buy a car in November, 1937 and

that $400 was withdrawn from the Hiss checking account a

few days before the purchase.  This is slim evidence on

which to base a criminal charge.  It certainly is not "over-

whelming corroboration" of guilt.

At trial the Hisses explained the withdrawal,

stating that it was to facilitate the purchase of furni-

ture for a new house they were renting at Volta Place,

Washington.*/    R. 1880, 1983-86, 2044-46, 2326, 2336-40,

2387-96.  The government brief finds this explanation un-

convincing because it claims that the trial record shows

---

*/  The government brief erroneously states that the
Hisses purchased the Volta Place house.  Govt. Memo. p. 23.
In fact, they only rented it.

-A-7-

that the Hisses had not yet closed the real estate transaction at the time of the withdrawal and that the Hisses
maintained checking and charge accounts and would not need
to make cash purchases of furniture. Govt. Memo. p. 23.

Hiss testified that his negotiations with the
real estate agent with whom the Volta Place house had been
listed began in early November and that by the time of the
$400 withdrawal on November 17th, he had a commitment from
the agent, satisfactory to him, that the deal would be closed
shortly. R. 1984-1986. In fact, the lease was signed on December 2nd, having been prepared a few days before. Govt. Memo. p. 69.

The government argument that Mrs. Hiss had charge
accounts at various stores and that there was no reason for
cash purchases hardly rises to the level of requiring a response. Mrs. Hiss testified that she often bought furniture
in stores in which she did not have charge accounts. All
of us make cash purchases, even with the ubiquity of checking
accounts and charge accounts, and such practice can hardly
be cited as evidence of conduct so irrational as to defy
belief.

The fact is that the Hisses had very little money and the suggestion that they would have loaned Chambers, who was constantly borrowing small sums from his friends and never repaying them, a sum as large as $400 was most unlikely. The Hisses had just purchased an automobile on the installment plan; only a few weeks later they had to borrow $300 from the bank. A loan of $400 to Chambers in these circumstances is on its face most improbable.

At the trial the defendant argued that Chambers' story about the loan was a fabrication inspired by his knowledge that the Hisses had, in mid-November, withdrawn $400 from their bank account. Hiss may have been unable at the trial to establish this charge to the satisfaction of the jury; however, information received from the FOIA proceeding makes possible a reconstruction of the circumstances which raises substantial doubt as to the validity of Chambers' story.

During pre-trial depositions of the Baltimore libel suit, Chambers was questioned at some length regarding the purchase of a 1937 Ford. He did not mention any loan from Hiss. Esther Chambers was questioned in the same proceeding on the same subject. She said that Chambers' mother had "probably" loaned the money to the Chambers to make the purchase of the car possible. Balt. Depos. Trans., pp. 423-426; 674-76.

We now know that from January 4th to mid-April, 1949 Chambers met with FBI agents almost daily for the purpose of preparing his testimony. On January 18, during these interviews, the New York field office of the FBI requested the Washington field office to check Alger Hiss' bank account in Washington to see if it reflected any transfer of funds to New York. CN Ex. 130. The Washington office responded that Alger Hiss maintained a savings account at Riggs National Bank but that bank officials were "reluctant to furnish records of the account without a subpoena." CN Ex. 131. We have no information as to whether the FBI agents were given an opportunity to examine the records of the account at that time.

However, on January 27th the New York field office transmitted the requested subpoena to Washington, and on February 7, 1949, the Washington office obtained photographs of the accounts of Alger and Priscilla Hiss. These records reflected that on November 19, 1937, Priscilla Hiss had withdrawn $400 from the savings account.  CN Ex. 132.

A week later Chambers first mentioned the loan in an FBI interview in New York.  CN Ex. 133.    He then stated that he needed $500 for the car; that Bykov suggested he borrow the money from Hiss and that he did so, in early 1938.  Chambers further said that he never paid Hiss back the $500.  Id. It would not be unusual for an FBI agent preparing Chambers' testimony to have questioned him concerning the source of the funds for the purchase of the Ford in 1937; it would not have been unusual for an agent, knowing of the withdrawal from the bank, to have asked Chambers whether there was any connection between that withdrawal and his purchase of the car; it certainly would not have been un- usual for Chambers, anxious to make a more credible case against Hiss, to have seized upon the idea that such a loan had been made.

Even Chambers' confusion about the amount of the loan might well have been brought about by lack of complete communication between an FBI agent who did not want to put words into his witness' mouth and Chambers' recollection that he needed $500 to purchase the car. */ In giving his trial statement to the FBI, he accordingly stated that the amount was $500, accompanied by considerable embellishment intended to corroborate that story. CN Ex. 21, pp. 126, 127.

By the time of the trial, however, Chambers was fully aware that the amount allegedly borrowed from the Hisses was $400. His testimony on redirect is as follows:

> Question: Now you say that Mr. Hiss loaned you $400 on or about the time you bought this automobile in Randallstown?
>
> Answer: This is right.
>
> Question: And your testimony was then and is now that Mr. Hiss loaned you $400?
>
> Answer: That is correct.

---

*/ The purchase price of the car was $811.75 which was paid by a trade-in allowance of $325 for the Chambers' 1934 Ford, and $486.75 in cash. R.614-616; Govt. Ex. 40.

Question:   Not $401 or $399 but $400?

Answer:     $400.

Question:   In cash?

Answer:     That is right.

R.626.

Chambers, of course, was never called upon to reconcile the $500 loan he reported to the FBI and the $400 loan concerning which he testified because the defense never knew of Chambers' earlier statements that he had borrowed $500.

At the second trial when defense counsel suggested that Chambers had learned of the withdrawal and then fabricated the story of the loan, Murphy requested the FBI to review its files and to prepare a memorandum as to the dates on which the FBI contacted the Riggs Bank.  CN Ex. 134.  A memorandum prepared for Murphy by the Washington field office dated December 5, 1949, in the midst of the second trial, reviewed the facts with respect to the dates when the FBI learned of the withdrawal from the Hiss account, and concluded that "it is not probable that the New York office would have any information, particularly the documents in question, in their possession as of February 14, 1949."  CN Ex. 135.

Whatever may have been "probable" with respect to the transmission of the records to New York before February 14th, it is certainly not unlikely that a diligent FBI attorney anxious to prepare his witness thoroughly might have had knowledge of the withdrawal in time to have suggested the loan to Chambers by February 14th.

"Overwhelming proof?" It probably would not have appeared so overwhelming had the defense been fully equipped with the varying statements of Chambers respecting the amount of the loan and with the knowledge that the FBI knew of the withdrawal by early February or possibly the end of January.

C.  Chambers' Films

On December 2, 1948, Chambers delivered to HUAC two
rolls of developed film and three rolls of undeveloped film,
which he had hidden in a hollowed-out pumpkin.  The developed
film contained photographs of State Department documents
which were introduced into evidence by the prosecution as
corroboration of Chambers' testimony.  The government brief
in opposition to the petition herein cites this evidence as
another item of "immutable proof", claimed to establish
Hiss' guilt.  Govt. Memo. at p. 17.

Much evidence was offered at the trial by both the
government and the defense concerning these documents and we
do not propose to repeat all of that evidence here.  It would
be well, however, to start out with a fundamental question:
how strong was the government's evidence that Hiss ever gave
these documents to Chambers?  Chambers testified that he had
no independent recollection of the person who had given him
the documents, except as he "reconstruct[ed] the event."
R. 662-663.  Henry Julian Wadleigh, who was an employee in
the Trade Agreement Division of the State Department, testified that he gave "in the neighborhood of 400" documents to
Chambers, but that he had an "absence of recollection" of

having given Chambers documents involved in the Hiss case
(R. 1145, 1228-29). However, he said that he might have
given Chambers most of the documents produced from the pumpkin. (R. 1216-19; 1229.) With such inconclusive identification, one might well argue that the documents should not have
been admitted at all. But we are not now reviewing possible
errors at the trial - we rather are addressing ourselves to
the question of whether the government's "immutable proofs"
in this instance were really immutable, or were merely documents for which a very shaky foundation had been laid at the
trial.

The evidence submitted in the trial with respect
to this point while extensive, is not decisive. The two
rolls of film consisted of 58 frames, each frame being a
photograph of a page of a State Department document. Enlargements of these frames were introduced in evidence as
Baltimore Exs. 48 and 50-55. The 58 frames of film comprised eight documents; Baltimore Exs. 48 and 50-53 (48
frames in all) were five memoranda dealing with trade agreement negotiations with Germany and Exhibits 54 and 55 (10
frames) comprised a group of three mimeographed information
copies of incoming telegrams initialed by Hiss and stamped

by the office of Assistant Secretary of State Frances Sayre,
Hiss's superior. Chambers, while unable to recall who gave
him the documents, said that a single person gave him all of
the filmed documents. (R. 568.)

The government argued that since three of the documents (Baltimore Exs. 54 and 55) bore Hiss's initials and all
of the documents came from a single person, it followed that
Hiss gave Chambers all of the documents, having somehow secured possession of the other five documents. (R. 3237.)
The defense, on the other hand, argued that since five of
the documents originated in the Trade Agreements Division of
the State Department and would not have been accessible to
Hiss, it followed that Wadleigh (or someone else in the same
Division) gave Chambers all of the documents, having somehow
secured possession of the three papers that bore Hiss' initials (R. 3160 53.) When we add to this evidence the testimony that Wadleigh was in the habit of wandering through
the various offices of the State Department (R. 1446-47),
the testimony makes it somewhat more likely that it was Wadleigh rather than Hiss who was the source of the documents.
Certainly the testimony can hardly be characterized as immutable.

However, the government argued that the Trade Agreement documents which were photographed and became Baltimore Exhibits 48 and 50-53 were, in fact, available to Hiss; it followed, the prosecution said, that Hiss was the source of all of the documents. Hence, the "immutable proof".

It is true that some Trade Agreement documents were available to Hiss but <u>not</u> the documents that were photographed.

The testimony was undisputed in some respects. The ribbon copies of a group of Trade Agreement documents were sent to Sayre's office in a single transmission as about January 9, 1938, and were available to Hiss. Those ribbon cop= ies may or may not have been accompanied by carbons but in any event the documents, having served their purpose, were filed in the regular course of business.

The Baltimore Exhibits, however, were not photo-graphic copies of the documents that went from the Trade Agreement Division to Sayre's office. Many of them were not even photographs of carbon copies of those documents. They were, instead, pictures of carbon copies of another "run" of the documents sent by the Trade Agreement Division to Sayre. They differed from the original documents not in content but in form. The photograph of the "chit" (Baltimore Ex. 48)

which accompanied the documents from the Trade Agreement section to Sayre's office was not a photograph of the original document but was a photograph of a carbon copy of the chit retained in the Trade Agreement Division. (R. 1086-1087, 1336-37.) Most of the pages of the Baltimore documents, Exs. 50-53, were not conformed copies of the papers sent to Sayre's office - they were a different run and in some cases lacked the hand written corrections which were made in the official ribbon copy. (R. 830-32, 1087-90, 1336-37, 1092-93.)

It is clear, therefore, that the documents photographed to make up Baltimore Exs. 50-53 were not papers which ever came into Sayre's office. Indeed, one of them, Exhibit 52, was the text of a diplomatic note in German, and not even a copy of that document was ever sent to Sayre's office. Exhibit 52 like the other filmed papers were copies of working copies of Trade Agreement Division papers. There is no evidence that they ever left the Division, and it is absurd to argue that an espionage agent with easy access to the original documents would have photographed carbon copies of working copies housed in another office.

No immutable proof here!

# TABLE OF CASES

# TABLE OF CASES

Page

Page

Page

Page

*EXHIBITS*

UNITED STATES DISTRICT COURT
SOUTHERN DISTRICT OF NEW YORK

------------------------------------X
        In re             :      78 Civ. 3433 (RO)

    ALGER HISS,          :

        Petitioner.     :      AFFIDAVIT

------------------------------------X

STATE OF NEW YORK )
COUNTY OF NEW YORK) ss.:

        JAMES M. PRUITT, being duly sworn, deposes and says:

        1.  Annexed hereto are copies of Exhibits 85-88,
90-135 (there is no Exhibit 89) which are cited in Petitioner's
Memorandum of Law in Support of Petitioner's Motion to Grant
Writ of Error Coram Nobis, dated July 8, 1980.  These exhibits
are true copies of documents provided petitioner by the Federal Bureau of Investigation ("FBI") and the Department of
Justice, or are true copies of pleadings and docket sheets
of cases filed in the United States District Court for the
Southern District of New York.  A few of the exhibits, where
indicated, are true copies of papers maintained in petitioner's
counsel's file compiled in the course of legal representation.

        2.  Except where otherwise noted or where apparent
from the context, the handwritten notations on the face of
the exhibits were made by researchers and clerical assistants
who were assisting petitioner.

        3.  Exhibit 110, "Correlation," was prepared by me

-1-

192

based upon my review of the records of wiretapping of petitioner provided by the FBI, and is accurated to the best of my
knowledge.

JAMES M. PRUITT

Sworn to before me this
8th day of July, 1980.

UNITED STATES DISTRICT COURT
SOUTHERN DISTRICT OF NEW YORK

------------------------------------x

        In Re           :

    ALGER HISS,         :

       Petitioner.    :

------------------------------------x

                  78 Civ. 3433 (RO)

EXHIBITS TO AFFIDAVIT
OF
JAMES M. PRUITT
(CN Exs. 85-88, 90-135)

# Federal Bureau of Investigation
## United States Department of Justice
### New York, N. Y.

IN REPLY, PLEASE REFER TO
FILE NO. _____

MEMORANDUM:

Re: JAY DAVID WHITTAKER CHAMBERS, with aliases
ALGER HISS, et al;
PERJURY
ESPIONAGE - R

Set forth herein are certain instructions which are to take effect immediately. Also set forth are clarifications of instructions already in effect.

The overall supervision of the case is the direct responsibility of the writer. Special Agent J. T. Hilsbos is charged with the immediate supervision of the case. The case is assigned to Special Agent J. K. Kelly, who has the same responsibilities he would have as in any case assigned to him. It will be his responsibility to see that reports emanating from this office are prepared and submitted with logical frequency. He is also responsible for the daily teletype to the Bureau setting forth the pertinent developments of each day's investigative activities, including Grand Jury developments.

Special Agent T. G. Spencer, along with Special Agent F. X. Plant, has the responsibility of handling and thoroughly and completely interviewing WHITTAKER CHAMBERS. It is their responsibility to obtain from him over a period of time, and as soon as possible, every iota of information in his possession regarding Communism and Russian espionage.

Special Agent J. J. Ward is to analyze Bureau letter dated January 3, 1949, and is to coordinate information obtained from CHAMBERS. He will check the office files and where necessary have the Bureau files checked on names developed through the interviews with CHAMBERS, and will see that teletype leads are set forth for appropriate offices to conduct the necessary investigations; and will see that lead cards are made where necessary for the purpose of conducting investigation in this area.

Special Agent L. W. Spillane will daily review the testimony of the Grand Jury and will have lead cards prepared and teletype leads set forth as developments require. He will also prepare a complete comprehensive summary of all the information available in this office on WHITTAKER CHAMBERS, including in that report information furnished to this office by the Bureau, Baltimore, and the Washington Field Offices, which have been requested to furnish

AJT:RAA
65-14920

*3 p memo assigning to various agents responsibilities for investigating numerous individuals involved in the Hiss case w/ instructions (p 2 -)*

F.B.I.
65-14920-947 A
JAN 11 1949
N.Y.C.

ROUTED TO     FILE

EX 95

196

information in their files to this office. Of course any information furnished by other offices regarding CHAMBERS should likewise be set out in this report. Agent Spillane will also thoroughly review and analyze the pertinent testimony developed at the hearings of the House Committee on Un-American Activities, and will see that leads are set forth to conduct any logical investigation developed in those hearings.

Special Agent D. E. Shannon is charged with the direct supervision of all the investigation in this area and //// elsewhere in connection with obtaining typewriting specimens of the missing Woodstock typewriter formerly owned by the HISS', as well as the supervision of the investigation pointing towards the location of said typewriter.

It is intended that a lead card will be made on such individuals deemed worthy of vigorous attention and investigation. Agents will be assigned certain individuals and it will be their responsibility to see that all the necessary logical investigation regarding these individuals is conducted and reported. As pointed out in Bureau letter of January 3, 1949, in addition to corroborating the two counts of the indictment against HISS in this case, the additional purpose of the investigation is to develop evidence of all ramifications of the activities of various persons in this case for possible subsequent prosecution. It will be the responsibility of agents to whom individuals are assigned to completely review all the references in this office on these individuals, as well as to obtain from other offices and the Bureau any information in their files. A most complete, thorough, comprehensive investigation of these individuals is expected. It must not only be thorough, but must be intelligent and prompt. An agent will be expected to know everything there is to know about an individual assigned to him. Photographs, complete physical descriptions, the adult life histories, and a complete account of these individuals' activities, employments, residences, associations, education, etc., is required.

For the moment the following individuals are assigned to the agents designated. Other individuals subsequently deemed worthy of special attention will likewise be assigned, and the same instructions set forth herein will apply as to those individuals.

| | | | |
|---|---|---|---|
| Alger Hiss | Kelly | Whittaker Chambers | Spencer, Plant |
| Priscilla Hiss | Shannon | Henry H. Collins | Gallant |
| William W. Pigman ) | | Henry J. Wadleigh | Spencer |
| George L. Pigman ) | Shimmers | | |
| David V. Zimmerman | Martin | Abraham G. Silverman | Gallant |
| Franklin V. Reno | O'Keefe | Philip Reno | O'Keefe |
| Alexander Stevens | O'Keefe | Eleanor Nelson Soyring | O'Keefe |
| Boris Bykov | McCarthy | Felix A. Inslerman | Danahy |
| Laurence Duggan | Danahy | Unsub "Bernie" | Martin |
| Unsub "Keith" | Martin | Azemov | Martin |
| Schevesnikov | Martin | Cynthia Jones | Sullivan |

AJT:RAA
65-14920

New York, N. Y.

| | | | |
|---|---|---|---|
| John Loomis Sherman | Ward | Donald Hiss | Kelly |
| Max Bedacht | Spillane | Grace Hutchins | O'Keefe |
| Rubin Schmeitz | O'Keefe | Hans Inslerman | Danahy |

     As you know, this case is of the utmost importance to the Bureau, and it is imperative that each agent handle his assignments according to the highest Bureau standards. Besides the peculiar knowledge of the individuals assigned, you are of course expected to know the entire case thoroughly, to keep abreast of pertinent developments daily, and to be so equipped with a knowledge of the case that you will be able to handle any assignment and conduct any interview that might arise on moment's notice. You should thoroughly read and digest Bureau letter dated January 3, 1949, as well as any instructions subsequently coming from the Bureau or the desk. If at any time a certain phase of the investigation assigned to you develops to the point where you cannot handle it as thoroughly and as promptly as it should be handled, the desk should be notified immediately so that additional personnel can be assigned to assist you in that particular phase of the investigation.

                                 A. J. TUOHY,
                                   Supervisor

READ, INITIAL AND RETURN:

cc -

Danahy
Gallant
Hilsbos
Kelly
Martin
O'Keefe
Shannon
Skinner
Spencer
Spillane
Sullivan
Plant
McCarthy
Ward

Blount
Bracken
McCovey
Neagle

-3-

Assistant Attorney General Alexander M. Campbell
Criminal Division

January 31, 1949

Director, FBI          CONFIDENTIAL

JAY DAVID WHITTAKER CHAMBERS, WAS.,
ALGER HISS, ET AL
PERJURY
ESPIONAGE - R

There are transmitted herewith the following additional reports in
connection with instant investigation:

Report of:

Special Agent James L. Kirkland dated 1-11-49 at Philadelphia, Pennsylvania
Special Agent Edwin O. Johnson dated 1-12-49 at Denver, Colorado
Special Agent John J. O'Toole, Jr. dated 1-12-49 at Albany, New York
Special Agent Mahlon F. Coller dated 1-12-49 at Detroit, Michigan
Special Agent Francis X. McBride dated 1-13-49 at New Haven, Connecticut
Special Agent Raymond L. Faist dated 1-13-49 at Springfield, Illinois
Special Agent Howard P. Winter dated 1-14-49 at New Haven, Connecticut
Special Agent Robert T. Gryan dated 1-14-49 at Buffalo, New York
Special Agent James T. Haverty dated 1-17-49 at New Haven, Connecticut
Special Agent John C. Carr dated 1-17-49 at New Haven, Connecticut
Special Agent Harold F. Dodge dated 1-17-49 at Los Angeles, California
Special Agent James C. Kennedy dated 1-18-49 at San Antonio, Texas
Special Agent Mahlon F. Coller dated 1-19-49 at Detroit, Michigan
Special Agent G. Parnell Thornton dated 1-19-49 at St. Paul, Minnesota
Special Agent Edward E. Johnson dated 1-19-49 at Salt Lake City, Utah
Special Agent J. Phillip Claridge dated 1-19-49 at El Paso, Texas
Special Agent Harold F. Dodge dated 1-20-49 at Los Angeles, California
Special Agent G. Parnell Thornton dated 1-20-49 at St. Paul, Minnesota
Special Agent Arthur R. Stevens dated 1-20-49 at New Haven, Connecticut
Special Agent Henry A. Snow dated 1-20-49 at Birmingham, Alabama
Special Agent Leonard H. Walters dated 1-20-49 at Richmond, Virginia
Special Agent Paul R. Alker dated 1-20-49 at Newark, New Jersey
Special Agent Edward E. Kachelhoffer dated 1-20-49 at St. Louis, Missouri
Special Agent Joseph M. Kelly dated 1-21-49 at New York, New York
Special Agent Francis X. McBride dated 1-21-49 at New Haven, Connecticut
Special Agent Francis X. McBride dated 1-21-49 at New Haven, Connecticut
Special Agent John P. Manton dated 1-21-49 at Cleveland, Ohio
Special Agent Harry F. Howard dated 1-21-49 at Indianapolis, Indiana

1735

Special Agent Robert T. McIver dated 1-21-49 at Kansas City, Missouri
Special Agent Mahlon F. Coller dated 1-21-49 at Detroit, Michigan
Special Agent John E. Davis dated 1-21-49 at Atlanta, Georgia
Special Agent J. Hugh Smith dated 1-22-49 at Charlotte, North Carolina
Special Agent Mahlon F. Coller dated 1-24-49 at Detroit, Michigan
Special Agent Frederick M. Connors dated 1-24-49 at Boston Massachusetts
Special Agent Robert E. Dowd dated 1-24-49 at Omaha, Nebraska
Special Agent Carl L. Sherwood dated 1-25-49 at Pittsburgh, Pennsylvania
Special Agent Clark E. Lovrien dated 1-25-49 at Milwaukee, Wisconsin
Special Agent Edward F. Hummer dated 1-25-49 at Washington, D. C.

As other reports are received, they will be made available to you promptly.

STANDARD FORM NO. 64

*Office Memorandum* • UNITED STATES GOV

JEH

FBI 11-23-48
3-15-76

TO : The Director, Federal Bureau of Investigation    DATE: November 23, 1948

FROM : Alexander M. Campbell, Assistant Attorney General,    AMC:TJD:DJ (a second one)
(Criminal Division)

SUBJECT: Testimony of Whitaker Chambers Before Grand Jury

On November 19, 1948, Solicitor General Perlman informed me that he had received a message from William L. Marbury, 1000 Maryland Trust Building, Baltimore, Maryland, an attorney who is representing Alger Hiss in in the civil suit in Federal court at Baltimore against Whittaker Chambers.

I contacted Mr. Marbury by telephone and he advised that the matter was of considerable importance and he did not wish to discuss it on the telephone. Mr. Russo, Mr. Schedler, and myself met with Mr. Marbury and Mr. Evans, who represent Alger Hiss, and with Messrs. Richard F. Cleveland and William D. MacMillan, 2500 O'Sullivan Building, representing Whittaker Chambers, and Mr. Harold R. Medina, Jr., 15 Broad Street, New York City, representing Time Incorporated, at 4:00 o'clock in the afternoon of Friday, November 19, 1948. Mr. Marbury stated that as attorneys for Alger Hiss they had taken a deposition from Whittaker Chambers on Wednesday, November 17th. The attorneys for Whittaker Chambers and Mr. Medina, the attorney for Time Magazine, were also present at the taking of this deposition.

Mr. Marbury said that he had consulted with Alger Hiss and Hiss was desirous that this information be brought to the attention of the Government. Chambers brought to Mr. Marbury's office a number of documents, totaling approximately 162 pages, purporting to be confidential documents of the State Department. In his deposition Chambers stated that these documents had been given to him by Alger Hiss to be delivered to a Russian Colonel by the name of Bukoff (phonetic). Mr. Marbury fixed the time as about 1937 and 1938. It is noted that the deposition had not been transcribed by the official reporter at the time of this interview since the attorneys for both Hiss and Chambers were desirous of consulting with the Department of Justice prior to having this done.

Mr. Marbury said that Mr. Hiss commented that he thought summaries of some of these documents were in his handwriting but he is quite positive in stating that he never turned these documents over to Chambers.

The attorneys agreed by stipulation with the approval of the court to delay any further proceedings in this civil action for a period of two weeks in order that the Department of Justice might take whatever action it deems appropriate.

EX. 86

The photostatic copies of the documents, which are in the possession of Mr. Cleveland, will be made available to the FBI. The originals are in the custody of the Clerk of the Court.

Chambers testified before a Federal grand jury in the Southern District of New York to the effect that he had no information concerning espionage activities involving Alger Hiss. It is also noted that he did not inform the grand jury or the FBI that he had these documents in his possession. In his testimony before the grand jury he stated that neither Alger Hiss nor any other individuals, whom he claimed he had been in contact with, had turned over any Government documents to him.

It is desired that an immediate investigation be conducted so that it can be determined whether Chambers has committed perjury. In this connection the photostatic copies of these documents should be obtained together with a copy of the deposition given by Chambers.

Chambers was asked a general question in the grand jury as to whether he could furnish any further information that would be helpful to the grand jury. In response to this question he stated that perhaps there was a point that should be brought out and that about 1937 or early in 1938 J. Peters introduced him to a Russian who also went under the name of Peter. Chambers went on to testify that he learned from comparing notes with Kravitsky that this was a Colonel Bukoff, which he explained was a phonetic spelling, and Bukoff had been with Kravitsky in Italy. He went on to say that Bukoff was interested in the apparatus in Washington. He described him as a rather dreadful character from the slums of Odessa who lived in constant fear of the American secret police. Chambers further stated that there was a jurisdictional rivalry between J. Peters and Peter Bukoff, and J. Peters was anxious that Bukoff should not know what was going on in Washington because he feared the Russians would try to take over the Washington group. Chambers said the last he saw of Bukoff was shortly before he left the Communist Party the last time. Chambers was then asked a question in the grand jury whether he received any further information than that which he related to the grand jury which indicated that Bukoff was engaged in espionage activities. Chambers responded to this question that he could only say from inference. He was then asked the question whether he had related this information concerning Bukoff to the FBI. He answered that he did as nearly as he could remember it. Chambers gave no further testimony concerning Bukoff and made no reference whatsoever to having contacts with Bukoff for the purpose of turning documents over to him.

It is also requested that Mr. Marbury be contacted for the purpose of obtaining his permission to interview his client, Alger Hiss. Upon the interview with Alger Hiss he should be questioned concerning the allegation of Chambers that he, Hiss, turned these documents over to Chambers. All information concerning the documents should also be

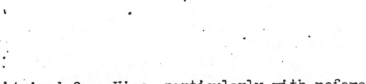

obtained from Hiss, particularly with reference to his handling
these documents in the State Department. If possible, a signed
statement should be obtained from Hiss. In this connection, it is
contemplated that Hiss might be questioned before the grand jury in
the Southern District of New York with reference to these allegations. It is noted that when Hiss testified before the grand jury he
denied that he furnished any confidential information to any unauthorized persons and he also denied that he knew Whittaker Chambers.

It is further noted that the term of the New York grand jury
will come to a close on December 15, 1948, and since it is likely that
it will be necessary to present further testimony before them, it is
important that this investigation be given expeditious attention.

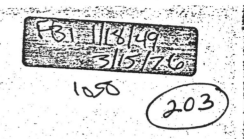

C- pre-trial preparations ← File

FBI Investig ← copy-filed    1-18-49.

203

1050

ASH FROM NEW YORK 97    18

RECTOR    URGENT    1-p telex report'g

O

AY DAVID WHITTAKER CHAMBERS, WAS., ET AL, PERJURY, ESP DASH R.

HAMBERS INTERVIEWED TODAY FOR APPROXIMATELY FIVE HOURS AND ENTIRE

IME SPENT IN DICTATION AND PROOFREADING OF MATERIAL PREVIOUSLY

YPED.  INTERVIEW CURTAILED FOR SEVERAL HOURS IN VIEW OF FACT THAT CHAMBE

AS WITNESS AT GJ TODAY.  INTERVIEW CONTINUES TOMORROW.

1050

Ex. 87

1) WC— pre-trial preparation
2) FBI Investig  (204)
3) "Felix"

JAN 20 1949
TELETYPE

CONF 3 STNS

WASHINGTON AND WFO   52   BALTIMORE  5

DIRECTOR AND SACS      URGENT

JAY DAVID WHITTAKER CHAMBERS, WAS., ETAL, PERJURY, ESP. - RE CHAMBERS
APPEARED BEFORE GJ TODAY AND SUBSEQUENT THERETO WAS INTERVIEWED FOR
APPROXIMATELY FOUR HOURS.  TIME SPENT AT INTERVIEW TODAY UTILIZED IN
EDITING AND CORRECTING INFORMATION PREVIOUSLY DICTATED.  IN CONNECTION
WITH LOCATION OF APARTMENT IN BALTIMORE THAT CHAMBERS USED TO PHOTO-
GRAPH DOCUMENTS AS MENTIONED IN NY TEL YESTERDAY, CHAMBERS PRESENTLY
OF OPINION THAT STREETCAR LINE TURNS OFF OF CALVERT STREET AT REED
STREET.  HE IS QUITE DEFINITE THAT APARTMENT NOT LOCATED ON THIS
STREET BUT RATHER AT INTERSECTION OF STREET ABOVE OR BELOW REED STREET
WHERE THEY INTERSECT CALVERT STREET.  ALSO STATED THAT REMOTE POSSI-
BILITY EXISTS THAT NAME OF INDIVIDUALS IN WHOSE NAME THIS APARTMENT
WAS LISTED WAS "GLAZER".  CHAMBERS ALSO RECALLED THAT OFFICE REFERRED
TO ON FIRST FLOOR OF APARTMENT BUILDING OF "WOOD PRODUCTS CO.".
INTERVIEW WITH CHAMBERS WILL CONTINUE TOMORROW.

SCHEIDT

1211

1- p tele re statements of WC about
location in baltimore of photography Felix's apt

WC — pre trial preparations
FBI Invstg

FBI 1/21/49
3/15/26
1219    (205)

File: ①
Copy filed: ②

CONF 2 STNS

WASHINGTON    48    BALTIMORE    4

DIRECTOR AND SAC    URGENT

JAY DAVID WHITTAKER CHAMBERS, WAS., ETAL. PERJURY, ESP. R. CHAMBERS
INTERVIEWED TODAY FOR APPROXIMATELY FIVE HOURS AND PLANS TO DEPART
FOUR THIRTY PM FOR WESTMINISTER, MARYLAND. IS SCHEDULED TO APPEAR
TEN AM JAN. TWENTYFIFTH, FORTYNINE, BEFORE GJ. WILL BE INTERVIEWED
LATER THAT DAY IN CONTINUATION OF OBTAINING MATERIAL FOR SIGNED STATE-
MENT. ENTIRE TIME TODAY SPENT IN CORRECTING AND ADDING TO INFOR-
MATION PREVIOUSLY GIVEN. CHAMBERS RELATED TODAY THAT SOME TIME,
PROBABLY IN NOVEMBER OR DECEMBER, FORTYEIGHT, HE RECEIVED A LETTER FROM
AN INDIVIDUAL WHOSE NAME HE DOES NOT NOW RECALL BUT WHO PROBABLY WAS
A CONTRIBUTING EDITOR TO THE FARM JOURNAL, PUBLISHED IN PHILA., PA.
THIS LETTER CONCERNED THIS INDIVIDUAL-S KNOWLEDGE OF ALGER HISS.
CHAMBERS RELATED AFTER THE INSTIGATION OF THE LIBEL SUIT BY HISS,
HE TURNED THIS LETTER OVER TO HIS LAWYER, MR. CLEVELAND IN BALTIMORE
AND THAT ONE OF MR. CLEVELAND-S INVESTIGATORS INTERVIEWED THIS INDI-
VIDUAL. CHAMBERS RELATED THAT CLEVELAND HAS A FULL REPORT ON THIS
MATTER AND IS OF THE IMPRESSION THAT HISS CORRESPONDED WITH THIS
END OF PAGE ONE

INDEXED - 14

1219

— p they in WC states about
letter he received in Nov 1948
— AH

BULKY EXHIBIT

Date received___1-20-48___

JAY DAVID WHITTAKER CHAMBERS, et al

___65-14920 - 1B___
(Title of case)

Submitted by Special Agent___T. G. Spencer and F. X. Plant___

Source from which obtained___Steno. - Dorothy E. Stremel___

Address_____

Purpose for which acquired___Evidence___

Location of bulky exhibit___In cabinet with file___

Ultimate disposition to be made of exhibit___Retain___

Estimated date of disposition - Undetermined.

List of contents:

114.  Stenographer's notes on changes and additions to statement of
      JAY DAVID WHITTAKER CHAMBERS on 1-17-49.   (See Exhibit 1 B113)

#30

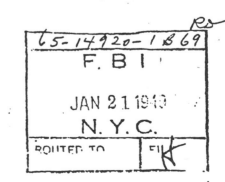

65-14920-1 B 69

F. B I

JAN 21 1949

N. Y. C.

ROUTED TO

BULKY EXHIBIT


Date received __1-3-49__

__JAY DAVID WHITTAKER CHAMBERS, et al__

__65-14920 - 1B__
(Title of case)


Submitted by Special Agent_____T. O. Spencer_____

Source from which obtained_____Steno. Helen Reynolds_____

Address_____

Purpose for which acquired_____Evidence_____

Location of bulky exhibit_____In cabinet with file_____

Ultimate disposition to be made of exhibit_____Retain_____

Estimated date of disposition – Undetermined

List of contents:


192. Stenographer's notes of statement of JAY DAVID WHITTAKER CHAMBERS,
1-3-49.


#33


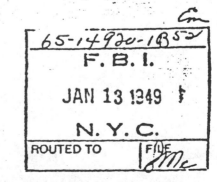

65-14920-1B
F. B. I.

JAN 13 1949

N. Y. C.

ROUTED TO    FILE

JN EDGAR HOOVER
DIRECTOR

(208)

FBI 8/18/41
10/4/76
WC-6

Federal Bureau of Investigation

United States Department of Justice

Washington, D. C.

PJN:MES
62-62107

August 18, 1941

MEMORANDUM FOR E. FOXWORTH

(A 27)

RE: (1) WHITTAKER CHAMBERS; — 1942 Statement
(2) Ludwig Lore, Confidential Informant;
ESPIONAGE - R
(3) FBI pre-48 investig's   (4) Balt Docs

A review of the Bureau indices reveals the following
information concerning the above-named individual:

On September 16, 1940, Confidential Informant ▓▓▓▓▓▓
submitted to the New York City Field Office information to the effect
that a confidential informant, Ludwig Lore, knew an individual who
"has been a high GPU officer for eight years abroad and for seven
years in this country."

deletion
6-7-D

On May 9, 1941, pursuant to Bureau instructions, Special
Agent George J. Starr, after several futile attempts to contact Lore,
finally succeeded in interviewing him regarding the unknown OGPU agent.
At that time Lore advised the OGPU agent above-referred-to, is a native
born American, married and has two children about eight and eleven years
of age; that the OGPU agent is employed on the editorial staff of a
popular magazine.  Lore further advised that this individual is afraid
to reveal the true story of his OGPU activities in the United States,
believing he will encounter serious trouble.  Lore also stated that this
individual was in contact with two girls who were private secretaries to
Assistant Secretaries of State and was also in touch with a girl who was
employed in a secretarial capacity with one of the high officials of
the Department of Commerce; that the OGPU agent obtained from the latter
girl all necessary statistical data.   RECORDED

WC-6

Mr. Lore also advised that the practice in preparing confidential correspondence in the Department of State was to make three
copies of the correspondence, one original and two carbon copies; that
the above-mentioned contacts of the OGPU agent in the Department of State
would prepare two extra copies of pertinent letters which would be
delivered to the OGPU agent (and who) Lore at that time described the OGPU agent
as a supervisor who had approximately seventy OGPU agents and other
individuals working under his supervision.  Lore also advised that this
OGPU agent had received information to the effect that a list of employees
of the United States Government had been submitted to the President of
the United States; that this list contained the names of various employees
of the Government who were Communists or possessed pro-Russian political

and
who

COPIES DESTROYED ▓▓▓▓▓▓▓

COPIES DESTROYED

5 6 OCT 1 6 1973

4-p memo detailing interview w/ Lore, who
said that W.C. ---

Ex.88

sympathies to the extent that their employment would be a serious menace to the Government; that the above-mentioned list had been on the President's desk for several weeks and that nothing had been done about it.

Lore also advised that the OGPU agent had informed him, Lore, that this case had been discussed with the Director some six or seven months prior to the interview; that when the intermediary suggested a guarantee of immunity regarding the OGPU agent, the Director stated no such agreement or guarantee could be arranged.

On May 16, 1941, the New York Office was advised that the Director was never approached regarding a guarantee of immunity in connection with this individual.

On August 3, 1941, the Bureau was advised that Mr. Lore had been reinterviewed by Special Agent Starr, at which time Lore stated in strictest confidence that the man he referred to as being a former OGPU supervisor is Whittaker Chambers, an associate editor of "Time" magazine; that Chambers spends Thursdays, Fridays and Saturdays of each week at the offices of the above-mentioned publication. During this interview Lore repeated his previous statement that until fairly recently Chambers had held an important position in the OGPU; that he definitely handled arrangements for placing agents in the Government service at Washington or for making contacts through which the OGPU agents could obtain information at Washington. Lore also reiterates the fact that he understood Chambers had approached either the Director or someone representing the Director to ascertain whether he could secure some sort of a promise of immunity; that Chambers had been told it would be necessary for him to furnish the information before any such matter could be discussed. The New York City Office advised that "unless instructions to the contrary are received from the Bureau, arrangements will be made to interview Chambers."

An examination of the Bureau files indicates Chambers is the author of a short story entitled "Can You Hear Their Voices?" published by the Internation Pamphlets, 799 Broadway, New York City. The pamphlet bears number twenty-six. It is noted that the above-mentioned short story bears a subcaption "The Arkansas Farmers' Fight for Food" and concerns itself with the difficulties experienced by the Arkansas dirt farmers during a severe drouth. The article suggests that Communism is a solution to the evils of economic inequality. A brief note appearing on the last page of the pamphlet indicates the story was first published in the March, 1931 issue of the "New Masses" and was rendered into a play produced at Vassar College and by a number of workers' dramatic groups. According to a list of articles appearing on the back page of

FBI   2/16/49
12/12/75

(210)

TO : The Director

DATE: February 16, 1949

FROM : D. M. Ladd

File under Crane
memo by JE 42236

SUBJECT: JAY DAVID WHITTAKER CHAMBERS, was., et al
PERJURY
ESPIONAGE - R
INTERNAL SECURITY - R

4- Page #
Summarizing ongoing
Investy of Crane

FBI

## ALLEGATIONS OF CHAMBERS REGARDING WILLIAM EDWARD CRANE, was., FORMERLY KNOWN AS UNKNOWN SUBJECT KEITH

Whittaker Chambers has advised that one of the photographers in his underground apparatus was known to him as "Keith" which name was a party pseudonym. He stated that "Keith" was connected with Colonel Bykov in New York City and came to Washington in 1937 for a short time to do some photographic work for Chambers in an apartment located in the Northwest Section of the city. He recalled that "Keith" came East from California. Chambers stated that he was introduced to "Keith" by Colonel Bykov. Chambers also advised that in 1935 his then superior "Bill" sent him to San Francisco with a money belt for the use of unknown individuals on the West Coast. He said he registered at the Golden Gate YMCA under the name Lloyd Cantwell and by pre-arrangement was contacted by "Keith" whom he then met under the name "Pete." Subsequently "Keith" introduced him to an elderly man named Volkoff who has since been identified as Isaac Wolkoff well known Communist on the West Coast. He stated that Volkoff was connected with the Pan-Pacific Trade Union Secretariat. Chambers said he was not certain whether he delivered the money belt to "Keith" or Volkoff. He said it was his understanding that the Pan-Pacific Trade Union Secretariat was then operating a courier system to Japan and he assumed that the money was for underground purposes. Chambers was not certain as to how much money he carried to the West Coast.

Chambers subsequently advised that he had a vague recollection that "Keith's" real name may have been Crane; that "Keith" was connected with John Loomis Sherman and that Sherman may have brought "Keith" into the apparatus when Sherman was on the West Coast. The San Francisco Office advised that in May, 1945, it was learned through a technical surveillance on the residence of Isaac Folkoff that an inquiry was made of Folkoff as to whether he knew this fellow Ed Crane or Bill Morgan." Folkoff stated that he had not seen him for two years but that he was "okay." It was further determined that the Ed Crane mentioned by Folkoff was identical with William Edward Crane, a Communist on the West Coast. A photograph of this individual was displayed to Whittaker Chambers on February 1, 1949 and he identified Crane as the individual known to him as "Keith."

## INTERVIEWS WITH WILLIAM EDWARD CRANE

William Edward Crane has been interviewed by the Los Angeles Office intermittently since February 7, 1949. He has furnished the following information in substantiation of Chambers' allegations.

Crane stated he joined the Communist Party in San Francisco about 1932 and shortly thereafter he was singled out by "Pop" Folkoff (Isaac

FLJ:ofm

2236   EY 90

ACTION:

       The above is being brought to your attention at this time inasmuch
as Crane has substantiated to a large extent Chamber's allegations concerning
his involvement in Soviet espionage. The interviews with him are continuing
and he will undoubtedly be a valuable witness in the case against Alger Hiss
because of his knowledge of the apparatus which was handled by Colonel Bykov,
of which Alger Hiss allegedly was a part thereof. You will be kept informed
of any further pertinent developments as a result of the interviews with Crane.
All leads growing out of the above information furnished by Crane are being given
expeditious attention as are all other leads in this case.

- 4 -

*Mr. Tamm*

*A. K. Bowles*

*FELIX AUGUST INSLERMAN*
*IS-R*

② TW Specimens

    *Pursuant to telephonic request from Domestic Intelligence Division 2/22/54, the Laboratory report on the listed evidence received from the Albany office 2/22/54, is set forth below for attention of Domestic Intelligence Division.*

Q1   *One sheet of torn white paper containing a portion of a typewritten letter beginning "is somebody else of the same breed....," ending "...you do not seem to know it." (Purported to be the copy of a portion of a letter given to Inslerman by Chambers in 1933 for delivery probably to "Ben.")*

    *The typewriter used to type Q1 was equipped with type corresponding most closely to the standard maintained in the Laboratory for Corona elite style of type spaced 12 letters to the inch. This style of type was first used on Corona typewriters May 1, 1924.*

    *Q1 bore the watermark "Superior Opaque-Rag Content Bond." Superior Opaque Bond is registered for the American Pad and Paper Company, 83 Winter Street, Holyoke, Massachusetts. White bond paper showing this watermark has been used since before 1938.*

    *The typewriting on Q1 was compared with the typewriting on the Baltimore Documents in the Alger Hiss case,      and the known standards of typewriting made on the Hiss typewriter and it was concluded Q1 was typed by the use of a different typewriter.*

    *Evidence attached.*

RECOMMENDATION:

    *That this memorandum and attached evidence, Q1, be forwarded for the immediate attention of the Domestic Intelligence Division.*

memo re Q1

Attachment

CC: Mr. Branigan
    Room 1527

RCF:jsb

53 MAR 11 1954

NOT RECORDED
159 MAR 3 1954

INITIALS ON ORIGINAL

113

Ex.

RECORDED - 40

1/13/76
2856
filed Woodstock
FBI-Lab

(213)

# FEDERAL BUREAU OF INVESTIGATION
## WASHINGTON D.C.

To:

SAC, Philadelphia                                          April 8, 1949

There follows the report of the FBI Laboratory on the examination of evidence received from your office on April 8, 1949.

*J. Edgar Hoover*
John Edgar Hoover, Director

Re:      JAILBI

YOUR FILE NO.
FBI FILE NO.
LAB. NO.

Examination requested by:

Philadelphia

Reference:

Letter dated April 6, 1949

Examination requested:

Document

Specimens:

K736   A two-page letter typewritten on letterhead stationery of The Northwestern Mutual Life Insurance Company of Milwaukee, Wisconsin, dated at Philadelphia, Pennsylvania, July 24, 1929 to Mr. Harry L. Martin, c/o Mr. M. A. Carroll, 505 Algoma Blvd., Oshkosh, Wisconsin, signed THOMAS L. FARGLER.

RESULTS OF EXAMINATION:

The typewriting listed above as specimen K736 was compared with the typewriting appearing on specimens Q5 and Q6 through Q69. The conclusion was reached that specimen Q5 was not typed by the same machine which typed K736. Inasmuch as there are nine years intervening when K736 and specimens Q6 through Q69 were typed a definite conclusion could not be reached in regard to a comparison of K736 with Q6 through Q69. A machine could develop numerous defects in nine years of use. Specimens Q6 through Q69 show many typewriting defects which do not appear in the typewriting K736. However, there are several defects appearing in the typewriting K736. Due to the fact that these defects are of minor nature and there are other defects in the questioned specimens which do not appear in K736 the known specimen cannot be definitely eliminated or identified with Q5 through Q69.

K736 will be photographed and returned to the Philadelphia office in the next several days.

APR 8 1949 P.M.

2 - New York
1 - Baltimore
2 - Washington Field

EX 91 A

12-10-49

*1-p telex reporting that*

OFFICE WAS ADVISED THAT THOMAS GRADY RESIDES AT TWO ONE TWO SIX ... WAUWATOSA, WISCONSIN. THAT HE IS AN EMPLOYEE OF THE L. C. ELLIS EQUIPMENT COMPANY OF CHICAGO, ILLINOIS, WITH OFFICES AT SEVEN FOUR THREE WEST FOURTH STREET MILWAUKEE. BUSINESS PHONE MARKET EIGHT SEVEN FOUR ONE TWO. HOME PHONE ONE FOUR ... ... ... . FOR INFO MILWAUKEE THOMAS GRADY SOLD A NEW (WOODSTOCK)

(TYPEWRITER) TO THE (FANSLER-MARTIN) PARTNERSHIP THEN SPECIAL AGENTS FOR THE NORTHWESTERN MUTUAL LIFE INSURANCE COMPANY, AND WHICH PARTNER-SHIP WAS LOCATED IN THE BULLITT BUILDING ON SOUTH FOURTH STREET, PHILA. THIS SALE WAS MADE PROBABLY DURING NINETEEN TWENTYSEVEN. HARRY MARTIN OF AFORE-MENTIONED PARTNERSHIP, WAS ADVISED TODAY THAT GRADY WAS OF UNRELIABLE CHARACTER AND THAT POSSIBILITY EXISTS THAT GRADY OBTAINED THIS WOODSTOCK ILLEGALLY FROM THE WOODSTOCK AGENCY IN PHILA AND SOLD IT TO FANSLER-MARTIN SUBSEQUENT TO THE TERMINATION OF GRADYS EMPLOYMENT WITH WOODSTOCK WHICH OCCURRED ON DECEMBER THREE, TWENTY SEVEN. OTHER INFO RECEIVED TO DATE ... TO ... THAT ... ... TYPEWRITER MAY NOT HAVE BEEN PURCHASED FROM ... ... ... ... ... TWENTYEIGHT OR NINETEEN TWENTYNINE. ... ...

IMMEDIATELY THOROUGHLY INTERVIEW GRADY FOR ALL INFO IN HIS POSSESSION ... PAGE ONE

3 DEC 17 1948

DEC 28 1948

183 1 ...

EX91B

TELETYPE

12-10-49

(ILLEGIBLE) NEW YORK FROM PHILA

   (ILLEGIBLE) NEW YORK TO MILWAUKEE

JAY DAVID WHITAKER CHAMBERS, WAS, PERJURY, ESPIONAGE R. CHICAGO
OFFICE HAS ADVISED THAT THOMAS GRADY RESIDES AT TWO ONE TWO SIX
(ILLEGIBLE) RIVER PARKWAY, WAUWATOSA, WISCONSIN, THAT HE IS AN EMPLOYEE
OF THE R. C. ELLIS ENGINEERING COMPANY OF CHICAGO, ILLINOIS, WITH
OFFICES AT SEVEN FOUR THREE WEST FOURTH STREET MILWAUKEE. BUSINESS
PHONE MARKET EIGHT SEVEN FOUR ONE TWO. HOME PHONE SPR FOUR NAUGHT SIX
THREE SEVEN. FOR INFO MILWAUKEE THOMAS GRADY SOLD A NEW WOODSTOCK
TYPEWRITER TO THE FANSLER-MARTIN PARTNERSHIP THEN SPECIAL AGENTS
FOR THE NORTHWESTERN MUTUAL LIFE INSURANCE COMPANY, AND WHICH PARTNER-
SHIP WAS LOCATED IN THE BULLITT BUILDING ON SOUTH FOURTH STREET,
PHILA. THIS SALE WAS MADE PROBABLY DURING NINETEEN TWENTYSEVEN. HARRY
MARTIN OF AFORE-MENTIONED PARTNERSHIP, HAS ADVISED TODAY THAT GRADY
WAS OF UNRELIABLE CHARACTER AND THAT POSSIBILITY EXISTS THAT GRADY
OBTAINED THIS WOODSTOCK ILLEGALLY FROM THE WOODSTOCK AGENCY IN PHILA
AND SOLD IT TO FANSLER-MARTIN SUBSEQUENT TO THE TERMINATION OF GRADYS
EMPLOYMENT WITH WOODSTOCK WHICH OCCURRED ON DECEMBER THREE, TWENTY
SEVEN. OTHER INFO RECEIVED TO DATE TENDS TO INDICATE THAT THE WOODSTOCK
TYPEWRITER MAY NOT HAVE BEEN PURCHASED FROM GRADY BEFORE EITHER
NINETEEN TWENTYEIGHT OR NINETEEN TWENTYNINE. MILWAUKEE SHOULD
IMMEDIATELY THOROUGHLY INTERVIEW GRADY FOR ALL INFO IN HIS POSSESSION
END PAGE ONE

216

PAGE TWO.

REGARDING THE SALE OF THIS TYPEWRITER TO FANSLER-MARTIN. ADVISE
NEW YORK AND PHILA. NO FURTHER INFO DEVELOPED TODAY WHICH WOULD SHOW
PRESENCE OF ADDITIONAL DOCUMENTS HERE.

                                        BOARDMAN

FEDERAL BUREAU OF INVESTIGATION
U. S. DEPARTMENT OF JUSTICE
COMMUNICATIONS SECTION

JAN 5 - 1949

TELETYPE

FBI 45749
3/15/76

772

217

WASHINGTON AND WFO 5 NYC 2 FROM PHILA 1-5-49 12.36 PM

DIRECTOR AND SACS   2-p teletex tracing out FBI investig & conducting

JAY DAVID WHITTAKER CHAMBERS, - ETAL, ESPIONAGE-R, PERJURY. REBUTEL

YESTERDAY, OPINION OF PHILA OFFICE THAT PROPER SEARCH FOR WOODSTOCK

TYPEWRITER BE LIMITED TO MACHINES MANUFACTURED BETWEEN JANUARY ONE,

TWENTYSIX, AND DECEMBER TTHIRTYONE, FORTYSEVEN, BASED ON FOLLOWING --

THOMAS GRADY, WHO SOLD WOODSTOCK TYPEWRITER TO FANSLER-MARTIN PARTNER-

SHIP, RESIGNED FROM WOODSTOCK CO. ON DECEMBER THREE, TWENTYSEVEN. JOHN

CAROW, MANAGER OF PHILA AGENCY DURING ALL OF TWENTYSEVEN, AND FOR A

NUMBER OF YEARS THEREAFTER, HAS ADVISED THAT THERE WERE NO INVENTORY

SHORTAGES PRIOR TO THIRTYTHREE. THIS WOULD ELIMINATE THE POSSIBILITY

THAT GRADY STOLE A TYPEWRITER AND SOLD IT TO FANSLER-MARTIN DURING

LATER YEARS OF PARTNERSHIP. LIKEWISE GRADY STATES THAT HE SOLD A

WOODSTOCK TO FANSLER-MARTIN, SHORTLY AFTER THAT PARTNERSHIP COMMENCED.

LETTER OBTAINED BY MILWAUKEE OFFICE DATED JULY TWENTYTHREE, TWENTYSEVEN

K-TWELVE/, AND FORWARDED TO LABORATORY FOR COMPARISON INDICATES ACTIVE

PARTNERSHIP COMMENCED APPROXIMATELY AUGUST ONE, TWENTYSEVEN. THEREFORE,

MACHINE WAS OBVIOUSLY MANUFACTURED BEFORE GRADYS RESIGNATION FROM WOOD-

STOCK ON DECEMBER THREE, TWENTYSEVEN. WOODSTOCK SERVICE MANUAL RE-

FLECTS SERIAL NUMBER CURRENT AS OF JANUARY ONE, TWENTYEIGHT AS ONE

TWENTYSEVEN THOUSAND ONE HUNDRED. JOHN GALLAGHER, WHO WAS REPAIRMAN

FOR WOODSTOCK AT PHILA DURING PERIOD OF SALE TO FANSLER-MARTIN, AND

58 JAN 17 1949

EX91C

(218)

PAGE TWO

SUBSEQUENTLY BECAME MANAGER OF WOODSTOCKS PHILA AGENCY HAS
STATED THAT MACHINES DID NOT REMAIN ON AGENCY INVENTORY FOR LONG
PERIODS BEFORE SALE.  IN HIS OPINION, NOT LONGER THAN THREE MONTHS.  TO
ALLOW MARGIN OF ERROR IN GALLAGHERS MEMORY, IT APPEARS LOGICAL THAT
ASSUMING A NEW MACHINE WERE ON THE INVENTORY AS MUCH AS EIGHTEEN
MONTHS PRIOR TO THE SALE TO FANSLER-MARTIN, THIS WOULD MAKE THE MANU-
FACTURE DATE OF SUCH MACHINE, NOT PRIOR TO JANUARY ONE, TWENTYSIX, OR
SERIAL NUMBER ONE ~~NUMBER FIFTYNINE THOUSAND THREE HUNDRED~~ FortyFive Thousand, AS REFLECTED
IN SERVICE MANUAL.  INVESTIGATION REPORTING ABOVE FACTS IS REFLECTED
IN REPORTS OF SA J. L. KIRKLAND AT PHILA DATED DECEMBER SEVEN, SEVENTEEN
AND TWENTYTHREE LAST, AND OF SA CLARK E. LOVRIEN AT MILWAUKEE, DATED
DECEMBER TWENTYONE LAST, PAGE FIVE, PARAGRAPH THREE, AND IN CHICAGO
TELETYPES DECEMBER FOURTEEN AND TWENTYTWO LAST.

BOARDMAN

CORRECTION  SECOND PAGE EIGHTH LINE PLEASE READ AS FOLLOWS
"SERIAL NUMBER ONE FORTYFIVE THOUSAND, AS REFLECTED"

3-15-76

536

(219)

No. 1

CASE ORIGINATED NEW YORK

FILE MEMcG

| RT MADE AT | DATE WHEN MADE | PERIOD FOR WHICH MADE | REPORT MADE BY |
|---|---|---|---|
| HILADELPHIA, PA. | DEC. 23 19 | 12-16,18,20/23-48 | JAMES L. KIRKLAND |

| | CHARACTER OF CASE |
|---|---|
| AY DAVID WHITTAKER CHAMBERS, AS., ET AL | PERJURY ESPIONAGE - R |

OPSIS OF FACTS:

Attempts to locate records of sale of Woodstock Typewriter to FANSLER-MARTIN partnership and to identify serial number of this typewriter unsuccessful. Laboratory has identified specimens submitted by Phila. as written on same typewriter as some of questioned specimens. Additional specimens submitted. Investigation Norristown, Pa. re RUSSELL INGRAM negative.

② Woodstock Typewriter

③ Typewriting Specimens

- ◼◼◼ -

ENCES:

Bureau File ◼◼◼◼
Report of SA JAMES L. KIRKLAND, dated at Philadelphia, Pa., 12-17-48.
Bureau teletype to New York, Boston, Baltimore, and Philadelphia, dated 12-20-48.

IS:

## AT PHILADELPHIA, PA.

This is the joint investigation of SA JOSEPH E. FLAHERTY, PHILIP KOCHENDERFER, WILLIAM H. NAYLOR, and the writer.

HARRY L. MARTIN, former partner of THOMAS FANSLER, has been re-interviewed regarding the possible existence of partnership records. MARTIN explained that the FANSLER-MARTIN partnership was a partnership "in name only," that no partnership agreement papers were drawn,

ED AND
ARDED: L. V. Boardman    SPECIAL AGENT IN CHARGE

DO NOT WRITE IN THESE SPACES

536

EX91D

whose typewriters contained serial numbers which would have been manufactured
around 1927. These names were indicated to the reporting agent, and investigation concerning them will be set forth in a later section of this report.
The list in question has been forwarded to the Milwaukee Office with the request that it be exhibited to THOMAS GRADY. In the event GRADY is able to
identify any of the names as customers to whom he sold a new WOODSTOCK typewriter
in 1927, attempts will be made to determine the serial numbers of these
machines, having in mind that the identification of such serial numbers might
be of assistance in narrowing the group of serial numbers in which the machine
purchased by FANSLER-MARTIN is contained.

       By teletype dated December 21, 1943 the Dallas Office advised
that H. N. WEBSTER, now WOODSTOCK TYPEWRITER COMPANY Southwestern Zone Manager,
had stated that in 1946 he had closed out eight eastern offices of the WOODSTOCK
COMPANY, including the office at Philadelphia. According to WEBSTER, all old
records at Philadelphia, consisting of repair records, were burned, and only
current records at that time were kept and inventory stock records were returned
to the factory in Woodstock, Illinois. WEBSTER has stated that these are
the instructions he gave to GALLAGHER at Philadelphia, and that this procedure
was made by him and of the company due to the shortage of file space.

       By teletype dated December 20, 1943 the Chicago Office advised
that Mr. MELVIN O. JOHNSON, Secretary-Treasurer of the WOODSTOCK TYPEWRITER
COMPANY, at Woodstock, Illinois, had been unable to locate Philadelphia branch
records, and did not recall the receipt of stock records from Philadelphia
although he believed that some records had been received and were later destroyed.
A search of the available files pertaining to stock, service and sales,
revealed no pertinent records. Mr. JOHNSON had indicated that he would make
further inquiries at the plant and exhaust all possibilities concerning the
location of Philadelphia Agency records.

       JOHN O. CAROW, 5313 Locust Street, Philadelphia, presently
employed by the REMINGTON-RAND COMPANY, advised that he had come to Philadelphia on November 26, in either 1926 or 1927, from Detroit, where he had
been Manager of the local branch of the WOODSTOCK TYPEWRITER COMPANY. He
had been assigned to Philadelphia by the company to manage the Philadelphia
Agency. He further said he recalled THOMAS GRADY, the salesman, and said
that he had hired GRADY shortly after he, CAROW, had come to Philadelphia,
and that GRADY had remained in the employ of the Philadelphia Agency for
seven or eight months but that it had been necessary to ask for GRADY's
resignation due to a lack of sales volume on his part. He indicated that
GRADY's record had been clean, and that all machines charged to him had
been returned to the company at the time of his resignation. He insisted
that the only reason for GRADY's dismissal was lack of sales volume.

- 4 -

536

CAROW was questioned concerning the possibility that any typewriters might have been missing from the records of the typewriter agency and advised that he had never experienced the loss of a typewriter through theft at the Philadelphia Agency prior to 1933.

CAROW was asked to identify all persons who had been in charge of the Philadelphia Agency from 1925 until the time the agency closed. He furnished the following identities:

SAM WARD
JOHN CAROW
CHARLES PARKER
JOSEPH GWYN
H. E. STEINKE
JACK KREIFELS
JOHN GALLAGHER

CAROW advised that SAM WARD might be located by investigation at St. Louis, Missouri, and that JOSEPH GWYN was believed to be with REMINGTON-RAND at Birmingham, Alabama. He likewise furnished the location of STEINKE at Philadelphia. CAROW could give no information concerning the whereabouts of CHARLES PARKER. CAROW likewise advised that monthly reports had been submitted to the home office of the WOODSTOCK TYPEWRITER COMPANY, and that it had never been the practice to have an outside agency audit the records at Philadelphia, nor, to his knowledge, had an internal audit ever been conducted by the company. He said that all records received by him were, in turn, turned over to CHARLES PARKER, his immediate successor, and that he retained absolutely no records in his possession or know of no records which would assist in the identification of a sale of a typewriter to the FANSLER-MARTIN partnership.

By teletype dated December 21, 1948, the St. Louis Office advised that it had located SAM V. WARD, now a realtor in St. Louis, who had advised that he had been Branch Manager for the WOODSTOCK TYPEWRITER COMPANY from September 1922 until October 1926, that THOMAS GRADY had been employed by him as a sales representative, and that he considered GRADY a reputable and highly intelligent employee. He said that the office force consisted of approximately eight employees, and that there had been considerable turnover. According to WARD, he had left all records in the possession of JOHN CAROW and JAMES HACKNEY, who was then Sales Manager. WARD believed that HACKNEY was now employed as a Portable Sales Representative for the REMINGTON-RAND COMPANY at Buffalo, New York. He further advised that upon the completion of each month all typewriters sold on trial or on loan were a matter of record, which record indicated the name of the purchaser, and that these records were directed each month to the WOODSTOCK TYPEWRITER

- 5 -

536

WASH 19 AND NEW YORK 5 FROM PHILA          8          Schmall #40

DIRECTOR AND SAC NEW YORK CITY                URGENT

JAY DAVID WHITTAKER CHAMBERS, WAS, PERJURY, IS - R. REMYTEL DECEMBER

SEVEN. HARRY MARTIN HAS ADVISED RESULTS OF INTERVIEW TODAY WITH HORACE

SCHMAHL WHO CAME TO MARTIN-S OFFICE ALONE FROM NEW YORK PARTICULARLY

FOR THIS INTERVIEW. SCHMAHL QUESTIONED MARTIN AND HIS ATTORNEY, SIDNEY

ORLOFSKY WHO WAS PRESENT DURING INTERVIEW AT GREAT LENGTH CONCERNING

POSSIBLE WHEREABOUTS OF DOCUMENTS WRITTEN ON WOODSTOCK TYPEWRITER.

MARTIN FURNISHED INFORMATION IN RESPONSE TO DIRECT QUESTIONS AS TO

POSSIBILITY OF A WILL BEING WRITTEN ON THE TYPEWRITER THAT FANSLER

DID HAVE A WILL WRITTEN IN NINETEEN FORTY. ORLOFSKY TOOK SCHMAHL TO

CITY HALL WHERE WILL WAS EXAMINED. SCHMAHL INDICATED HE DID NOT

BELIEVE IT WAS WRITTEN ON THE WOODSTOCK AND MADE NO EFFORT IN ORLOFSKY-

PRESENCE TO OBTAIN THE ORIGINAL WILL OR HAVE A COPY MADE. SCHMAHL

ASKED IF INCOME TAX RETURNS WERE TYPED ON THE WOODSTOCK AND MARTIN

BELIEVES THIS WAS PROBABLE FOR ALL YEARS OF THE PARTNERSHIP. SCHMAHL

INQUIRED AS TO EXISTENCE OF DOCUMENTS AT HEAD OFFICE OF NORTHWESTERN

MUTUAL LIFE INSURANCE CO. AND MARTIN CLAIMS HE ATTEMPTED TO CONVINCE

SCHMAHL THAT THERE WOULD NOT BE ANY SUCH DOCUMENTS IN EXISTENCE. RE

MILWAUKEE LETTERS TO BUREAU DECEMBER SEVEN WITH INSTANT CAPTION.

143

EX 91E

MARTIN HAS EXAMINED PHTOTOSTATS OF THE FOUR ORIGINAL LETTERS
OBTAINED AND UPON OBSERVING STENO-S INITIALS ON LETTER DATED NOVEMBER
FOUR, NINETEEN TWENTYSEVEN NOW RECALLS THAT A STENO NAMED KATHERINE
LOGERMAN WAS FANSLER-S SECRETARY AT INCEPTION OF PARTNERSHIP IN
NINETEEN TWENTYSEVEN. THROUGH INQUIRY TODAY MARTIN HAS LOCATED
KATHERINE SHOTWELL, NEE LOGERMAN WHO ADVISED HIM THAT SHE WAS
PARTNERSHIP SECRETARY UNTIL APPROXIMATELY MIDDLE OF NINETEEN TWENTY
EIGHT AND THAT DURING HER ENTIRE TENURE THE ONLY TYPEWRITER WAS A
ROYAL. MARTIN THEN RECALLED THAT WOODSTOCK WAS OBTAINED SOMETIME
AFTER NEW STENO, ANNE C. COYLE WAS EMPLOYED AT TIME KATHERINE LOGER-
MAN RESIGNED AND THAT AT TIME WOODSTOCK WAS PURCHASED THE ROYAL WAS
EITHER TRADED IN OR SOLD IN A MANNER UNKNOWN TO HIM. AFTER EXTEN-
SIVE INQUIRY MARTIN HAS LOCATED THE FORMER ANNE COYLE NOW MRS. THOMAS
C. FOX AS RESIDING NEAR VINELAND, N.J. NOT WILLIAMSTOWN AS SET FORTH
IN REFERENCE TELETYPE. MARTIN PLACED PHONE CALL TO MRS. FOX BUT WAS
ADVISED SHE WILL NOT BE AVAILABLE UNTIL THURSDAY AM. HE WILL CALL
HER AGAIN AT THAT TIME. MARTIN AND HIS ATTORNEY BOTH GAINED IMPRESSION
FROM SCHMAHL THAT THREE IS SOME DOUBT IN HIS MIND AS TO HISS-S INNO-
CENCE SINCE SCHMAHL TOLD THEM THAT HISS-S STORY CONCERNING THE TYPE-
WRITER AND QUOTE SEVERAL OTHER POINTS UNQUOTE HAS BEEN FOUND TO BE
INACCURATE. HE DID NOT ELABORATE ON THE NATURE OF THE OTHER POINTS

- PAGE THREE -

NOR DID HE SAY DIRECTLY THAT HE DOUBTED HISS-S INNOCENCE BUT
BOTH MARTIN AND ATTORNEY GAINED THE IMPRESSION THAT THIS WAS WHAT HE
MEANT. SCHMAHL DID STATE THAT IF HISS WERE PROVEN WRONG ON QUOTE ONE
MORE THING UNQUOTE HIS FIRM WOULD WITHDRAW FROM THE CASE. MARTIN HAS
ALSO ADVISED SCHMAHL IN ANSWER TO DIRECT QUESTIONS THAT DOCUMENTS
PREPARED ON THE WOODSTOCK ARE POSSIBLY IN EXISTENCE AT SEVERAL OTHER
SOURCES SUCH AS FANSLER-S CHURCH AND ATTORNEY. SCHMAHL APPEARED AT
PHILADELPHIA OFFICE THIS PM WHILE AGENT HANDLING THIS CASE WAS WITH
MARTIN AND WAS INTERVIEWED BY COMPLAINT AGENT. WAS IN CONSIDERABLE
HURRY TO CATCH TRAIN TO NEW YORK AND GAVE SUBSTANTIALLY THE SAME
INFO AS MARTIN HAS ADVISED HE GAVE SCHMAHL. IT NOW APPEARS THAT ALL
THREE LETTERS DATED IN NINETEEN TWENTYSEVEN FORWARDED BY MILWAUKEE TO
LABORATORY AND POSSIBLY THE FOURTH LETTER DATED IN NINETEEN TWENTY-
NINE WERE WRITTEN ON THE ROYAL TYPEWRITER USED BY THE PARTNERSHIP
OF FANSLER - MARTIN BEFORE THE WOODSTOCK WAS OBTAINED SOMETIME DURING
THE EMPLOYMENT OF ANNE C. COYLE AS PARTNERSHIP STENO. SCHMAHL DOES
NOT POSSESS INFO RE ACTUAL WHEREABOUTS OF MRS. FOX, NEE COYLE NOR DOES
HE KNOW ABOUT ROYAL TYPEWRITER AND FORMER STENO LOGERMAN SINCE THIS
INFO WAS DEVELOPED SUBSEQUENT TO INTERVIEW BETWEEN SCHMAHL AND MARTIN
AND HIS ATTORNEY. INVESTIGATION AT PHILADELPHIA WILL BE GUIDED BY
    - END PAGE THREE -

3

?

- PAGE FOUR -

RESULTS OF MARTIN-S CONVERSATION WITH MRS. FOX TOMORROW.  BUREAU MAY
DESIRE TO OBTAIN INCOME TAX RETURNS OF FANSLER FOR YEARS NINETEEN
TWENTY EIGHT THROUGH NINETEEN THIRTYFIVE FOR COMPARISON WITH DOCUMENTS
PRODUCED BY CHAMBERS.

FBI 12/13/48
3/15/7?

(226)

12/3?/48

31

240

TELETYPE

SH 17, NEW YORK 6 FROM PHILA     13     7-45 PM EST

DIRECTOR AND SACS NEW YORK, WASH FIELD AND MILWAUKEE

RE WHITTAKER CHAMBERS, WAS, PERJURY, ESPIONAGE DASH R.   MRS. KATHERINE

GERMAN SHOTWELL, FORMERLY STENO TO FANSLER-MARTIN IN TWENTYSEVEN

AND PART OF TWENTYEIGHT, NOW STATES THAT SHE WAS MISTAKEN ABOUT A

ROYAL TYPEWRITER BEING IN OFFICE-- THAT IT WAS A WOODSTOCK TYPEWRITER

AND HAD BEEN THERE PRIOR TO THE FORMATION OF FANSLER-MARTIN WHILE

FANSLER WAS IN PARTNERSHIP WITH ANOTHER PERSON.   MRS. SHOTWELL LIKE-

WISE STATES IT IS POSSIBLE THAT THE TYPEWRITER WAS TRADED IN FOR A

NEW ONE DURING TWENTYSEVEN OR TWENTYEIGHT, BUT THAT SHE CANNOT RECALL

THIS FACT.   DOES NOT RECALL THOMAS GRADY.  LETTER OBTAINED TODAY FROM

FREE LIBRARY, PHILA., WHO THEN EMPLOYED DAISY FANSLER, SISTER OF

PRISCILLA HISS, WHICH MAY HAVE BEEN WRITTEN ON THOMAS FANSLER-S WOOD-

STOCK TYPEWRITER.   THIS LETTER, DATED DECEMBER SIX, THIRTYONE, HAS

BEEN FORWARDED TO LAB FOR COMPARISON PURPOSES.   NO CORRESPONDENCE

AVAILABLE BRYN MAWR COLLEGE RE PRISCILLA HISS OR GEORGE SCHOOL RE

TIMOTHY HOBSON.   RE MILWAUKEE TEL TODAY.  THOMAS GRADY ON REINTERVIEW

ATTEMPTS TO FIX DATE OF SALE OF WOODSTOCK TO FANSLER-MARTIN BY RECALL-

ING STENO COYLE EMPLOYED BY FANSLER-MARTIN.   IT IS POINTED OUT THAT

GRADY COULD NOT HAVE KNOWN COYLE AT TIME OF SALE SINCE HE RESIGNED

3 DEC 17 1948

50 DEC 28 1948 369

END PAGE ONE

240

EX91F

FROM WOODSTOCK DECEMBER THREE, TWENTYSEVEN, WHEREAS COYLE DID NOT

BEGIN EMPLOYMENT UNTIL FALL OF TWENTYEIGHT.  HOWEVER, COYLE WAS STILL

MARTIN-S STENO IN GENERAL AGENCY WHEN HE, GRADY, PURCHASED LIFE

INSURANCE POLICY IN NINETEEN THIRTY AND LATER WHEN HE, GRADY, WAS

EMPLOYED BY NORTHEASTERN MUTUAL IN EARLY NINETEEN THIRTIES.

    BOARDMAN

END

(228)

UNITED STATES
DEPARTMENT OF JUSTICE

Room 1404, U. S. Court House
Foley Square, New York, N.Y.

PERSONAL

January 27, 1950

J. Edgar Hoover
Director
Federal Bureau of Investigation
U. S. Department of Justice
Washington, D. C.

Dear Mr. Hoover:

I would like to express to you my deep appreciation for the excellent work performed by the personnel of the FBI in the Alger Hiss case.

It is my sincere conviction that the successful conclusion of this case is attributable to the sedulous efforts of the Bureau. An outstanding instance is the identification and location by the Baltimore Office of Edith Murray. It is apparent that her testimony as a Government witness had a tremendous influence on the Jury.

It is difficult to single out any particular individuals for commendation. The agents that I had contact with in New York City were all outstanding and I realize that there were many other agents working on the case in other Field Offices whose work was of the same high calibre. It can be best summed up by stating that it is another example of an outstanding job done by a splendid organization.

I am enclosing, for your information, a copy of a letter that I have sent to the Attorney General.

Sincerely yours,

Thomas F. Donegan

THOMAS J. DONEGAN
Special Assistant to
the Attorney General

4529

EX.92

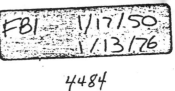

*Edith Murray*
*Priscilla Hiss*
*Mike Catlett*

FEDERAL BUREAU OF INVESTIGATION
U. S. DEPARTMENT OF JUSTICE
COMMUNICATIONS SECTION

JAN 17 1950

4484

229

TELETYPE

WASHINGTON 16 FROM NEW YORK     17     4-47 P

DIRECTOR     URGENT

AHAM.  HISS TRIAL SUMMARY, AM SESSION, JAN. SEVENTEEN.   IN FURTHER RE-
BUTTAL STANLEY RUSSELL TESTIFIED RE RENTAL OF WOODSTOCK TYPEWRITER TO DEFENSE ATTYS
FROM FEB. TO MAY LAST.  AUGUST CLAESSENS, OF THE SOCIALIST DEMOCRATIC
FEDERATION, TESTIFIED HE WAS NYC ORGANIZER FOR SP IN THIRTYTWO AND THAT
DURING THAT YEAR APPLS FOR MEMBERSHIP IN SP FILLED OUT CARDS FROM WHICH
WERE MADE UP OFFICE FILE CARDS.  HE THEN IDENTIFIED SUCH FILE CARD
BEARING NAME AND ADDRESS OF PRISCILLA HISS AND SAME IN EVIDENCE OVER
OBJECTION.  WITNESS TESTIFIED THERE WAS A MORNINGSIDE BRANCH OF SP IN
THIRTYTWO.  ONLY INQUIRY ON CROSS BROUGHT OUT THAT WITNESS LEFT SP IN
THIRTYSIX.  FRANCES O. BOOTH THEN TESTIFIED RE MIKE CATLETT AND TWO
WHITE MEN COMING TO HER WASHINGTON RESIDENCE ONE NIGHT LAST MARCH, SAID
MIKE TOLD HER THEY WERE FBI MEN AND THAT HE WAS WORKING WITH FBI.
SHE TOLD HIM AND THE MEN THAT SHE REMEMBERED A TYPEWRITER IN THE CATLETT
RESIDENCE.  MIKE RETURNED NEXT DAY AND TOLD HER TO SAY NOTHING OF
VISIT PREVIOUS EVENING.  ON CROSS WITNESS TESTIFIED SHE NEVER HAD
POSSESSION OF THE TYPEWRITER BUT DID SEE IT IN CATLETT HOME IN LATE
SUMMER OF THIRTYNINE WHEN SHE ROOMED THERE.  SHE THEN NAMED ALL THE

EX. 93

4484

PAGE THREE

RECENTLY SOME ONIONSKIN COPY SHEETS AND SAID SHE SECURED SAME AT HER
HOME AND THAT THEY HAD BEEN PURCHASED BY HER FATHER IN THE EARLY THIR-
TIES. SA JOHN S. MC COOL, OF NYO, WAS SWORN AND STEPPED DOWN FROM WIT-
NESS STAND AND AT REQUEST OF MURPHY MADE COPY ON ONE OF SHEETS PUT IN
EVIDENCE THROUGH MISS REYNOLDS OF BALTO DOCUMENT THIRTYTWO ON THE WOOD-
STOCK TYPEWRITER IN EVIDENCE. COPY TYPED BY SA MC COOL THEN PUT IN EVI-
DENCE. NO CROSS. SA FRANCIS J. DUANE, OF WFO, THEN IDENTIFIED PHOTO-
GRAPHIC ENLARGEMENTS OF FIVE ADS HE LOCATED IN WASHINGTON NEWSPAPERS FOR
SALE OF VOLTA PLACE HOUSE. MURPHY EXPLAINED TO JURY THAT DATES OF SUCH
ADS WERE OCT. SEVENTEE, TWENTYSIX, TWENTYSEVEN, TWENTYEIGHT AND DEC.
FIFTH, NINETEEN THIRTYSEVEN. ON CROSS WITNESS TESTIFIED HE DID NOT KNOW
THAT LEASE SIGNED BY HISSES FOR VOLTA PLACE HOUSE WAS DATED DEC. SECOND,
THIRTYSEVEN. LAST WITNESS OF AM WAS EDITH MURRAY, WHO TESTIFIED SHE
WORKED AS A MAID FOR MR. AND MRS. LLOYD CANTWELL AT THEIR ST. PAUL ST.
AND EUTAW PLACE RESIDENCES IN BALTO AND THAT SHE REMEMBERED THEIR LITTLE
GIRL, NAMED ELLEN. SAID CHAMBERS WAS HOME ONLY WEEKENDS AND THAT SHE
RECALLS ONLY TWO VISITORS TO CHAMBERS RESIDENCE ON EUTAW PLACE. SHE
THEN POINTED OUT PRISCILLA IN THE COURTROOM AND SAID SHE WAS THE LADY
END PAGE THREE

AGE FOUR

HO VISITED MRS. CHAMBERS AT THAT HOUSE AND SAID SHE RECALLS PRISCILLA
COMING THERE ON A TOTAL OF FOUR OCCASIONS. ONE OF WHICH WHEN SHE WAS
ACCOMPANIED BY ALGER, WHOM SHE THEN POINTED OUT IN THE COURTROOM.
SAID SHE RECALLS DISTINCTLY ONE VISIT MADE BY PRISCILLA WHEN SHE STAYED
OVERNIGHT AT CHAMBERS APT. BECAUSE MRS. CHAMBERS HAD TO GO TO NYC FOR
PRENATAL CARE. WITNESS SAID PRISCILLA TOLD HER SHE WAS FROM WASHING-
TON AND THAT SHE HAD A LITTLE BOY. SAID SHE CALLED MRS. HISS "MISS
PRISCILLA" AND THAT LAST NOV. FBI TOOK HER TO FARM NEAR WESTMINSTER
WHERE SHE IDENTIFIED MR. AND MRS. CHAMBERS AS BEING THE CANTWELLS FOR
WHOM SHE WORKED. SHE THEN IDENTIFIED AN OLD PHOTO OF PRISCILLA
ALREADY IN EVIDENCE. ON CROSS WITNESS TESTIFED CHAMBERS FAMILY OCCU-
PIED THIRD FLOOR APT. ON ST. PAUL ST. WHEN SHE BEGAN WORKING FOR THEM
IN THE FALL OF THIRTYFOUR AND SHE HAS NO RECOLLECTION RE DOORBELL OR
MAILBOX. SAID CHAMBERS LEFT THAT ADDRESS FOLLOWING SPRING AND IN THAT
FALL, WHICH WAS THIRTYFIVE, SHE AGAIN WORKED FOR THEM AT EUTAW PLACE
UNTIL THE FOLLOWING SPRING, AND HAD NOT SEEN THEM AGAIN UNTIL NOV.,
FORTYNINE AT THE FARM. REITERATED SHE SAW PRISCILLA AT EUTAW PLACE ON
FOUR DIFFERENT OCCASIONS WHICH SHE CAN RECALL AND SAID IT WAS POSSIBLE
END PAGE FOUR

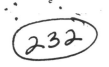

PAGE FIVE

SHE HAD BEEN THERE MORE TIMES. SAID ALGER CAME WITH PRISCILLA ONE
EVENING TO THE EUTAW PLACE APT. AND THAT WAS ONLY TIME SHE HAD EVER
SEEN HIM. SAID SHE IDENTIFIED HISSES ON NOV. SEVENTEEN, LAST IN COR-
RIDOR OUTSIDE COURTROOM IN NYC. SAID SHE HAD PREVIOUSLY SEEN PHOTO-
GRAPHS OF THEM, AS WELL AS OF CHAMBERS AND WIFE. FIRST SAW FBI ONE
SUNDAY LAST NOV. AND NEXT DAY WAS TAKEN TO CHAMBERS FARM. INSISTED
FBI AGENTS NEVER MENTIONED NAME HISS TO HER AND THAT THEY SIMPLY
ASKED HER WHEN EXHIBITING PHOTOS IF SHE COULD IDENTIFY THEM. SAID SHE
HAS NOT READ NEWSPAPERS SINCE FORTYTWO EXCEPT COMICS, AND DENIED
HAVING SEEN ANY NEWSREEL PICTURES OF HISSES. SHE WAS QUESTIONED RATHER
CLOSELY BUT REMAINED FIRM IN HER TESTIMONY. SAID SHE HAS NOT WORKED AS
A DOMESTIC SINCE FORTYTWO AND THAT FIRST PHOTO OF PRISCILLA SHOWN HER
WAS A PROFILE. SHE WAS QUESTIONED CLOSELY ABOUT HER REACTION WHEN SHE
FIRST SAW THIS PHOTO AND SHE SAID SHE THOUGHT TO HERSELF THAT SHE HAD
SEEN THAT WOMAN BEFORE, BUT WAS NOT SURE IF SHE HAD SEEN HER IN THE
MOVIES, OR WHERE IT HAD BEEN. SHE CONTINUED TO INSIST THAT SHE WAS
NEVER TOLD ANYTHING IN ADVANCE BY AGENTS WHEN VARIOUS PHOTOS WERE DIS-
PLAYED TO HER AND SAID THEONLY TIME SHE SAW ANY PHOTOS WAS INITIAL
VISIT FROM FBI ONE SUNDAY LAST NOV. SAID SHE NEVER EVEN HEARD THE NAME
HISS UNTIL SHE IDENTIFIED ALGER AND PRISCILLA IN NYC. SHE THEN DES-
END PAGE FIVE

233

BED CHAMBERS AS SHE REMEMBERED HIM FROM THIRTYFOUR AND THIRTYFIVE

COULD NOT RECALL IF HE EVER HAD A MUSTACHE. THIS WITNESS WAS VERY

ECTIVE AND BECAME EVEN MORE SO AS CROSS EXAMINATION CONTINUED.

ENSE COUNSEL VOLUNTEERED INFORMALLY AFTER LUNCHEON RECESS WAS CALLED

AT THIS WITNESS HAD BEEN EXTREMELY DAMAGING TO THEIR CASE. REMAIN-.

G REBUTTAL WITNESSES TO BE HEARD THIS PM ARE MRS. TALLEY RE LEASE OF

LTA PLACE AND JOHN FOSTER DULLES.

SCHEIDT

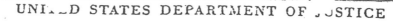

UNITED STATES DEPARTMENT OF JUSTICE

FEDERAL BUREAU OF INVESTIGATION

WASHINGTON, D.C. 20535

(234)

January 4, 1978

Ms. K. Randlett Walster
Attorney at Law
Rabinowitz, Boudin and Standard
30 East 42nd Street
New York, New York   10017

Dear Ms. Walster:

        The enclosed FBI documents were found in a search
of the files maintained by the United States Attorney
for the Southern District of New York and were forwarded
to us for a determination of releasability pursuant to the
Freedom of Information Act.

        A total 68 documents were forwarded to the Bureau
for review and all are releasable except one document
which is being denied in total under Title 26, United States
Code, Section 6103 and Title 5, United States Code, Section
552 (b)(3).   In addition, three documents have minor deletions
and are otherwise released in their entirety.   Detailed
explanations of the denied material are enclosed with
this release.

        These documents have been reviewed for inclusion
in the public records maintained by the United States
Attorney for the Southern District of New York and are
also being made available to you without charge.

                        Sincerely yours,

                        *Allen H. McCreight Jr.* (signature)

                        Allen H. McCreight, Chief
                        Freedom of Information-
                          Privacy Acts Branch
                        Records Management Division

Enclosures (71)

Ex.94

September 28, 1949

I, Mrs. Ellwood F. Murray, also known as Mrs. Edith Gland Murray, 342 Bloom Street, Baltimore, Maryland, wish to furnish the following information voluntarily to Special Agents Joseph R. Marszalek, Edward G. Gough and Frank G. Johnstone of the Federal Bureau of Investigation.

Sometime in the fall of 1934 I first met Mr. and Mrs. Cantwell who were then residing in a second floor apartment at 903 St. Paul Street, Baltimore. At that time I was referred to the Cantwells by their former maid and the Cantwells hired me as their new maid. I worked for the Cantwells as their maid at 903 St. Paul Street through the winter months and until the spring of 1935. In the spring of 1935 the Cantwells left Baltimore and told me they were going to New York City.

In the fall of 1935 I met Mrs. Cantwell on the street near my home, which was then at 1113 Madison Avenue, Baltimore, and Mrs. Cantwell rehired me as their maid. Mrs. Cantwell told me then that they were living at that time in Washington, D. C. but gave me no further details. I first cleaned up the Cantwells' new apartment on the second floor at 1617 Eutaw Place, Baltimore before they moved into it. I remember that the Cantwells disposed of the furniture they had at 903 St. Paul Street when they moved out of town and recall definitely that they gave me three chairs at that time. I do not know where the Cantwells got the furniture for 1617 Eutaw Place, whether they bought it all or had some given to them. I do remember that when they moved in at this address, several days after Mrs. Cantwell

FD-141
(7-1-48)

BULKY EXHIBIT

Date received _____ 11-19-49

JAHAM

65-14920 - 1B
(Title of case)

Submitted by Special Agent _____ T. G. Spencer

Source from which obtained _____ Baltimore Office - See Serial #5232

Address _____

Purpose for which acquired _____ Investigation

Location of bulky exhibit _____ In cabinet with file

Estimated date of disposition _____ Retain, pending conclusion of case

Ultimate disposition to be made of exhibit _____ To be decided by Agent

List of contents:

541. One (1) original signed statement of Mrs. EDITH GLAND MURRAY, 342
Bloom Street, Baltimore, dated November 18, 1949.

*The original signed statement
is in the U.S. Attorney's office, S. D. N. Y.
#12*

65-14920-1L-323

FBI : NEW YORK
FEB 3 1950

EX 95

① *Priscilla Hiss*

② *Typewriting Specimens*

### FEDERAL BUREAU OF INVESTIGATION · WASHINGTON D. C.

Se 26 - 3/15/76 (237)

FBI 1/25/49
3/15/76
1359

January 25, 1949

To: SAC, Washington .

There follows the report of the FBI laboratory on the examination requested in your teletype dated January 19, 1949.

Re:

J. D. *ALGER HISS*
with aliases, et al
Perjury; Espionage - R
Internal Security - R

*John Edgar Hoover, Director*

YOUR FILE NO.

FBI FILE NO.

LAB. NO.

Examination requested by:

Reference: Washington

Examination requested: Teletype dated 1-19-49

Specimens: Document

*- p tely plus 1-p lab report indicating Prisc. Hiss typing*

Request of a comparison of the corrections, handlettering, spelling, typographical errors, et cetera in 132, 137, Q665, 741, 2249, R646, 1159 and 1157 with those in 45 through 467.

Result of Examination:

A comparison of the corrections, handlettering, spelling, typographical errors, et cetera, in specimens 45 through 467 with those in 137, 132, 741, Q665, 1159, 1157, 2257 and 1449 does not disclose individual characteristics or habits sufficient for a conclusive identifying or eliminating as to who as the person who typed or corrected the questioned documents 45 through 467.

It is believed . . . handprinted specimens of PRISCILLA HISS would be of no . . . certain with the limited handprinting appearing on 45 through 467.

3 - New York
1 - Philadelphia
1 - Communications

1359

EX. 96

# REPORT
## of the
## FBI
## Laboratory

## FEDERAL BUREAU OF INVESTIGATION
### WASHINGTON D.C.

To: SAC, Washington                                      January 25, 1949

There follows the report of the FBI Laboratory on the examination requested in your teletype dated January 19, 1949.

                                        John Edgar Hoover, Director

Re: J.D. Whitaker Chambers
    with aliases, et al                  Your File No.
    Perjury; Espionage - R               FBI File No.
    Internal Security - R                Lab. No.

Examination requested by: Washington

Reference: Teletype dated 1-19-49

Specimens: Document

Request of a comparison of the corrections, handlettering, spelling, typographical errors, et cetera in K32, K17, Kc60, K41, K249, K156, K159 and K157 with those in Q5 through Q69.

Result of Examination:

A comparison of the corrections, handlettering, spelling, typographic errors, et cetera, in specimens Q5 through Q69 with those in K17, K32, K41 Kc60, K156, K159, K157 and K249 does not disclose individual characteristi or habits sufficient for a conclusion identifying or eliminating Mrs. Hiss as the person who typed or corrected the questioned documents Q5 through Q

It is believed that the handprinted specimens of Priscilla Hiss would be of no (illegible) comparison with the limited handprinting appear on Q5 through Q69.

2 - New York
1 - Philadelphia
1 - (Illegible)

(4)

WASHINGTON AND NEW YORK FROM WASH FIELD    1-19-49

DIRECTOR AND SAC, NEW YORK

J. D. WHITTAKER CHAMBERS, WAS, ETAL, PERJURY, ESP - R, IS - R.

RE FBI LAB REPORT JANUARY EIGHTEEN, LAST, REFLECTING EXAMINATION OF

SPECIMEN K THREE NAUGHT THREE.  *K303*  PARAGRAPH TWO OF THIS REPORT DEALS WITH A

COMPARISON OF THE CORRECTIONS, HAND LETTERING, SPELLING, TYPOGRAPHICAL

ERRORS, ETC. IN K THREE NAUGHT THREE  *K303*  WITH THOSE IN Q FIVE THROUGH Q SIXTEEN. *Q5 > Q69*

IT IS REQUESTED FBI LAB MAKE A SIMILAR EXAMINATION IN REGARD TO SPECIMENS

K THIRTYTWO, K SEVENTEEN, KO SIXTY, K FORTYONE, K TWO FOUR NINE, K ONE FIVE SIX,   *K32  K17  K60  K41  K249  K156*

K ONE FIVE NINE, K ONE FIVE SEVEN, WHICH ARE TYPEWRITING OF MRS. HISS.   *K159  K157*

IF FBI LAB FEELS ADDITIONAL HANDWRITING SPECIMENS OF PRISCILLA HISS WOULD

BE OF ASSISTANCE, IT IS BELIEVED THAT SAME CAN BE OBTAINED BY WFO.

1359

4

*Office Memorandum* • UNITED STATES

TO : Director, FBI    ATT: (FBI LABORATORY)    DATE: December 10, 1948

FROM : SAC, New York

SUBJECT: JAY DAVID WHITTAKER CHAMBERS
PERJURY; ESPIONAGE - R

*① typewriting specimens*
*② Hiss lawyers*

Reference is made to a letter from the New York Office to the Bureau dated December 7, 1948, wherein specimens of typewriting furnished by Mr. EDWARD C. MC LEAN, attorney for Mr. ALGER HISS, were furnished to the Laboratory for examination and comparison purposes. There was furnished at that time a copy of a letter dated January 30, 1933, 378 Central Park West, New York City, addressed to WALTER L. TIBBETTS, ESQ., 1216 Atlantic National Bank Building, Boston, Mass.

Today, Mr. EDWARD C. MC LEAN furnished the original copy of the letter addressed to WALTER L. TIBBETTS, ESQ., 1216 Atlantic National Bank Building, Boston, Mass. Mr. MC LEAN advised that the letter had actually never been sent and it is unsigned. Mr. MC LEAN stated that he was furnishing it to this office for examination in an effort to determine if it was typewritten on the questioned typewriter. The Bureau requested the Boston Office to attempt to ascertain this original copy of the letter. Boston has been advised that the letter was furnished by Mr. MC LEAN to this office today.

*1-P memo to JEK, W all lab report .*

There is also enclosed herewith a carbon copy of a letter dated February 17, 1933, 378 Central Park West, New York, New York. This letter was addressed to WALTER G. SCHELKER, Assistant Secretary, The Equitable Life Assurance Society, 393 Seventh Avenue, New York, New York.

The Laboratory is requested to examine these specimens and compare the results of the examination with the typewriting on the documents furnished by Mr. WHITTAKER CHAMBERS, who states that the documents were furnished to him by Mr. ALGER HISS and copied on the HISS typewriter. It is requested that upon the completion of the examination, the results and the specimens be forwarded to the New York Office.

Mr. MC LEAN has been advised that the results of this examination will not be furnished to him, but he has insisted that these specimens be returned to him. He was unable to offer any explanation why the original copy of this letter was in Mr. HISS' possession, when it was not mailed to the addressee, and he also advised that he does not know whether these specimens were typed on the typewriter which Mr. HISS had in his possession.

Encs.(2) -    SPECIAL DELIVERY
             REGISTERED MAIL - RETURN RECEIPT REQUESTED

RECORDED - 

E x 97

# REPORT
## of the
### FBI LABORATORY

## FEDERAL BUREAU OF INVESTIGATION
### WASHINGTON D.C.

December 14, 1943

To: SAC: New York

There follows the report of the FBI Laboratory on the examination of the evidence received from your office on December 10, 1943.

*John Edgar Hoover, Director*

Re: [illegible]

YOUR FILE NO.

FBI FILE NO.

LAB. NO

Examination requested by: New York

Reference: Letter dated December 10, 1943

Examination requested: Document

Specimens:

[illegible — faded typewritten text]

REPORT
of the
FBI
Laboratory

FEDERAL BUREAU OF INVESTIGATION
WASHINGTON D.C.

To: SAC, New York                                    December 14, 1948

There follows the report of the FBI Laboratory on the examination
of the evidence received from your office on December 13, 1948.

John Edgar Hoover, Director

Re: Jay David Whittaker Chambers
    Perjury; Espionage - R

Your File No.
FBI File No.
Lab. No.

Examination requested by: New York

Reference: Letter dated December 10, 1948

Examination requested: Document

Specimens:
K17     (Photostats previously submitted) Original two-page typewritten
        letter dated January 30, 1933, beginning "Dear Walter, on reading
        over my policy last week .....", second page beginning:"(illegible)
        stating that I had 'always' lived in my ......". The letter is
        unsigned, and purportedly typewritten by MRS. ALGER HISS.

K33     Carbon copy of typewritten letter, dated February 17, 1933, addresse
        "Walter O. Schelker, Assistant Secretary, The Equitable Life Assurar
        Society, 393 Seventh Avenue, New York, New York", letter beginning:
        "This is in reply to your letter of .....".

RESULTS OF EXAMINATION:

        The conclusion was reached that the typewriting appearing on specime
K17 was typed by the machine which typed K32 and Q6 through Q69.

        The typewriting on K33 was not clear enough for a definite conclusio
to be made in a comparison with evidence in this case.

        The additional evidence, K17 and K33, is returned herewith to the Ne
York office, photographic copies having been made for the Bureau's file.

Enclosures - REGISTERED MAIL          1 - Philadelphia
1 - Milwaukee                         1 - Washington Field
1 - (Illegible)

UNITED STATES DISTRICT COURT
SOUTHERN DISTRICT OF NEW YORK

- - - - - - - - - - - - - - - - - x

UNITED STATES OF AMERICA,                :

              Plaintiff,    :

        -v-                   :    AFFIDAVIT

ALGER HISS,                              :

              Defendant.    :

- - - - - - - - - - - - - - - - - x

STATE OF NEW YORK    )
COUNTY OF NEW YORK    )  ss:

        THOMAS F. MURPHY, being duly sworn, deposes and
says:

        I am the Assistant United States Attorney in
charge of the above entitled matter and make this affidavit in opposition to the defendant's order to show cause
why an order should not be made pursuant to Rule 16 of the
Federal Rules of Criminal Procedure permitting the defendant to inspect and copy certain documents and to submit others to experts for testing as to quality, age and
characteristics.

        The requested documents fall into two categories:
(a) typewritten documents emanating from any typewriter
previously belonging to the defendant, and (b) typewritten
or handwritten documents emanating from persons not
parties to this proceeding, to wit, Whittaker Chambers
and his wife Esther Chambers.

that it will help him fix the date when he says he gave the
Woodstock typewriter to the Catletts. Oddly enough, the
defendant doesn't state this, but his attorney makes the
oath, thus avoiding possible cross-examination material.
It is respectfully submitted that an inspection of such
material is not for the spurious purpose alleged, but merely
to learn in advance what material the Government has in its
possession to confront and confuse the defendant when he
takes the stand and offers the story of the gift of the
typewriter to the Catletts. Obviously, the typewritten
specimens from the Corona typewriter could not help fix the
date of the alleged gift of the Woodstock typewriter. The
defendant has already testified under oath that he gave it
to the Catletts prior to January 1, 1938.

The second category of documents requested are
those typewritten and handwritten documents of the witnesses,
Whittaker Chambers and Esther Chambers. The defendant's
attorney says that these are needed so as to help in the
determination of who the operator of the Woodstock machine
was at the time the "Baltimore papers were written". This
category falls outside of the scope of Rule 16 since there
is no affirmative showing that these documents belong to
the defendant or were seized from others or obtained by
process. Even if such a showing was made, it strains one's

imagination   see how that would tend   prove who the operator of the Woodstock typewriter was.  It can hardly be claimed that an expert could tell what individual typed a certain instrument by having a specimen of his typing since the impressions are made by a mechanical means, and how handwriting could help in determination of who was the operator who typed a certain instrument seems more incredulous.

-3-

FBI 12/4/41

MCO:veh　　　1437 K Street, Northwest
101-606　　　　Washington, D. C.
　　　　　　　December 4, 1941

Mr. Vincent C. Burke
Postmaster
Washington, D. C.

　　　　　　　　　Re: ALGER HISS
　　　　　　　　　INTERNAL SECURITY
　　　　　　　　　HATCH ACT

Dear Sir:

　　　　　　In connection with an official investigation
being conducted in this office, it is requested that a
fifteen-day mail cover be placed on all mail received at
3415 Volta Place, N. W., Washington, D. C.

　　　　　　In any communications regarding this matter,
please refer to our file number 101-606.

　　　　　　　　　Very truly yours,

　　　　　　　　　S. K. McKEE
　　　　　　　　　Special Agent in Charge

1-p memo instructing

EX 98A

101-606-4

(247)

# FEDERAL BUREAU OF INVESTIGATION

| | DATE WHEN MADE | PERIOD FOR WHICH MADE | REPORT MADE BY |
|---|---|---|---|
| WASHINGTON, D.C. | 4-19-45 | 3/23-4/11/45 | LOGAN J. LANE |

CASE OR ORIGINATED AT BUREAU

FILE NO. 100-17,162

4-19-45

CHANGED:

PHILIP JACOB JAFFE, with aliases; et al

CHARACTER OF CASE

STRICTLY CONFIDENTIAL

92079

SYNOPSIS OF FACTS:

Background information

ALGER HISS

1) AH Re '78 Surveillance

2) Philip Jaffe Amerasia Case

AT WASHINGTON, D.C.

5 p's of 17 pyprts on Philip Jaffe Notes AH toll calls were monitored undept 43 also cause reference to mail cover

DETAILS DESTROYED
72 FEB 11 1961

100-267360-113

INDEXED

COPIES OF THIS REPORT

5 - Bureau
2 - New York
2 - Washington Field

EX 99

## ALGER HISS

The files of the Civil Service Commission were reviewed by the writer on March 28, 1945, with reference to ALGER HISS. It is noted that HISS resides at 3210 P Street, N. W., Washington, D. C., telephone Michigan 0811. The files of the Civil Service Commission reflect that HISS was born on November 11, 1904, at Baltimore, Maryland. He received his preparatory education in the Baltimore Public Schools and at Powder Point Academy, Duxbury, Massachusetts. He received his A. B. degree in 1926 from Johns Hopkins University, where he was also a member of Phi Beta Kappa. He specialized in political science and foreign languages. He received his LLB degree from Harvard University in 1929 with honors. He is a member of the bar of the States of Massachusetts and New York. While at Harvard he pursued studies, among others, in international law. He was employed as secretary to Justice HOLMES of the U. S. Supreme Court from 1929 to 1930. He was employed as an associate in the office of CHOATE, HALL and STEWART, Boston, Massachusetts, from October, 1930, to April, 1932, and as an associate in the office of COTTON, FRANKLIN, WRIGHT and GORDON in New York City from April, 1932, to May, 1933. He was employed as assistant to the General Counsel of the Agricultural Adjustment Administration in May, 1933, which was his first Government employment. From August, 1934, to August, 1935, he was employed as legal assistant to the Senate Munitions Committee and from the beginning of this employment to April, 1935, he was on assignment to the Committee from the Agricultural Department.

He was employed as a special attorney in the Office of the Solicitor General, Justice Department, from August, 1935, to August, 1936, and was then employed as assistant to an Assistant Secretary of State on September 1, 1936. On September 13, 1939, he was detailed to the Office of the Advisor on Political Relations, Dr. HORNBECK. His duties were in reference to the Far East (China, Japan, Thailand, Philippines), where it was his duty to maintain liaison with the Executive Assistant to the President on matters relating to China, and with officers of the Army and Navy. He also was to maintain direct liaison with the Department of Justice in all legal matters regarding the trade agreements program. On January 13, 1942, the Civil Service Commission approved his appointment as Special Assistant to the Advisor on Political Relations, Department of State.

The service records of the Civil Service Commission regarding ALGER HISS reflect the following Government employment:

| Date | Position | Salary | Agency |
|------|----------|--------|--------|
| 5-12-33 | Principal Attorney | $6000 | Agricultural Dept., A.A.A. |
| 3-21-34 | Discharged without prejudice | | |
| 3-22-34 | Special Attorney | $6800 | " " " |

100-267360-113

4/19/50

| Date | Position | Salary | Agency |
|------|----------|--------|--------|
| 7-1-34 | Re-adjustment | $6500 | Agricultural Dept., A.A.A. |
| 10-4-34 | Discharged without prejudice | | |
| 10-5-34 | Special Attorney | $6500 | " " " |
| 4-4-35 | Resigned without prejudice | | |
| 8-15-35 | Special Attorney | $6000 | Justice Department |
| 7-1-36 | Promoted | $7500 | " " |
| 8-31-36 | Resigned without prejudice | | |
| 9-1-36 | Assistant to an Assistant Secretary of State | $5600 | State Department |
| 6-1-39 | Promoted | $5800 | " " |
| 1-1-42 | Promoted (with Mr. ACHESON) | 6000 | |
| 1-16-42 | Special Assistant to Advisor on Political Relations (HORNBECK) | $6500 | State Department |
| 11-16-44 | Deputy Director, Office of Special Political Affairs | $8000 | State Department |

It is noted that an article appeared in the Washington Evening Star on April 6, 1945, which stated that ALGER HISS, Director of the Office of Special Political Affairs, State Department, is to be Secretary General of the forthcoming San Francisco Conference on world security. This appointment is to a permanent post, according to the article, and he was so designated by the President on April 6, 1945.

By cover letter dated April 2, 1945, the telephone toll calls from the telephone listed to ALGER HISS at MIchigan 0811 from September 20, 1943, to December 14, 1944, were furnished to the Bureau.

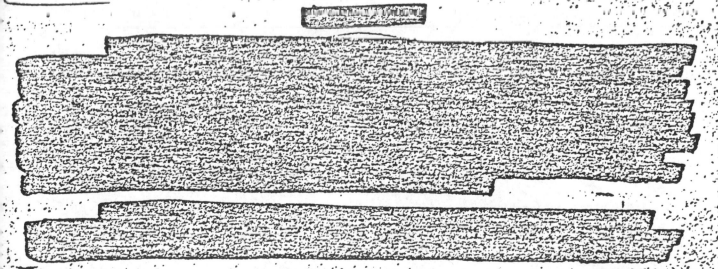

100-267360-113

4/19/45

A mail cover placed on mail delivered to the residence of ALGER HISS, 3210 P Street, N. W., reflected the following return addresses:

Congress of the United States
Senator CARL HAYDEN

American Society for International Law
700 Jackson Place, N. W.
Washington, D. C.

United China Relief, Incorporated
1720 Eye Street, N. W.
Washington, D. C.

100-267360-13

FEDERAL BUREAU OF INVESTIGATION

Form No. 1

This Case Originated At NEW YORK, NEW YORK    File No. 100-17493

| Report Made At | Date When Made | Period For Which Made | Report Made By |
|---|---|---|---|
| WASHINGTON, D. C. | 10 APR 1946 | 12/17/45- 3/14/46 | W. ALBERT STEWART, JR. WAS:MCP |

| Title | Character of Case |
|---|---|
| NATHAN GREGORY SILVERMASTER, was, Et Al | ESPIONAGE - R |

SYNOPSIS OF FACTS:

Long distance telephone calls and telegrams, covering 1945, of the following subjects are hereinafter set out:

ALGER HISS

REFERENCE:     Bureau File 65-56402.

COPIES DESTROYED

Approved and Forwarded:                    Special Agent in Charge        Do Not Write In These Spaces

Copies of this Report
  5 - Bureau
  3 - New York
  2 - Washington Field

| Number of Times Called | Date | Place Called | Number Called |
|---|---|---|---|
| 1 | 10/17/45 | New York City | CIRcle 6-9882 |

Information received from confidential sources indicated that the above call was a collect call from CIRcle 6-9882 made by TIMOTHY HOBSON to ALGER HISS at MIchigan 0811.

By letter dated January 23, 1946, the New York Field Division advised that New York telephone number CIRcle 6-9882 is listed to DANIEL L. BOWEN, 45 West 56th Street, New York City.

The following telegrams were charged to the telephone number of ALGER HISS, MIchigan 0811:

On September 24, 1945, a telegram was directed to Mrs. JOHN ALFORD, 35-A Charles Field Street, Providence, Rhode Island, and read as follows:

"Am spending Tuesday night in New York.
Arriving Providence Wednesday afternoon.
Signed - SUE FANSLER".

WFO 100-17493

A telegram dated November 11, 1945, was dispatched to Mrs.
CHARLES ALGER HISS and Miss ANNA HISS, Atlantic City, which read as follows:

"Delighted you are having rest in Atlantic
City and appreciate your thoughtful
invitation. Stop. Unfortunately it would
be impossible for me to be away this week.
Love and Thanks. ALGER ".

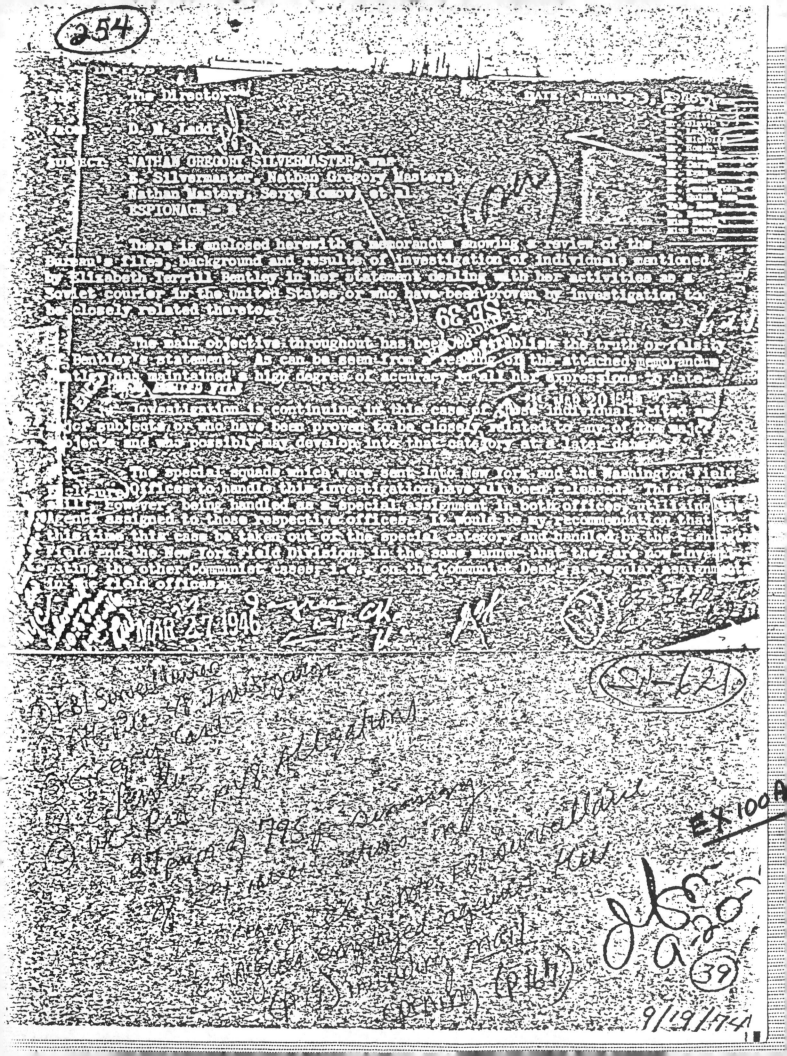

254

TO: The Director                           DATE: January 3, 1946

FROM: D. M. Ladd

SUBJECT: NATHAN GREGORY SILVERMASTER, was.
N. Silvermaster, Nathan Gregory Masters,
Nathan Masters, Serge Komov, et al
ESPIONAGE - R.

There is enclosed herewith a memorandum showing a review of the Bureau's files, background and results of investigation of individuals mentioned by Elizabeth Terrill Bentley in her statement dealing with her activities as a Soviet courier in the United States or who have been proven by investigation to be closely related thereto.

The main objective throughout has been to establish the truth or falsity of Bentley's statement. As can be seen from a reading of the attached memorandum she has maintained a high degree of accuracy in all her expressions to date.

Investigation is continuing in this case of those individuals cited as major subjects or who have been proven to be closely related to any of the major subjects and who possibly may develop into that category at a later date.

The special squads which were sent into New York and the Washington Field Offices to handle this investigation have all been released. This case is, however, being handled as a special assignment in both offices, utilizing the Agents assigned to those respective offices. It would be my recommendation that at this time this case be taken out of the special category and handled by the Washington Field and the New York Field Divisions in the same manner that they are now investigating the other Communist cases; i.e., on the Communist Desk as regular assignments in the field offices.

MAR 27 1946

TO:       The Director                    DATE: January 3, 1946

FROM:     D. M. Ladd

SUBJECT:  NATHAN GREGORY SILVERMASTER, was
          E. Silvermaster, Nathan Gregory Masters,
          Nathan Masters, Serge Komov, et al
          ESPIONAGE - R

There is enclosed herewith a memorandum showing a review of the Bureau's files, background and results of investigation of individuals mentioned by Elizabeth Terrill Bentley in her statement dealing with her activities as a Soviet courier in the United States or who have been proven by investigation to be closely related thereto.

The main objective throughout has been to establish the truth or falsity of Bentley's statement. As can be seen from a reading of the attached memorandum Bentley has maintained a high degree of accuracy in all her expressions to date.

Investigation is continuing in this case of those individuals cited as major subjects or who have been proven to be closely related to any of the major subjects and who possibly may develop into that category at a later date.

The special squads which were sent into New York and the Washington Field Offices to handle this investigation have all been released. This case is still, however, being handled as a special assignment in both offices, utilizing the Agents assigned to those respective offices. It would be my recommendation that at this time this case be taken out of the special category and handled by the Washington Field and the New York Field Divisions in the same manner that they are now investigating the other Communist cases; i.e., on the Communist Desk, as regular assignments in the field offices.

RE: NATHAN GREGORY SILVERMASTER, with aliases
E. Silvermaster
Nathan Gregory Masters
Nathan Masters
Serge Komov: Et Al
ESPIONAGE - R.

Jan 3, 1946

For index see
end of Part 2

621

2

## RESULTS OF INVESTIGATION

Through a mail intercept it was determined that Mrs. Alger Hiss informed her son Timothy Habson, 45 West 56th Street, New York City, that Alger Hiss expected to sail from the United States for London around the 27th or 28th of December. According to this same source, it was determined that both Mr. and Mrs. Alger Hiss have been studying the problem of atomic energy. Mrs. Hiss stated that she daily attends the Senate hearings on the atomic power question, and she and her husband Alger have been attempting to read and understand the Smythe report.

On November 28, 1945, a man and woman were observed to visit the Hiss home and subsequently on the same evening Alger Hiss and his wife accompanied this man and woman in their automobile. There persons have been identified as Mr. and Mrs. Ben T. Moore, 3101 P Street, N.W., Washington, D. C. The physical surveillance reflected that Ben T. Moore and his wife visited at the Hiss residence on December 4, 1945.

On December 10, 1945, Alger and Priscilla Hiss were guests in the home of Lawrence Meredith Clemson Smith at 3230 Reservoir Road, N.W., Washington, D. C. On this same occassion an automobile which is listed to the Polish Embassy was observed to park alongside the Smith residence.

37895

FEDERAL BUREAU OF INVESTIGATION

Form No. 1
This Case Originated At NEW YORK, NEW YORK   File No. 100-17493

| Report Made At | Date When Made | Period for Which Made | Report Made By |
|---|---|---|---|
| WASHINGTON, D. C. | 4/15/46 | 3/16-31/46 | LAMBERT G. ZANDER - LGZ:JAG |

| Title | Character of Case |
|---|---|
| NATHAN GREGORY SILVERMASTER with aliases et al | ESPIONAGE - R |

EX 100 B

SIL 1019

COPIES DESTROYED

Approved and
Forwarded

Copies of This Report
5 - Bureau
3 - New York
3 - Washington Field

29

WFO 100-17493

Information was received from a highly confidential source to the

to Mr. ALGER HISS, which read as follows:

"December 24, 1945

"Dear Mr. HISS:

"In accordance with our conversation the other day about the UNO, I am writing you a brief resume of my background. I have also filed application with Mrs. SELVIG as you suggested. I am particularly interested in the trusteeship council, to which I believe my experience, background, and interests logically point. I have been in Washington since 1942 in various Government capacities.

"I first came in as a Senior Analyst with the Board of Economic Warfare in the United Nations Division and worked chiefly on lend-lease matters, especially relating to China and India. Within a few months I was detailed to the staff of the White House as an assistant to LAUCHLIN CURRIE on various international questions, mainly in the Far East and including Korea and Indo-China. After more than a year in the White House, I returned to FEA to work on problems of rehabilitated areas in both Europe and Asia, and including relaations with UNRRA. In 1944 I was Chief of the Southeast Asia Section under RUPERT EMERSON, dealing specifically with such independent areas as India, Malaya, Indo-China, and the Philippines. Subsequently, I became Chief of the Government Controls Section of the Enemy Branch engaged in planning for military occupation in Germany and Japan. My current assignment is to GHQ-SCAP (Supreme Command Allied Powers), Tokyo, to help work out policy problems connected with changes in the Japanese government and with the Allied Control Council.

"Before coming to Washington I was with the Institute of Pacific Relations in New York as a member of its International Secretariat. I shared administrative responsibility for planning and procedures at the various international conferences held periodically by the IPR. These conferences were attended by both Government officials and public figures from Britain, U.S.S.R., China, France, Holland, India, Philippines, etc. I helped prepare agenda, draw up reports, act as rapporteur of panels and commissions, especially those dealing with colonial problems. In between conferences I assisted the Secretary General, E.

32

WFO 100-17493

"Mr. EDWARD C. CARTER, on secretariat matters. When in 1941 Mr. OWEN LATTIMORE left for China, I succeeded him as managing editor of "Pacific Affairs."

"Previous to the IPR, I was a Research Fellow at Harvard University and at Cambridge University, England. At Cambridge where I graduated with high honors (a double first), I was elected a Fellow of Trinity College. At Harvard I was a Joseph H. Choate Fellow. My Ph.D. thesis was on International Relations in the Far East.

"My languages are French, Spanish, German, and some elementary Chinese. I have traveled extensively in Europe and Asia and slightly in Latin America and North Africa.

"I expect to stay in Tokyo for several months and would then be available. Of course, anything you might be able to do for me would be most appreciated.

"Sincerely yours,

/s/ MICHAEL GREENBURG"

Several penciled changes appeared on this letter, among which were a change of date from December 24, 1945, to March 20, 1946, and the last paragraph of the letter changed to read :

"I expect to be in New York next week and would appreciate any suggestions you might make. Should it be possible for you to put me in touch with principal UNO people, I would appreciate it duly."

FEDERAL BUREAU OF INVESTIGATION

Form No. 1
This Case Originated At  NEW YORK, NEW YORK

File No.  100-17493

| Report Made At | Date When Made | Period for Which Made | Report Made By |
|---|---|---|---|
| WASHINGTON, D. C. | 12/13/45 | 11/24 – 11/30/45 | FLOYD L. JONES  FLJ:JAG |

| Title | Character of Case |
|---|---|
| NATHAN GREGORY SILVERMASTER, with aliases et al | ESPIONAGE - R |

STRICTLY CONFIDENTIAL

Synopsis:  Following individuals have been under surveillance in Washington, D. C.:

ALGER HISS.

107 pdf 202 p investigative report
on subjects in the Gregory Case
summarizes results of 1945 physical
surveillance of A. Hiss + ~~FBI~~ cover
placed on his mail.

COPIES DESTROYED  1/5/54

Approved and                Special Agent
                            In Charge

Do Not Write In These Spaces

RU 17

234

517

Copies of This Report

5 - Bureau
   - New York
   - Washington Field

10 JUN 7 3 1946

EX 101

100-17493

ALGER HISS (Also known as EUGENE HISS)
Residence: 3210 P St., N.W., Washington, D. C.
Employment: State Department, Washington, D.C.

A cover on the mail going to ALGER HISS, 3210 P St., N.W., Washington, D. C. was placed November 28, 1945. No affirmative results have been had from this cover as yet, but future results will be reported as received.

From the Register of the State Department, 1941, the following information was obtained:

ALGER HISS was born at Baltimore, Md., 11/11/1904. He graduated from Baltimore City College; Powder Plant Academy; Johns Hopkins University, BA degree 1926; Harvard University, LLB degree 1929; member of the Bar of both Massachusetts and New York; Secretary and Law Clerk to Supreme Court Justice 1929-30; law practice 1930-33; Assistant to General Counsel and Assistant General Counsel, Agricultural Adjustment Administration, 1933-35; Legal Assistant, Special Senate Committee investigating the munitions industry 1934-35; Special Attorney, Department of Justice, 1935-36; appointed Assistant to the Assistant Secretary of State at $5600 per year, September 1, 1936; married.

The November, 1945 State Department directory contains the following:

"ALGER HISS, Office of Special Political Affairs, Room 164, Main State Department Building, Branch 2941."

Selective Service Board #1, Washington, D. C. records reflect that ALGER HISS has Order No. 11, Serial No. 3048. He is classified as 4-A. His old address is given as 3415 Volta Place, N.W., Washington, D. C., and his present address is 3210 P St., N.W., Washington, D. C. The Selective Service records reflect his education as

1 year Powder Plant Academy, Duxbury, Mass.
4 years Johns Hopkins University – AB degree.
3 years Harvard University Law School – LLB degree.
Member of the Bar in Massachusetts, New York and
the U. S. Supreme Court.

100-17493

post of the Assistant Secretary of State, Mr. HISS from time to time attends meetings of the Executive Committee on commercial policy.

There is also a letter from the State Department to Local Draft Board #1, Washington, D. C., dated May 16, 1941, signed by EDWARD YARDLEY, Director of Personnel at the State Department, asking for HISS' deferment for the reason that HISS was still employed as Assistant to Dr. STANLEY HORNBECK, Advisor of Political Relations.

PHYSICAL SURVEILLANCE

Surveillance instituted 11/26/45 and conducted through the period of this report, 11/30/45, developed on 11/26/45 HISS' 1937 Plymouth light gray coach, bearing tags 98-027, parked on P St. between Wisconsin Ave. and 32nd St., N.W. from 9:40 to 10:00 am. At 5:10 pm, an unidentified woman entered the HISS home with a key, accompanied by a 3 to 4 year old boy. She appeared to be between 30 and 40 years of age, 5'-5", slender build, with reddish-brown bushy hair.

At 7:45 pm, a woman and a man, probably HISS and his wife, were observed to leave the HISS home and enter the car which was parked near 31st St. This car was driven down P St. toward 30th, but was later lost in traffic. HISS did not return home up to 9:15 pm that evening, when the surveillance was discontinued.

On 11/27/45, Agents ~~and~~ ~~~~ at 9:05 am observed HISS and Mrs. HISS enter the car and drive to the State Department where HISS entered the State Department building. His wife drove the auto away. A surveillance maintained at the State Department developed no activity on HISS' part during the morning and afternoon of that day.

At 5:00 pm, a spot check at the HISS home, 3210 P St., N.W., developed that HISS' car was parked there. At 7:07 pm, HISS was observed to enter his home, approaching from the street car line. Another unidentified man, whose description is in the surveillance log, was observed at the HISS home, but information concerning him will not be set out in this report until it is developed that he is of pertinent interest to this investigation.

At 10:50 pm, this unidentified man left the HISS home and walked to 3100 Dumbarton Ave., N.W. The City Directory shows at this address SAMUEL BRUMMER and ROLAND SEVRY are supposed to reside. There is no record of either one in the Washington Field Division indices.

100-17493

On November 28, 1945, Agents ~~████~~ and ~~████~~ observed TONY HISS, age 4, leave his home for school in a Buick bearing D.C. 1945 tags 105-005, registered to GEORGE M. WILSON, Jr., 3827 S St., N.W., 1941 Buick sedan.

At 9:15 am, HISS left his home in his car with his wife for the State Department, carrying a large manila envelope. At 9:26 am he was observed to get out of this car at 17th and Pennsylvania Ave., N.W., and enter the West door of the State Department, his wife driving the car away from the State Department. HISS was not observed to leave the State Department which has numerous exits, and a spot check at 5:35 pm at the HISS home by Agent ~~████~~ developed that the HISS family car was parked there. At 7:07 pm, HISS approached his home from Wisconsin Ave., and entered carrying an envelope. There appears to be a colored woman working at the HISS home.

On November 28, 1945, HISS was observed by Agent ~~████~~ at 8:57 am on the porch of his home at 3210 P St., N.W. At 9:09 am, Mr. and Mrs. HISS were observed by Agent ~~████~~ to leave there home and drive their car east on P St. HISS was carrying a large envelope. At 9:16 am, HISS and his wife were observed by Agent ~~████~~ to arrive at 17th and Pennsylvania Ave., N.W. Mrs. HISS was observed to drive the car away and HISS was observed to enter the West side entrance of the State Department carrying this envelope.

The Agents maintained a surveillance of this entrance of the State Department and at 1:06 pm Agent ~~████~~ observed HISS leave the West side entrance of the State Department in company with another man. The two walked to Pennsylvania Avenue and then to 17th and H Sts., N.W., where they entered the Metropolitan Club at 1:10 pm, presumably for lunch. HISS and his companion were observed to leave the Metropolitan Club in company with another man who was in uniform at 2:04 pm. At 2:11 pm, HISS and his two companions entered the West side entrance of the State Department.

A description of the civilian companion as furnished by Agent ~~████~~ is as follows:

| | |
|---|---|
| Age | 40 to 50 |
| Height | 6'-?" |
| Weight | 150 - 160 lbs. |
| Build | Slender |
| Chin | Pointed |
| Face | Slender |

|  |  |
|---|---|
| Shoulders | Hunched forward |
| Dress | Brown hat, brown suit, brown shoes, brown overcoat |

The companion in uniform was described by Agent ~~████~~ as follows:

|  |  |
|---|---|
| Age | 35 - 40 |
| Height | 6'-2" |
| Weight | 180 lbs. |
| Build | Rangy |
| Dress | Officer's cap |
|  | Officer's Trench Coat |
|  | Carried a light tan leather brief case. |

At 2:39 pm Agent ~~████~~ observed the uniformed companion leave by the front door of the State Department. At 6:35 pm, and unknown man was observed to approach the HISS home from Wisconsin Avenue and enter the HISS home. At 6:45 pm, this same man left and walked to 3101 P. St., N.W. This man is described as follows:

|  |  |
|---|---|
| Age | 35 to 40 |
| Height | 6'-0" |
| Weight | 150 lbs. |
| Dress | Blue overcoat, gray felt hat, brim turned up. |

It is not known whether this individual has any connection with this case.

At 7:00 pm, HISS entered his home, approaching from WISCONSIN Avenue. At 8:30 pm, a man and woman were observed to cross P St from 32nd St. and enter HISS' home. At 8:45 pm, this same man and woman together with HISS left the HISS home and crossed to the Northwest corner of 32nd and P Sts. where they entered a car and drove to Wisconsin Ave. and P St., N.W. The surveillance was lost in traffic at this time. The lisence of the car was not obtained, but it was a Ford sedan, 1940 or 1941, light in color, carrying District of Colombia tags.

At 10:59 pm, HISS and this man and woman returned to the HISS home from the direction of 32nd St. At 11:12 pm this man and woman were observed by Agent ~~████~~ to leave the HISS home and walk to 3101 P St., N.W., where they entered.

100-17493

The woman is described as follows:

| | |
|---|---|
| Age | About 35 |
| Height | 5'-4" |
| Weight | 130 lbs. |
| Dress | Wearing a tan coat; bare-headed |

On November 30, 1945, Mr. and Mrs. HISS were observed in their car at 17 and Pennsylvania Ave., N.W. at 9:16 am by Agent ▓▓▓▓▓ HISS got out of the car at this point and walked to the West entrance of the State Department while Mrs. HISS went away. HISS was not observed leaving any of the entrances of the State Department during the day and at 7:10 pm HISS was observed by Agent ▓▓▓▓ getting off the street car and entering his home at which time he was carrying a large brief case, tan in color.

At 8:50 pm, HISS was observed by Agents ▓▓▓▓▓ and ▓▓▓▓▓ leaving his residence and walking to the Potomac Pharmacy, 1564 Wisconsin Ave., N.W., and on leaving the store was carrying a package which appeared to be a bottle wrapped in paper. He returned to the HISS home at 8:57 pm.

At 9:10 pm, a man and a woman were observed by ▓▓▓▓▓ and ▓▓▓▓▓ to come to the HISS home and enter. They came in 1941 Plymouth sedan bearing D.C. 1945 tags 84368. They remained at the HISS home until 11:35 pm when they drove off in this same car. They drove to 3744 Huntington Ave., N.W., which is the residence of HAROLD W. STEIN to whom the D.C. license tag is issued. LORIN S. STEIN is listed as the wife of HAROLD W. STEIN in the City Directory. The Washington Field Office indices contain no information on HAROLD W. STEIN or LORIN S. STEIN.

A description of ALGER HISS as furnished by Special Agents ▓▓▓▓▓ and ▓▓▓▓▓ is as follows:

| | |
|---|---|
| Race | White |
| Age | 41, born 11/11/04, Baltimore, Md. |
| Height | 6'-0" |
| Weight | 154 lbs. |
| Build | Slender |
| Hair | Dark brown |
| Eyes | Blue |
| Complexion | Dark |

F_____ _____EAU OF IN_____ON

Form No. 1
THIS CASE ORIGINATED AT WASHINGTON, D. C.      105592      FILE 100-17493

| REPORT MADE AT | DATE WHEN MADE | PERIOD FOR WHICH MADE | REPORT MADE BY |
|---|---|---|---|
| WASHINGTON, D. C. | 10/17/46 | 9/16-30/46 | LAMBERT G. ZANDER      LGZ:JAG |

49257

| TITLE | CHARACTER OF CASE |
|---|---|
| NATHAN GREGORY SILVERMASTER with aliases et al | ESPIONAGE - R |

SYNOPSIS OF FACTS:                    STRICTLY CONFIDENTIAL

APPROVED AND FORWARDED

SPECIAL AGENT IN CHARGE

DO NOT WRITE IN THESE SPACES

COPIES DESTROYED 11/3/55 #24

65- 56402 -1638X

5 - Bureau
1 - New York (info)
3 - Washington Field

15 DEC 80 1946

RECORDED INDEXED
7 EX 33

EX 102

100-17,493

1C5648

RE: ALGER HISS

The following investigation was conducted by Special Agent R. W. McCASLIN.

Mail cover on Mr. ALGER HISS, 3210 P Street, N. W., for the period of September 1 through September 30, 1946, reflects the following:

| Sender | Addressee | Postmark |
|---|---|---|
| J. Blaise de Sibour & Co. 1700 I Street, N. W. Washington, D. C. | ALGER HISS 3210 P Street, N.W. Washington, D. C. | 9-12-46 Washington, D. C. |
| MARGARET R. 55 Randolph Street South Orange, N. J. | | 9-23-46 South Orange, N. J. |

Confidential Informant advised that on September 3, 1946, KATHY believed to be KATHERINE HISS, was in contact with PRISCILLA HISS, and mentioned that she, KATHY, had just returned from the Cape.

Later on, according to informant, KATHY advised ALGER HISS that she had a good publisher for "that book". ALGER evidenced pleasure upon hearing this.

The informant advised on September 5, 1946, that BEN DORE contacted ALGER HISS and advised that he had returned the preceding evening from his vacation. BEN accepted an invitation to the HISS home on Saturday for dinner for him and his wife, MARGO.

According to informant, ALGER HISS was contacted later on that day by ANNA KRISS. ANNA advised she had arrived that afternoon from Baltimore and that she was planning on leaving for Texas in two days. She mentioned she would like to see ALGER and DONNY, believed to be DON TULAN. She stated she would like to have lunch with them so they would be able to have a talk. ALGER mentioned to ANNA that he would be able to get ahold of DONNY now, because he had returned from his vacation.

On September 6th, informant advised that HENRY ABBOTT contacted PRISCILLA HISS and advised he had been in the Naval Hospital for a week and was now out. HENRY mentioned that he transferred from the Navy to the State Department.

On September 9, 1946, the informant advised that PRISCILLA informed ALGER that there was a letter from one JACK SUTRO (phonetic) who was staying at the Pierre Hotel in New York City. PRISCILLA mentioned, according to informant,

## Physical Surveillance

On September 11, 1946, it was observed that Mrs. HISS contacted the clerk at the Georgetown Post Office Sub-Station. Later, inquiry was made of the ~~_____~~ by the writer, and it was determined that the HISS'S did not have any personal mail coming into that office. He stated that he felt perhaps HISS was receiving personal mail through his business office.

At 12:00 on September 11, 1946, HISS was observed leaving the State Department and proceeding to the Tally Ho Restaurant on 17th, between H and I Streets, where he joined his wife. After lunch, HISS returned to the State Department.

On September 12, 1946, HISS was observed as he left his home at 9:15 AM, proceeding to and entering the State Department. At 1 PM HISS was observed leaving the State Department by the front entrance and proceeding to the Greystone Cafeteria on 17th and H Streets. At 2:30 PM HISS left the Greystone Cafeteria and returned to the State Department building, where he was observed entering Room 164..

The doorplate on this room carried the following: Mr. HISS, Director of Office of Special Political Affairs.

# FEDERAL BUREAU OF INVESTIGATION

Form No. 1

THIS CASE ORIGINATED AT WASHINGTON, D. C.

| REPORT MADE AT | DATE WHEN MADE | PERIOD FOR WHICH MADE | REPORT MADE BY |
|---|---|---|---|
| WASHINGTON, D. C. | 5/10/47 | 3/14 - 32/17 | |

| TITLE | CHARACTER OF CASE |
|---|---|
| NATHAN GREGORY SILVERMASTER 0052074 with aliases et al | ESPIONAGE |

SYNOPSIS OF FACTS:

STRICTLY CONFIDENTIAL

HENRY HILL COLLINS, Jr., in contact with ~~████████████████~~ and ALGER HISS

~~████████████████████████████████~~ ALGER HISS

4 COPIES DESTROYED

DO NOT WRITE IN THESE SPACES

best copy available

New York
Washington Field

MAY 24 1947

EX. 103

drunkard and reportedly came to Preston from New York City.  They were
not known to have expressed any political opinions in this vicinity.
Because of the small size of the farm on which they reside, the informant
in Preston stated it was necessary that they have an outside income in
order to maintain their standard of living.  Mr. FANSLER at one time was
employed by the Preston News in Preston, Maryland, and by the Sears Company
in Cambridge, Maryland.

       The Baltimore Field Division has furnished the following informa-
tion on BARBARA RYAN ANDERSON and L. L. ANDERSON of Saint Michaels, Maryland,
who on several different occasions contacted subject ALGER HISS through
Telephone Number 41-M at Saint Michaels.

       At the present time Mr. and Mrs. ANDERSON reside at Calera 72,
Villa Obregon, Mexico, D. F., and the mail received by them at Saint
Michaels is forwarded to the tenant manager, Mr. GEORGE DEPIBAUGH, who
at the present time is maintaining the estate for the ANDERSONS.

       The Baltimore Field Division has furnished the following informa-
tion on H. K. DOUGLAS COTTON who has contacted subject ALGER HISS.

## PHYSICAL SURVEILLANCE

       A physical surveillance at the residence of ALGER HISS on
Sunday, March 9, 1947, revealed that subject HENRY HILL COLLINS was observed
to enter the Hiss residence carrying a brown leather briefcase.

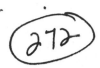

On the same date, MILLER tried to contact ALGER HISS at the Carnegie Endowment Institute. However, MILLER was advised that Mr. HISS was in New York and would not return until early next week. MILLER advised HISS' secretary to advise ALGER that he, MILLER, had seen Mr. PRESCOTT DENNET (phonetic) of the World Peace Foundation while he, MILLER, was in New York.

FBI - 11/28/45

SIL - 94

JOHN EDGAR HOOVER
DIRECTOR

102

OFFICE OF THE
RECEIVED
NOV 29 1945
ATTORNEY GENERAL

Federal Bureau of Investigation
United States Department of Justice
Washington, D. C.

November 28, 1945

PERSONAL AND CONFIDENTIAL

1- Pre 1948 Investigation
regory card

MEMORANDUM FOR THE ATTORNEY GENERAL

82223

In connection with this Bureau's investigation of Soviet espionage activity, it has been reported that Alger Hiss, 3210 P Street, N. W., Washington, D. C., phone, Michigan 0811, has been engaged in espionage for the Soviet Secret Intelligence (NKVD).

All-wiretaps

I recommend authorization of a technical surveillance on Hiss to determine the extent of his activities on behalf of the Soviets and for the additional purpose of identifying espionage agents.

Respectfully,

John Edgar Hoover
Director

ENCLOSURE

KEEP IN F. B. I. FILES

12/5/45  ε 75.

RECORDED  65-56402-94

EX-47  3  DEC 5 1945

SIL-94

FOR VICTORY
BUY
UNITED STATES
WAR
BONDS
AND
STAMPS

1945
& memo, JEH to Atty Genl
recommending wiretap on Hiss
w/ Atty Genl reply requesting info on Hiss.

EX 104

101

OFFICE OF
THE ATTORNEY GENERAL

DEPARTMENT OF JUSTICE

11/29

Mr. ~son
Mr. ~mm
Mr. Clegg
Mr. Coffey
Mr. Glavin
Mr. ~
Mr. Nichols
Mr. Rosen
Mr. Tracy
Mr. Carson
Mr. Egan
Mr. Gurnea
Mr. Hendon
Mr. Pennington
Mr. Quinn Tamm
Mr. Krase
Miss Gandy

Alger Hiss

Edgar :-

82252

Is this man now

employed at the State

Dep't - If so, what do

we have on him?

Edgar:-
    Is this man now
employed at the State Dept.
If so, what do we have on
him?        TCC

65-56402-94

EX-47

RECORDED

EX-47

Deletions                    46                                    FBI-11/30/45

2 75

Federal Bureau of Investigation

United States Department of Justice

Washington, D. C.

November 30, 1945                          SIL-122

IN REPLY, PLEASE REFER TO

FILE NUMBER_____    MEMORANDUM FOR THE ATTORNEY GENERAL

1-Pre 46 Investigation
1-Wiretap            Re:  ALGER HISS              65-56402
Gregory Case

       Reference is made to the note attached to my original recommen-
dation for authorization of a technical surveillance on Alger Hiss in
Washington, D. C., for the purpose of determining the extent of his activities on behalf of the Soviets and for the additional purpose of
identifying espionage agents.

       You asked, "Is this man now employed at the State Dept. If so,
what do we have on him?"

       Alger Hiss has been employed at the State Department but is now en-
gaged in activity on behalf of the United Nations Organization.

B-1

       Mr. Whittaker Chambers, now an editor of "Time Magazine," has advised
this Bureau that when he was engaged in Communist underground work for the
Soviet NKVD in Washington during the early thirties, Alger Hiss originally
employed by the Agricultural Adjustment Administration and subsequently by
the Department of State, was a member of the underground Communist espionage
group which included Charles Kramer and John Abt.

       Elizabeth Terrill Bentley has during this month, advised the Bureau
that she was the principal contact between the Soviets and the Communist underground espionage groups in Washington, D. C., one of which groups was identical
with the one reported to the Bureau by Whittaker Chambers. In connection with
the activities of the members of this group, she stated that Hiss in the State
Department had taken two or three of the members of the group with which John
Abt and Charles Kramer were connected and turned them over for direct control
by the Soviet representatives in this country.         65-56402    12 D
                                                                   SIL

       The information furnished generally by Chambers and the Bentley
woman has proved accurate under investigation, consequently, I wish to renew
my recommendation for a technical surveillance on Hiss.

1 p memo, Hoover to Atty Gen summarizing FBI info
re Hiss based on allegations of W.C. &
Bentley & renewing...

       Respectfully,

John Edgar Hoover
Director

EX 105

(276)

FBI 1/6/49
3/15/76
752

file Gregory Case

WASHINGTON AND WFO FROM NEW YORK    36    6    8-58½P

DIRECTOR AND SAC        URGENT

JAY DAVID WHITTAKER CHAMBERS, WAS, ETAL, PERJURY, ESPIONAGE, R..

REP SA LAMBERT Z. ZANDER, SEPTEMBER SEVENTEENTH, FORTYSIX AT WASHING-

TON, D.C. IN CASE ENTITLED "GREGORY".  IN REFERENCE REPORT, CONFIDEN-

TIAL INFORMANT ADVISED THAT ON AUGUST NINTH, FORTYSIX, TONY HISS WAS

ENROLLED IN THE MARGERY WEBSTER JUNIOR COLLEGE, SIXTEENTH AND COLUM-

BUS ROAD, N.W., WASHINGTON, D.C.  SUGGEST CONTACT BE MADE AT THIS

JUNIOR COLLEGE FOR ANY RECORD OF A TYPEWRITTEN SPECIMEN EMANATING

FROM THE HISS FAMILY.        RECORDED - 39                     752

308                 SCHEIDT            4  JAN 11 1949        -TWO COPIES WFO

JAN 14 1949
HOLD PLS.

EX 106.

3/15/76

277

FBI 1/6/49
3/15/26
757

BUREAU OF INVESTIGATION
U. DEPARTMENT OF JUSTICE
COMMUNICATIONS SECTION

TELETYPE

File Gregory Case

WASHINGTON AND WFO FROM NEW YORK 38 6 9-11P

DIRECTOR AND SAC URGENT

JAY DAVID WHITTAKER CHAMBERS WAS, ETAL, PERJURY, ESPIONAGE, R, INTER-
NAL SECURITY, R. REREP SA LAMBERT Z. ZANDER, DECEMBER SIXTH, FORTY
SIX, WASHINGTON, D.C. IN CASE ENTITLED "GREGORY". REFERENCE REPORT
INDICATES CONFIDENTIAL INFORMANT ADVISED THAT TONY HISS ENTERED MRS.
UDISKY-S ART CLASS AT NINETEEN TEN I STREET, WASHINGTON, D.C. SUGGEST
THIS MRS. UDISKY BE CONTACTED FOR ANY TYPEWRITTEN SPECIMENS EMANA-
TING FROM ANY MEMBERS OF HISS FAMILY.

SCHEIDT

757

HOLD PLS

RECORDED - 34

JAN 11 1949

Feb - 5.

INDEXED - 34

TWO COPIES WFO

HOLD PLS

FBI 1/7/49
3/15/76
769

file Gregory Case

WASHINGTON AND WFO FROM NEW YORK 66 7 10-OSP

DIRECTOR AND SAC URGENT

JAY DAVID WHITTAKER CHAMBERS, WAS, ALGER HISS, ETAL, PERJURY, ESP.

R. INTERNAL SECURITY, R. REREP SA LAMBERT G. ZANDER DATED MARCH

ELEVENTH, FORTYSIX AT WASHINGTON, DC, IN THE CASE ENTITLED "GREGORY".

REFERENCE REPORT INDICATES THAT ON FEBRUARY SIXTH, FORTYSIX ALICE

STRONG CONTACTED MRS HISS RE RAISING MONEY FOR NATIONAL CONFERENCE

OF CHRISTIANS AND JEWS. MRS. HISS AGREED TO WRITE LETTERS AND PER-

FORM ANY OTHER ACTION DESIRED IN ASSISTANCE TO THIS PROJECT. CONTACT

THIS ORGANIZATION FOR POSSIBLE TYPEWRITTEN SPECIMEN EMANATING FROM

MRS. HISS.

SCHEIDT

RECORDED - 39

769

4 JAN 11 1949

Feb 5

INDEXED - 39

50 JAN 368

FEDERAL BUREAU OF INVESTIGATION
U. S. DEPARTMENT OF JUSTICE
COMMUNICATIONS SECTION

JAN 8 - 1949

TELETYPE

WASH AND WASH FBXX FLD FROM NEW YORK 1    8    12-01 A:

DIRECTOR AND SAC        URGENT

JAY DAVID WHITTAKER CHAMBERS, WAS., ALGER HISS, ETAL, PERJURY, ESP R.
INTERNAL SECURITY R.  REREP SA LAMBERT G. ZANDER DATED OCT. SEVENTEENTH
FORTY SIX AT WASH., DC. IN CASE ENTITLED "GREGORY".
IN REFERENCE REPORT ADVISED THAT ON SEPT. TWENTY THIRD, FORTY
SIX PRISCILLA HISS STATED THAT A CLASSMATE OF HERS AT BRYNMAWR
COLLEGE WAS VISITING HER, HER NAME BEING CATHERINE NEILSON, EMPLOYED
AT THE MUSEUM IN BUFFALO, NY.  INTERVIEW CATHERINE NEILSON.  AS-
CERTAIN IF SHE WAS EVER A VISITOR IN THE HISS HOME IN WASH. OR
NY AND WHETHER SHE OBSERVED A TYPEWRITER IN THEIR HOME.  ASCERTAIN
TYPE OF TYPEWRITER AND OBTAIN MINUTE DESCRIPTION OF SAID TYPEWRITER.
ALSO OBTAIN FROM HER ANY TYPEWRITTEN SPECIMENS IN HER POSSESSION
EMANATING FROM ANY MEMBER OF THE HISS FAMILY.  SUTEL RESULTS.

SCHEIDT

BUFFALO ADVISED

RECORDED - 39

TWO COPIES

774

4 JAN 11 1949

The following investigation was conducted by SA ROBERT C. BLOUNT.

Information was received from the Washington Field Division that ALGER HISS had two file drawers of personal material and three shelves of books sent from the Carnegie Endowment in Washington, D.C. to the Carnegie Endowment in New York City.

MISS E. B. SAYRE, Assistant to the President, Carnegie Endowment for International Peace, 405 West 117th Street, advised that the above-mentioned personal material and books belonging to ALGER HISS were received by the Carnegie Endowment, New York City, sometime after Christmas, 1948, and that this material is now in the hands of MR. HISS' attorney, MR. EDWARD C. MC LEAN. MISS SAYRE advised that the box containing this material was not opened at the Carnegie Endowment and was turned over directly to MR. MC LEAN.

The records of Confidential Informant ~~~ reflect no correspondence from ALGER HISS. These files reflect that ALGER HISS paid his November, 1948 and January, 1949 bills by check but it was not possible to determine from these files which bank these checks were drawn.

The Bureau advised that MR. STEPHEN RAUSHENBUSH, formerly with the NYE Committee, has advised that MR. PAUL J. KERN and MR. LAWRENCE BROWN were with the NYE Committee and may have known ALGER HISS.

MR. PAUL J. KERN, attorney, 11 West 42nd Street, advised that he was employed by the NYE Committee and worked under MR. STEPHEN RAUSHENBUSH. He stated that he worked in New York City almost exclusively while employed by the NYE Committee and that he made only two or three trips to Washington, D.C. in connection with his work with the Committee. He stated that he is not acquainted with ALGER HISS and did not know that HISS had been employed by the NYE Committee until the HISS-CHAMBERS story appeared in the papers. He advised that he has received no correspondence from ALGER HISS and that he does not know WHITTAKER CHAMBERS.

MR. MATTHEW G. ELY, JR., HORACE ELY Real Estate Company, 76 Williams Street, advised that the last known address of LAWRENCE BROWN

Ex. 107

MI-SUMMARY

31673

10:55 AM
No cut

ALGER HISS to LEO PASSWALSKI (ph) at Brookings Institute. Made luncheon appointment for 1:00 PM Monday. ALGER apparently will come by for LEO and then they will walk to lunch.

10:58 am
Misc. 6491-3

ALGER HISS to GEORGE FINCH at Carnegie Endowment for International Peace. ALGER said Mr. DULLES had sent him a copy of his note to FINCH, saying that the 20th was convenient (for a meeting), that he was inviting Mr. DAVIS. ALGER said he noticed what he (DULLES) said about MALCOM DAVIS and SHOTWELL (ph). FINCH said he didn't understand from DULLES's letter whether he was sending out notices to the others. ALGER suggested FINCH write DULLES and find out whether the notices of the meeting had been sent, and if not to ask if he (FINCH) should send them out. ALGER said he wanted to prepare his schedule for the coming week. He mentioned he was going out to Des Moines the middle of the following week so he would like to get up to New York for a few days, the latter part of next week. ALGER said he wanted to come in Saturday morning and discuss the Budget matters and to also come in Monday and Tuesday to "700 Jackson Place" (Carnegie Endowment for International Peace) to discuss the same subject. FINCH said that would be fine. ALGER said HOWARD WILSON was coming down from New York and he would see him there Tuesday morning. He mentioned he didn't know what WILSON wanted. ALGER said he would go to New York Wednesday morning and that would give him Wednesday afternoon, Thursday, and Friday up there. They discussed office space for ALGER. FINCH asked if ALGER had sent his books over yet, and ALGER said he had checked with Mrs. RAWLINGS, his Secretary at the State Department, and she was finishing up the packing. ALGER said she was going to call FINCH's brother and he would have them picked up when she was ready. He mentioned that they were in a couple of packing cases. ALGER said the material is evenly divided between file material and books. About 2 drawers of a file case would be needed, and about 3 shelves of a book case. FINCH said he would have the necessary equipment put in ALGER's office. ALGER asked if there would be adequate stenographic help, as he had several letters he wanted to write Saturday morning. FINCH said there would be sufficient help.

EX 108

STANDARD FORM NO. 64

# *Office Memorandum* • UNITED STATES GOVERNMENT

TO : DIRECTOR, FBI     DATE: August 12, 1947

FROM : GUY HOTTEL, SAC, Washington Field

SUBJECT: JUSTIFICATION FOR CONTINUATION OF TECHNICAL OR MICROPHONE SURVEILLANCE

RE:    Title    GREGORY

Character of Case   ESPIONAGE – R (ALGER HISS)
Field Office    Washington Field Office
CONF. INFT. Symbol Number
Type of Surveillance: (Technical or Microphone)
Technical

1. Subject's name and address:

    ALGER HISS
    3210 P Street, N.W., Washington, D.C.

2. Location of technical operation:

    Chastleton Apartments
    16th & R Streets, N.W., Washington, D.C.

3. Dates of initial authorization and installation:

    Authorized – December 5, 1945
    Installed – December 13, 1945

4. Previous and other installations on the same subject (with dates and places):

    None

RECORDED
INDEX 65-56402-2755

5. Specific valuable information obtained since previous report with indication of specific value of each item and what use was made of each item of information involved:

    See attached page.

COPIES DESTROYED 11/2/58

53 SEP 4 1947

*[handwritten annotations:]*
1) AH Pre '48 Investigation –
2) Gregory Case
2) AH Wiretap
3) FBI Surveillance

Batch of docs indicating wiretap & physical surveillance of AH during '46 & '47

EX-55
DATE 5-16-80

EX109

6. Could above information have been obtained from other sources and by other means?

   No

7. Has security factor changed since installation?

   No

8. Any request for the surveillance by outside agency (give name, title and agency):

   No

9. Manpower and costs involved:

   Handled by a regularly established plant.

10. Remarks (By SAC):

    In the past this surveillance has furnished valuable information. During the major portion of the past 60 days, subject and his family have been away from Washington. They expect to move to New York this fall, probably in September. It is suggested the surveillance continue for the remaining time that subject resides in Washington.

11. Remarks (added at Seat of Government):

(284)

12.   Recommendation by Assistant Director:

It is recommended that this technical surveillance be continued
for an additional 60 days inasmuch as the Gregory Case is being
presented to a Federal Grand Jury in New York City.

13.   Recommendation by the Assistants to the Director:

100-17493
WHM:MB

285

WFO 100-17493

Number 5

May 18, 1947

One HARRY KEYES of Garden City, N.Y. contacted ALGER HISS concerning his forthcoming New York trip. During the conversation HISS mentioned that he and his family were driving up to Vermont in June to spend the summer. KEYES gave his home address as 114 Lee Road, Garden City, N.Y. This conversation provided new and hitherto unknown contact of ALGER HISS.

May 31, 1947

WALTER LIPPMANN, well known writer and columnist, talked to ALGER HISS concerning the proposal of former President HOOVER for a separate peace with the various former belligerent nations of World War II. LIPPMANN commented that such action would be a mortal blow to the United Nations. The two men then discussed the matter generally, LIPPMANN stressing that he felt HISS should assert his influence in the right direction, mentioning that he felt some one should go to JIMMY BYRNES on the matter. This conversation, although not important from an investigative standpoint, illustrates the acquaintanceship of WALTER LIPPMANN and ALGER HISS and further indicates that HISS still has contacts of considerable prestige and power in the State Department and elsewhere in the U. S. Government.

June 8, 1947

JO ABRAHAM spoke to ALGER HISS and his wife, PRISCILLA. During the conversation ALGER commented that he and his family hoped to spend all of July in Peacham, Vermont and probably a good portion of August at Dartmouth College. This conversation provided an indication of HISS' plans for the summer so that their activities might be followed intelligently.

June 15, 1947

ALEX LOWDEN (ph.) spoke to ALGER HISS and mentioned that he had an idea which he had discussed with SUMNER WELLES and Senator CONNOLLY and CONNOLLY had suggested that he talk to HISS about the matter with the idea of securing the support of the Carnegie Institute. The two men arranged to meet the following day at the Metropolitan Club. This conversation indicates the high regard in which HISS is still held by men instrumental in forming American policy.

COPIES DESTROYED 1/4/58
#23

65-56402-2755

ENCLOSURE

## Correlation

Dates for which there are no entries in the electronic
surveillance logs (Note: these dates do not correlate with
Hiss' absence from Washington):

### 1945

December 13, 1945

### 1946

January: 1, 2, 5, 6, 9, 12, 13, 19, 20, 24, 25, 26, 27

February: 1, 2, 3, 10, 15, 16, 22, 24

March: 4, 6, 9, 10, 15, 17, 22, 23, 26, 27

April: 3, 6, 7, 9, 10, 11, 13, 14, 15, 20, 21, 27, 28

May: 4, 5, 11, 12, 15, 16, 17, 18, 19

June: 12, 16, 23, 25, 29, 30

July: 1, 2, 3, 4, 5, 6

August: 3, 4, 11, 13, 17, 18, 22, 25, 26, 28, 30, 31

September: 1, 2, 7, 8, 22, 29

October: 1, 13, 14, 23, 27, 28

November: 1, 3, 7, 9, 10, 11, 12, 19, 20, 22, 25, 26, 27

December: 1, 4, 6, 12, 15, 16, 17, 25

### 1947

January: 1, 7, 16, 22, 24, 26, 27

February: 3, 4, 5, 10, 11, 12, 13, 14, 15, 17, 22

March: 2, 11, 12, 16, 17, 18, 20, 21, 22, 23, 25, 28

EX. 110

1947 (cont'd)

April:  1, 5, 8, 9, 12, 14, 15, 16, 17, 18, 21, 22, 23, 24, 25, 29

May:  1, 4, 5, 7, 8, 9, 10, 11, 12, 13, 14, 15, 17, 20, 21, 22,
      23, 24, 26, 27, 29

June:  3, 4, 5, 6, 7, 9, 10, 16

August:  entire month

September:  1, 2, 3, 4, 5, 9, 10


Information from wiretaps, reported in Summary Reports,

but not in wiretap logs:

| Summary Report (FBI Serial #) | Date of Wiretap Reported |
| --- | --- |
| 65-56402-1147 | 4-7-46 |
| 65-56402-1210 | 5-15-46 |
| 65-56402-1910 | 11-9-46 |
| 65-56402-1910 | 11-11-46 |
| serial unknown | 12-25-46 |
| 65-56402-2326 | 2-17-47 |
| 65-56402-2406 | 5-5-47 |
| 65-56402-2985 | 8-7-47 |

(288)

*jim - deletion file*

2554

*Count Two: traps*

FBI - 2/28/49
1/13/76
*Files FBI Survei*
~~FBI Survei~~

*Office Memorandum* • UNITED STATES GOVERNMENT

TO      :   Director, FBI                          DATE:   February 28, 1949

FROM    :   SAC, New Haven

SUBJECT:   AHAM
           PERJURY
           ESPIONAGE - R
           INTERNAL SECURITY - C

Re Bumemo 2/24/49.

This is to advise that technical surveillances have been installed on the residence telephones of the following subjects:

██████████████
██████████████
███████, Connecticut

Telephone - ██████████████████

Installation was completed at 9:00 A.M. 2/28/49.
Information will be reported under ████████████

---

██████████████
██████████████
████████, Connecticut

Telephone ████████████████

Installation was completed at 9:00 A.M. 2/28/49.
Information will be reported under ████████████

① FBI Surveillance
② FBI inv'stg

2554

EX111

*Office Memorandum* • UNITED STATES GOVERNMENT

TO : Director, FBI   Atten: Mechanical Section   DATE: 12/13/48

FROM : SAC, Baltimore

SUBJECT: JAY DAVID WHITTAKER CHAMBERS, was.
PERJURY; ESPIONAGE - R.

Through a highly reliable and confidential source, Agents of the Baltimore Office on Dec. 10, 1948, were given access to the personal effects of FRANKLIN VICTOR RENO, was Vincent Reno. These effects, which had been left by ████, in the custody of ████████████, Housing Manager of the Baldwin Manor Apartments at Aberdeen, comprised ten cardboard boxes, three trunks and one small black suitcase. Among the effects of RENO were numerous letters, mathematical formulas, photographs of individuals and miscellaneous names and addresses on scraps of paper. These items were photographed by Agents of this office and are being forwarded herewith to the Bureau for developing.. The photographs are contained on one roll of Photorecord film and five rolls of Kodak FX135 film.

Under the circumstances which these photographs were obtained, it was not possible to be selective of the documents. It is therefore suggested that the film be developed negatively only and not enlarged at this time. After the film has been developed it should be returned to the Baltimore Office for review, after which time the pertinent photographs will be returned to the Bureau for enlargement.

2 microfilm

2428

EX. 112

108

| NAME | ADDRESS | TO | ADDRESS | DATE OF COMMUNICATION | TYPE OF COMMUNICATION | NATURE |
|---|---|---|---|---|---|---|
| AUTH | No address | VIC | No envelope | April 14, 1946 | Personal | Mentions the University. "There is a rumor that the Legislature won't appropriate much money until some of the members of the faculty are removed namely the Red members! Later speaks of University of Illinois. |
| CATHARINE MERSHON DEDERICK | No address | | No envelope | No date | Invitation | Faculty and graduating class of Notre Dame of Maryland (June 7th, 1940.) |
| TENA | 3019 Seamoe Ave. Richmond, Va. | FRANK | No envelope | Nov. 17, 1935 | Personal letter | TENA is a school teacher. Talks about school. |
| MABEL | Providence, R.I. | Mr. F.V. REMO | Aberdeen, Md. | Sept. 9, 1940 | Post card | General conversation. |
| CLARA CHEW | Nashville, Tenn. | Mr.F.V. RENO | Aberdeen, Md. | Dec. 16, 1939 | Post card | General conversation. |
| WAYNE LOREN MAYER | 1319 Second Avenue Boulder, Colo. | VIC | No envelope | Dec. 20, 1943 | Personal letter | Asking favor of REMO. Wants recommendation for entering Navy V-12 program. States in case REMO doesn't know him he is RUTH'S son. |
| LILLIE Mrs. FLOYD WALTERS | 105 East 6th Lamar, Colo. | Mr. F.V. REMO | Bel Air Ave. Aberdeen, Md. | Sept. 7, 1938 | Personal letter | General conversation. States she is sorry to have hurt REMO. |
| C.L. CHRISTENSON Price Executive Machinery Branch | Office for Emerging Management Wash., D.C. La Salle Bldg. | Mr. FRANK V. RENO | Aberdeen Proving Gd. Maryland | June 2, 1944 | Business letter | Requesting REMO to answer questions in regard to applicant he is acquainted with. |
| MICHAEL COLDBERG Secretary | Bureau of Ordnance Navy Dep't. Wash., D.C. | Form letter Not addressed | No envelope | No date | 2 business letters | Letter entitled "The Mathematical Association of America, Md., District of Columbia, Virginia Section. REMO probably a member of this. Announcement of meetings-one in 1937, other in 1938. |
| PHIL | | VIC | No envelope | No date | Personal letter | States he is enclosing article about Soviet scientists. |
| PHIL RENO | | | No address on envelope | No date | Invitation | Senior class of University of Colo., commencement exercises. |

(291)                                                    1st ___ CLASS

# United States Post Office

IN REPLYING
MENTION INITIALS AND DAT

Chestertown, Md.          FBI    9.29.49
September 29, 1949

Special Agent in Charge,
Federal Bureau of Investigation,
Baltimore, Md.

1) FBI Surveillance Balt.
 Prob. 1380
2) Count II - Tyer
3) Richard Collins

Dear Sir:

    Have not received any information on the mail
cover of Mr. or Mrs. Richard Collins as yet but will
continue cover for 30 day period.

    Enclosed clipping is from the Aug. 5th issue of
the Kent County News which we have on file and may be of
some help.

                    Sincerely yours,

                    Harry C. Coleman, Jr.
                    Postmaster.

                                        65- 1642 -138 ?

Is  1p letter from Chestertown Postmaster
     to SAC Balt re mail cover on Richard
Collins

EX. 113

STANDARD FORM NO. 64

# Office Memorandum · UNITED STATES GOVERNMENT

TO : SAC

FROM : J. C. GARTNER, SA

SUBJECT: JAMAL

*1) FBI Pre-Trial Surveillance ✓*
*2) Count II Trips ✓ FBI*
*3) Nuclear ___ — Mrs. Richard H. Collins*

*9.27.49*          Sept. 27, 1949

~~_____~~ the following phone calls were made from May 22 thru Sept. 21, 1949, from phone Chestertown 114-R:

| | | | |
|---|---|---|---|
| May 22 | MUlberry 1600 | Baltimore, Md. | (Police Dept.) |
| May 23 | VErnon 2126 | Baltimore, Md. | |
| | Call made from 135-J and billed to 114-R | | |
| July 2 | Watkins 4-3162 | New York City | |
| July 2 | LExington 6-700 | Baltimore, Md. | (FBI office) |
| July 17 | TUxedo 8321 | Baltimore, Md. | |
| August 11 | Sudlersville, Md. | 2091 | |

*1 pg memos from Gartner re phone calls made from a Chestertown number*

65-1642

*Reported*
*Ser C22 ____ 1372*
*750*

*1 cc destroyed 2/66 date*

*initials*

*65 1642*

10/29/48

ence ████████ is a contract of ALGER HISS who is
charged with being a Communist ✓

However, refer-

124-869-5

EX. 114

1

10/29/48

T-5, a source of known reliability advised that ▓▓▓▓▓▓
was a contact of Mr. ALGER HISS. It is noted that Mr. WHITAKER
CHAMBERS, testifying under oath before the House Committee on Un-American
Activities, accused Mr. ALGER HISS of being a Communist Party member.

124-864-5

295

10/29/48

WFO 124-1328

ADMINISTRATIVE

(b)(7)(D)  T-15 is information gathered from monitory telephone contacts of
ALGER HISS which was reported in 100-17493-2631, page 61.

124-869-5

- 6 -

On May 10, 1945 Special Agents HARLAND F. DANNER and EDWARD F. HUMMER interviewed WITAKER CHAMBERS, one of the senior editors of Time Magazine in New York City. CHAMBERS advised that he was a courier in what he believed to be the Communist Party movement and that around 1935 he operated as such between ALEXANDER STEVENS (who was known to him as PETER) in New York City and HAROLD WARE, leader of a group of men composed of government employees in high-salaried positions who were Communist Party members (whose activities as such had ceased when they were transferred to the "underground" of the Communist Party). CHAMBERS explained that there were approximately eight individual members in the organization headed by WARE and that almost every one of these individuals was, himself, a leader of another underground unit operating in Washington, D. C. which consisted of some six or eight members. Each of these underground units were not aware of the identity or composition of any of the other units. CHAMBERS added that HENRY COLLINS who at that time was employed in the Forestry Department of the Department of Agriculture, was one of the persons who attended meetings of the WARE group. Others who attended these meetings were JOHN ABT, LEE PRESSMAN, NATHAN PERLO, CHARLES KRIVITSKY, was, CHARLES KRAMER, ALGER HISS, DONALD HISS and A. POST, NATHAN WITT and an unknown man who was the husband of ALICE WENDHAM. CHAMBERS advised that the WARE group met at various places in Washington, D. C. but the principal meeting place was the apartment of HENRY COLLINS on St. Mathew's Court over a garage. COLLINS, according to CHAMBERS was treasurer of the group and apparently collected a percentage of the salary each member which was then transmitted to PETER in New York. He added COLLINS had some regular way of sending money to New York which was known to CHAMBERS, but on several occasions when he supposed this system had broken down he, CHAMBERS, was instructed by COLLINS to deliver a package to PETER

3/9/48

## CONTACTS

Confidential Informant ~~████~~ who is in a position to report upon COLLINS' activities, advised that COLLINS is in frequent contact with ALGER HISS.

3/9/48

JULIUS J. JOSEPH, JOHN ABT and CHARLES KRAMER all of whom are a group allegedly engaged in Russian espionage according to Confidential Informant T-8.

101-1335-18

FBI 10/8/48

A-H-38
file

October 8, 1948

DIRECTOR, FBI

SAC, BALTIMORE

COGOO
ALGER HISS
INTERNAL SECURITY - C

(handwritten) FBI Pre-Indictment investig's.
A-H-~
Wiretaps

b-7-D

On September 13, 1948, confidentially advised Special Agent JAMES O. PONDER that an unknown woman whose telephone number is MOhawk 3752, on September 9, 1948, placed a call for ALGER HISS at Grammercy 34463, the address for this number being 22 E. 8th Street, New York City. The call was placed at 9:31 P. M. Inasmuch as HISS could not be located at this number and would not return there until Monday, the caller attempted to reach him at the Carlton Hotel in Washington, D. C. where the manager paged HISS. HISS was not located at the hotel.

On Sunday, September 12, the unknown caller again attempted to reach HISS. As of September 13, the call had not gone through.

The listing for telephone number MOhawk 3752 is in the name of CHARLES B. DUFF, 5504 Wexford Road, Baltimore, Maryland.

The indices of this office do not reflect any information concerning DUFF.

b-7-D

Inasmuch as the informant mentioned above ~~~~~~ it is absolutely essential ~~~~~~~ identity not be disclosed.

The above is being submitted to the Bureau and Washington Field office for its information.

JEF/JW

100-11794

cc - Washington Field

(handwritten) 1-p memo detailing attempts by an unknown & person to reach A-H via telephone

(handwritten) 101-26 A-H 38

FBI
65 OCT 11 1948

PAUL FROMM, C.S.R.
PLF. EXH. 13
DEF. ID.
6-19-80

EX 116

9

*Office Memorandum* • UNITED STATES GOVERNMENT 4642

TO : Director, FBI                    DATE: August 22, 1950

FROM : SAC, New York       ① FBI ~~Bradley~~               See

                            *Surveillance* 150

SUBJECT: ⓪ JAHAM

————————ESPIONAGE — R————————————————————

*1-p memo, indicating mail cover of A.H. by FBI, + attaching*

There is attached for the attention of the Bureau and the New Haven
Office a photostatic copy of a four-page letter that was made available to
Assistant United States Attorney THOMAS MURPHY by the New York Post Office
Department. Mr. MURPHY made this letter, which is a carbon copy, available
to this office. He advised that it had been forwarded to him by Mr. RICHARD
C. EGGLETON, Post Office Inspector in Charge, New York City. There was attached
to this carbon copy a note from the Post Office Department indicating that in
the event that Mr. MURPHY desired to know the circumstances under which this
letter was found, he should communicate with Mr. EGGLETON.

Mr. MURPHY stated that he did call EGGLETON and the latter informed
him that this letter came into the post office as "incoming mail." He further
explained that it would be impossible to tell just how the letter got into
the post office, but advised that this letter could have been found by someone
on the floor of one of the post office buildings and dropped into the outgoing
mail chute, or that it could have been put into a post office box on a street
corner and would then come into the post office when it was picked up by the
carrier. He explained to Mr. MURPHY that many of this type, wallets and other
material find their way into the post office after having been dropped in
either mail chutes in buildings, post office departments, or in the various
street corner mail boxes.

The attention of the Bureau and New Haven Office is called particularly to the third paragraph on the first page of this letter, which makes reference to one ~~xxxxxxxxxxx~~ Connecticut, and to ~~xxxxxxx~~ who, it
will be recalled ~~xxxxxxxxxxxxxx~~ of ALGER HISS.

MURPHY
~~xxxxxx~~ stated that at the present time he has no though of
bringing this matter to ~~xxxxxx~~ attention, but that he felt some investigation should be conducted into determining the author of this letter, as
well as some discreet inquiry relative to the identity and background of
~~xxxxxxxx~~

It will be noted this letter reveals that the author was for some
period of time a foreign service officer in the State Department. It will
be noted in the fourth paragraph on the first page of this letter, the writer
states: "I do not know who was in FE (Far East) in early 1938, as I was in
Peiping at that time, but for almost a year, beginning in July 1944, there
was a man of bad reputation in the China Division, and a connection between
him and Chambers can, I think, be shown."

EX. 117
4642

*Office Memorandum* • UNITED STATES GOVERNMENT

TO : D. M. LADD                                    DATE: September 29, 1950

FROM : A. H. BELMONT

SUBJECT: JAPAM
         ESPIONAGE - R

## PURPOSE

    To summarize a letter apparently directed to Alger Hiss by a former State Department employee identified by the State Department as ~~xxxxxxxxxxxxxxxxxxxx~~ who was attached to State Department establishments in the ~~xxxxxxxxxxxxx~~. Letter attached to New York instructing that information be furnished to U.S. Attorney.

## BACKGROUND

    Former Assistant USA Thomas Murphy who prosecuted the Hiss case made available to the New York Office a carbon copy of a letter which was furnished him by the Post Office Inspector in Charge, New York City. Murphy was advised that the letter had come into the post office as "incoming mail." The exact manner in which it reached the post office is unknown. The letter is addressed to "Dear Alger" and was apparently written at ~~xxxxxxxxxxxxxxxxxxxxx~~ Connecticut, January 29, 1950, and is unsigned.

    In the letter the writer alleges that through a reliable friend he had learned that a broker, Fisher Buell, who is described as an influential man, had stated to Judge Goddard "You find that man (Hiss) guilty - or else." The writer suggested that pressure on Goddard might explain why he dropped certain portions of the Judge's charge to the jury. He suggested that Buell has influence on the Judge's financial affairs.

    The writer also suggests that Larson (subject of the Amerasia case) may have been the man in the State Department who passed documents to Chambers. He suggested also that an employee of DCR in the State Department could have had access to such documents. In discussing a reason for Chambers' giving up his $30,000 a year job, the writer indicates that possibly Chambers' former employer would see to it that Chambers did not suffer thereby inasmuch as he "has proved to be such a gift from the Republican heaven."

    It is suggested also by the writer that another possible reason for Chamber's sacrificing the $30,000 a year job was that he had a "physical yen" for Hiss and upon being repulsed gave up his job in order to avenge himself against Hiss.

4640

FLJ:lfc

The writer also indicated that the State Department codes were insecure in the 1930's and that a man of Hiss' intelligence would never have filched at least some of the documents which were described in the press as having been turned over to Chambers. The writer forwarded to Hiss one hundred dollars as a contribution "toward the next trial" even though the date of the letter indicates that it was written subsequent to the second trial in the Hiss case.

## IDENTITY OF WRITER ACCORDING TO STATE DEPARTMENT

The New York Office when submitting the original information speculated that the writer might be identical with ~~—~~ formerly employed by the ~~————————————~~

## ACTION

There is attached hereto for your approval a letter to the New York Office advising of the apparent identification of ~~————~~ as the writer of the above-mentioned letter and instructing the New York Office to furnish this information to the U.S. Attorney. It is noted that the investigation has been conducted pursuant to the request of former Assistant U. S. Attorney Thomas Murphy who prosecuted the Hiss case in New York City.

- 2 -

119

**Federal Bureau of Investigation**

**United States Department of Justice**

New York, N.Y.

FBI 11/21/50

NY 3413

November 21, 1950

② FBI surveillance.

MEMORANDUM:

Re: JAHAM

On August 22, 1950, former AUSA Tom Murphy turned over to the writer a copy of a letter dated January 29, 1950, at Killingworth, Higganum, Connecticut. This copy was unsigned but was directed to ALGER HISS, and indicated that there was enclosed a check for $100 for HISS' defense fund. This letter also related that FISHER BUELL of Clinton, Connecticut, had made some remark relative to the fact that Judge GODDARD, who heard the second trial, had a preconceived notion of the guilt of ALGER HISS. This letter was turned over to MURPHY by the post office authorities. MURPHY requested the writer to determine, if possible, the identity of the writer of this letter, together with the identity of Mr. BUELL, and specifically stated that he had no intention of bringing this to the attention of Judge GODDARD or any of the Federal judges in this district, but was desirous, for the record, of determining the identity of the sender and of FISHER BUELL.

Through a check at the State Department and investigation at Higganum, Connecticut, it was determined that the author of this letter was Laurence Eustis Salisbury, a resident of Higganum and a former employee of the State Department. FISHER BUELL was identified as a former Wall Street broker, being a senior partner in the firm of Buell and Company, One Wall Street. This firm was dissolved some time in 1928 or 1929. This information was furnished the Bureau by New York letter of August 22, 1950. The Bureau answered this letter on September 29, 1950, and they point out on page 2 of their letter that the identity of the individuals mentioned above, as well as any other information developed, should be brought to the attention of the United States Attorney, but that "at that time the United States Attorney should be advised that none of the information concerning this matter has been furnished to the Department of Justice and that the Bureau would not do so unless the United States Attorney requested this action."

Reference is made to the report of Special Agent John W. Powell dated November 3, 1950, at New Haven, Connecticut, which sets forth background information concerning SALISBURY and FISHER BUELL. This report designated one copy for Mr. Donegan and one copy for the United States Attorney. At this time this report was received in this office the copies for Mr. Donegan and

GS:RAA
65-14920

2p memo noting that Murphy had obtained copy of letter to Hiss from postal authorities & that no mention of this should be made to Justice Dept.

65-14920-3413

FBI - NEW YORK
NOV 21 1950

TGS:RAA
65-14900

New York, N. Y.

the United States Attorney were sent to them directly by the receiving clerk. This report makes no mention of the basis for the investigation, nor does it have any reference to the letter in question.

Reference is made to the writer's report of November 17, 1950, which is to be furnished to the United States Attorney. This report contains no information relative to the above-mentioned letter except the fact that SALISBURY was the author of the letter dated January 29 directed to ALGER HISS. Mr. Donegan presently has all of the files of the HISS case that normally would be kept in the United States Attorney's office. The question of advising either Mr. Donegan or Mr. Saypol that the Bureau was not going to furnish copies of the report to the Department was discussed with Mr. Donegan on a confidential basis. He stated that it was his opinion that if this fact was brought to the attention of Mr. Saypol, the latter would immediately communicate with PEYTON FORD, and this might result in some embarrassment. He stated it was his suggestion that no mention of this be made to Mr. Saypol and that we allow the reports to go through since they appear to be very innocuous on the face and probably would not result in Saypol questioning the basis for the investigation in Connecticut. He stated that he would appreciate it if his suggestion was given to Mr. Belmont or Mr. Ladd at the Bureau as he was not quite sure of the purpose of the Bureau's suggestion relative to not giving copies to the Department. He stated that if the Bureau has some other idea in mind he would be of course willing to act in any way that the Bureau suggested regarding this matter.

T. G. SPENCER,
Special Agent

_I called L. L. Laughlin on this & we will go no further unless requested to do so._

_Whelan._

- 2 -

Copy

Mr. Alger/Hiss
22 East 8th Street
New York 3, N.Y.

My dear Mr. Hiss:

I have intended for weeks to write and say
to you and Mrs. Hiss that I regret the har-
rowing experience that you both have been
through. I firmly believe in your innocence,
and so do some of my very fine acquaintances
- not "Reds" at all. A

An indictment such as yours doesn't mean
anything at all to me in these days when
federal juries are "loaded" and intimidated,
and judges are being intimidated, and many
federal witnesses are professional ones
dragged from one coast to the other, or
are of the Louis Budenz and Elizabeth
Bentley type!

Integrity has been thrown out of the
window in our Justice and Immigration
Departments. Attorney General Tom Clark
set the pattern and Mr. McGrath is following
it assidously.

I fervently hope that you, Mr. Hiss, will
be vindicated during my lifetime.

With best wishes for better luck to you
both, I am

Very sincerely,

See 100-359916

351

100-359916-9

RECORDED: 9   INDEXED: 9

EX 118

(306)

② FBI Investig — post-trial  Rauley

STANDARD FORM NO. 64

FBI  12/2/49
1/13/76

file: ①  4293

# Office Memorandum • UNITED STATES GOVERNMENT

TO : Director, FBI                    DATE: 12/2/49

FROM : SAC, Newark

SUBJECT: ① JAHAM
Re DAVID SHERMAN
Plaza Hotel, Camden, N.J.

1-p memo re :  [Hiss Lawyers]

For the information of the Philadelphia and Miami Office, by teletype of 11/15/49, the New York Office advised th t a reliable confidential informant had furnished information that one DAVID SHERMAN, Plaza Hotel, Camden,
N.J., had sent a telegram to the Hiss Attorneys advising "have information
which may help Hiss. Call after 5 or write." The teletype requested this
office to discreetly ascertain the identity of DAVID SHERMAN through established confidential sources or by appropriate pretext.

On 11/17/49, A. J. LANGDON, Auditor, Plaza Hotel, Camden, N.J.,
advised that DAVID SHERMAN had resided there for a period of 4 or 5 months.
He stated that he left for a period of approximately 2 weeks in the latter part
of August, 1949, and had returned to the hotel on 9/7/49, and has occupied
Room #239 since that date.

LANGDON described DAVID SHERMAN as a white man, 38 to 40 years of age,
Height 5'9", weight 140, complexion medium. He stated that he did not see Mr.
SHERMAN often, that he apparently does not associate with anyone, and that he has
no information relative to his former address or his place of employment. He
stated that SHERMAN usually wore dark-colored work clothes and that he was of the
opinion that he has been unemployed for a period of several months.

Denied 2 p's
excisions } 67C

4293                    EX. 119

SAC, New York

Director, FBI          -4980                    March 3, 1952

① WC: break w/ CP
② WC: Translations
③ AH: M for NT
④ Hiss Lawyers

JAY DAVID WHITTAKER CHAMBERS, was.
et al
PERJURY
ESPIONAGE - R

One copy each of the following letters is enclosed
to New York and Baltimore:

      Letter dated December 14, 1951, from Paul Willert   —Balt
      to Mr. T. Roland Berner                                     1901

      Letter dated December 17, 1951, from Paul Willert   — Balt
      to Mr. Chester T. Lane                                      1900

      Letter dated February 19, 1952, from the Legal Attache,
      London, England.

deletions
b-1

      To the best of Willert's recollection, this
was in January or February, 1938. New York should interview Chambers
immediately and thoroughly in connection with this statement of Willert.
It is noted that New York advised by teletype February 21, 1952, that
Chambers planned to return to Baltimore on March 1, 1952. If Chambers
has returned, Baltimore should interview him immediately.

2-p memo ~~etc~~ cover for correspondence between
Chester Lane & Paul Willert, literary agent.

EX 120

New York should discuss this matter with the United States Attorney immediately to ascertain if he desires the Bureau to interview Vaudrin for any information he may have concerning Chambers' translation of Dr. Gumpert's book. It is noted that New York advised by teletype dated February 27, 1952, that Vaudrin was probably one of the editors at the Oxford University Press at the time he (Chambers) was translating material for Paul Willert. Chambers advised that he did not work for Vaudrin and recalled that he probably met Vaudrin at the most two or three times in his whole life.

14 Halsey Street,
London, S.W.3.

17th December, 1951.

Mr. Chester T. Lane,
Beer, Richards, Lane & Haller,
70 Pine Street,
NEW YORK 5., N.Y.

Dear Mr. Lane,

Your telegram reached me a few days after returning from
Spain. I had in the meantime collected in Paris a copy of your letter
addressed to me here. I must apologise for the delay.

My difficulty in the whole of this tortuous business, as I told
our mutual friend, is that I have no documentary evidence to support
my own memories as to when I met Chambers and when he told me that he
had definitely left the Communist Party and was in fear of his life.
It would appear to me, from my own recollection and from the date of
the publication of Dr. Gumpert's book, that these meetings must have
been just before or after Christmas 1937-8. It would be difficult, as
you will understand, for me, lacking documentary evidence, to swear to
this impression in a court of law. The best I could do would be to
repeat that fatal phrase "to the best of my recollection".

However, there is one way in which to support my memories one way
or the other; that is, to ask Dr. Gumpert on what date he handed back
his manuscript to me to be retranslated, or - and much more important -
to ask the then editor of the Oxford University Press, Philip Vaudrin,
when he first discussed this translation with Whittaker Chambers. It
was Philip Vaudrin who brought Chambers to my office for the purpose
of translating Dr. Gumpert's book. It would seem to me that these two,
far more important than myself, are in a position to state what date
Chambers began his work. It was during his work on the translation
that he told me of his fear of being murdered by the O.G.P.U. and
went into hiding in a way which embarrassed us very much. This would
be sufficient evidence to show when he said he had broken with the
Communist Party.

I am indeed sorry not to be more helpful and hope very much that
you will have some success with Gumpert and Vaudrin. I hope you
will not think that I am being uncooperative.

Yours very sincerely,

COPY

1) WK b/ul/CP
2) ANON front.
3) Paul Willert

Bolt 1901

14 Halsey Street,
London, S.W.3.

14th December, 1951.

My dear Ted,

Thank you so much for your letter and pleasant Christmas present of December 6th. I do hope none the less that you will succeed in obtaining your legal due as far as services are concerned, and express my regrets for technicalities which may in any way hold it up.

I am sending you a copy of a letter which I have written today to one of your colleagues, plus a copy of his letter to me. You will probably remember that long ago we did employ at the O.U.P. Whittaker Chambers. What you may not remember is that I got to know Whittaker Chambers quite well and was immensely intrigued by the fact that he went in obvious terror of his life, according to him, because he had left the C.P.; and on two occasions at least he spent the night with me in New York because it might be dangerous for him to go abroad. To the best of my memory this was in January or February 1938.

On the other hand I have no documentary evidence of this, and any possible value which my testimony might have in a court of law would depend on the corroboration of (a) Philip Vaudrin, who was the chief editor of O.U.P. at that time, and (b) Dr. Gumpert, the author.

I have no particular wish to be mixed up in this unsavoury matter, unless you and others feel that I could in any way help put right a serious miscarriage of justice.

All good wishes to you both for Christmas.

Yours ever,

Mr. T. Roland Berner,
30, Broad Street,
New York 4., N.Y.

# CRIMINAL DOCKET
## UNITED STATES DISTRICT COURT

*Cannella J*

61 Cr 1113

D. C. Form No. 100 Rev.

| TITLE OF CASE | ATTORNEYS |
|---|---|
| THE UNITED STATES | ~~DOCKET~~ T.18, Sec. 371 |
| vs. | Unlawfully conspiring to violate Section 1503 |
| CC..?.. ELLIOTT KAHANER — 1371 | U.S.Code by corruptly influencing, obstructing |
| CC.?.A.?.. ANTONIO CORALLO | & impeding & corruptly endeavoring to influence |
| C?..7-?-C-C- ROBERT M. ERDMAN | obstruct & impede the due |
| CC 5-?-?.? JAMES VINCENT KEOGH | ~~For Defendant~~ administration |
| 11-22-77 SANFORD J. MOORE ✓ 1305 | of justice in the U.S. Judicial District for the Eastern District of New York. |
| | ( ONE COUNT ) |

| STATISTICAL RECORD | COSTS | | | DATE | NAME OR RECEIPT NO. | REC. | |
|---|---|---|---|---|---|---|---|
| | | | | 1962 | (appeals) | | |
| J.S. 2 mailed ✓ | Clerk | | | 8/2 | Kahaner | 5 | |
| | | | | 8/2 | Keogh | 5 | |
| J.S. 3 mailed 1,2,4-3,5 | Marshal | | | 8/2 | Corallo | 5 | |
| | | | | 7/3. | 11 U.S.Treas | | |
| Violation | Docket fee | | | 7-4-64 | Erdman | 500 | |
| | | | | 8-7-64 | U.S.Treas | | 50 |
| Title | | | | 7-8-64 | Erdman | 580 | |
| | | | | 8-11-64 | U.S.Treas | | 35 |
| Sec. | | | | 6-10-67 | HANDELMAN | 5 | |
| | | | | 8-11-61 | U.S.TREAS | | |
| ROBERT M. ERDMAN — FINED — | $5,000. on 7-15-64. | | | 10-21-68 | HANDELMAN | 5 | |
| | | | | 11-15-68 | U.S.TREAS | | |
| | | | | 3/24/70 | HANDELMAN | 5 | |
| | | | | 3/25/70 | TREAS | | |

| DATE | PROCEEDINGS (See L. x Pa...) |
|---|---|
| 12-7-61 | Filed Indictment. |
| 12-7-61 | ANTONIO CORALLO - Warrant of arrest ordered. MacMahon, J. |
| 12-7-61 | ANTONIO CORALLO - Brought to Court on warrant. Pleads Not Guilty. (Atty present). Bail fixed at $50,000. Remanded in lieu of bail. Adj'd to 12-14-61 to fix date for making motions. MacMahon, D.J. |
| 12-7-61 | ANTONIO CORALLO-Bench warrant issued. [Ex 12] |
| 12-8-61 | ANTONIO CORALLO-Oral motion for reduction of bail denied. MacMahon, J. |
| 12-8-61 | ANTONIO CORALLO-Filed notice of appearance by Michael P. Direnzo, 253 B'way. |
| 12-8-61 | ANTONIO CORALLO - Filed consents and order (handwritten) enlarging the bail limits. So ordered. MAC MAHON, J. |

| DATE | PROCEEDINGS |
|------|-------------|
| 7-17-67 | JAMES VINCENT KEOGH - Docketed Answer on behalf of the Government, filed in opposition to the petitioner's application for a Writ of Error Cor |
| 7-17-67 | JAMES VINCENT KEOGH - Docketed Affidavits, filed 7/14/67 of William G. H John F. Lally, Charles Norman Shaffer. |
| 7-17-67 | JAMES VINCENT KEOGH - Docketed Memorandum, dated 5/22/67, endorsed on mot 5/10/67: " The within motion is respectfully referred to Judge CANNELLA, J." |
| 7-17-67 | JAMES VINCENT KEOGH - Docketed Defendant-Petitioner's Memorandum of Law filed 5/16/67). |
| 7-17-67 | JAMES VINCENT KEOGH - Docketed Reply Memorandum of Law of def't, filed 7/ |
| 7-17-67 | JAMES VINCENT KEOGH - Docketed Plaintiff Respondents Memorandum, filed in opposition to def't petitioner's Application for a Writ of Error Nobis. |
| 7-17-67 | JAMES VINCENT KEOGH - Docketed Opinion # 33822, filed 7/14/67 - WEINFELD " * * * * * Keogh now seeks a writ of error coram nobis to vacate judgment of conviction and for a new trial upon the grounds that prosecution knowingly (1) suppressed exculpatory evidence and (2 used and sponsored perjured testimony. * * * * * * The interest does not require a new trial. The petition is dismissed. WEINFELD (SEE Opinion) (Mailed notice 7/17/67). |
| 7/19/67 | Filed Transcript of record of proceedings, dated 6/5/67 |
| 8-10-67 | JAMES VINCENT KEOGH,- Filed notice of appeal from order dismissing petiti motion for a writ of error coram nobis., to the U.S.C. of Appeals fo 2nd circuit. |
| 9-8-67 | JAMES VINCENT KEOGH - Filed Notice that the Record on Appeal has been ce and transmitted to the U.S.C.A., on 9/8/67. |
| 3-12-68 | JAMES VINCENT KEOGH -Docketed Opinion and Judgment of the U.S.C.A., fil that the Order of the District Court is affirmed in part and vaca part and that the action be and it hereby is remanded for further in accordance with the opinion of this court. " Judgment entered 3/7/68 - John J. Olear, Jr., Clerk"     (Mailed Notice on 3/12/68). |
| 4-15-68 | JAMES VINCENT KEOGH: Filed affidavit & notice of motion for an order purs rule 34 of F.R.C.Procedure to examine, inspect and copy certain documents. (Ret. |
| 5-7-68 | JAMES VINCENT KEOGH: Memo endorsed on motion to inspect.-- Respectfully r to Judge Weinfeld, with his consent-                    PALMIE |
| 5-7-68 | JAMES VINCENT KEOGH: Before Weinfeld, J.- Hearing held on Petitioners' mo produce & concluded. Decision reserved. |

61 Crim.1113          Page 10          61 Cr 1113

| DATE | PROCEEDINGS |
|------|-------------|
| 4-15-68 | Filed Petitioner's memorandum of law |
| 4-15-68 | JAMES VINCENT KEOGH- Filed affdvt of J. Frank Cunningham Atty employed in the Criminal Division, U.S. Dept. of Justice, Washington, D.C. in support of respondent's opposition to petitioner's application for discovery and inspection of documents etc. Respondent's memorandum of law in opposition to petitioner's motion for discovery and inspection |
| 5-22-68 | Filed affirmation of Philip Handelman submitted in reply to the affdvt of respondent submitted in opposition to petitioner's motion for discovery etc. & petitioner's reply memorandum & endorsed respectfully referred to Judge Weinfeld- PALMIERI, J. |
| 5-22-68 | Filed affdvt of Emanuel Schaeffer |
| 5-22-68 | JAMES VINCENT KEOGH-/Filed memo endorsed on motion filed 4-15-68 * ** Accordingly, only the 1961 financial of Erdman in the possession of the Government will be subject to discovery and inspection under items 1 & 2 * * * If the further search referred to by the prosecutor upon the argument discloses additional reports which come within item 3, they, too, shall be made available to petioner for inspection and copying. In all other respects the motion is denied- WEINFELD, J |
| 6-20-68 | JAMES VINCENT KEOGH- Filed notice to take deposition of Ruth Wexler on 7-10-68 Room 60 |
| 7- 5-68 | JAMES VINCENT KEOGH: Filed affdvt & show cause order-quash subpoena duces tecum and notice to take deposition of Ruth Wexler be vacated, w/memo of law-Ret. 7-9-68. |
| 7-9-68 | JAMES VINCENT KEOGH: Filed affdvt of Philip Handelman in opposition to Government's application to quash the subpoena duces tecum (Judge Weinfeld) |
| 7-9-68 | endorsement on order to show cause filed 7-5-68-respectfully referred to Judge Weinfeld with his consent. EDELSTEIN, J |
| 7-10-68 | James Vincent Keogh,/Filed memo endorsed on motion filed 7-9-68 -Motion granted. Apart from the delay in the service of the supoena and notice to take deposition, and the ill health of the witness, the Court deems it desirable if her testimony is to be taken, that it be before the Court, so that it can have the benefit of her demeanor testimony. WEINFELD, J |
| **** SEE BELOW...... | |
| 7-25-68 | JAMES VINCENT KEOGH: Filed affdvt. & notice of motion to quash subpoena duces tecum served by petitioner upon the F.B.I. Ret. 7-24-68 in room 906. |
| 7-25-68 | JAMES VINCENT KEOGH: FIled memorandum of law in support of Govts. motion to quash. |
| 7-25-68 | JAMES VINCENT KEOGH: Filed MEMO ENDORSED on motion to quash subpoena. "Since all pertinent records have already been delivered to petitioners counsel, the motion is granted. (Mailed notices-7-29-68) WEINFELD,J. |
| 7/24/68 | HEARING BEGUN ON A MOTION FOR CORUM NORBIS |
| 7/25/68 | Hearing continued |
| 7/29/68 | Hearing continued |
| 7/30/68 | Hearing continued and concluded....Decision reserved.... WEINFELD, J. |

/////////////

continued on Page 11

61 Cr 1113      Page 12

| DATE | PROCEEDINGS |
|---|---|
| 4-27-70 | JAMES VINCENT KEOGH - Filed Affidavits and Motion for an extension of time within which to respond to James Vincent Keogh's second petition for a writ of error coram nobis 28 days from 5/4/70 to 6/1/70. (Motion pursuant to Rule 45(b), F.R.Cr.P. (Motion ret. 4/28/70, 10 A.M., before Weinfeld,J.) |
| 4-28-70 | Filed memo endorsed on order to show cause filed 4-27-70-MOTION GRANTED. Answering affdvts to be served by June 1, 1970     WEINFELD, J. (mailed notice) |
| 6-1-70 | Motion filed 1-21-70 is repsectfully referred to Judgw Weinfeld with his consent. WY of J. Frank Cunningham, Atty for Criminal Div. XXXXXXXXXX o |
| 6-1-70 | JAMES VINCENT KEOGH: Filed affdvt/in opposition to petition for writ of error coram nobis & memorandum of law. (Weinfeld J) |
| 6-1-70 | JAMES VINCENT KEOGH: Filed Govt's motion to dismiss the Petition for a writ of Error nobis. (Weinfeld J) |
| 6-15-70 | JAMES VINCENT KEOGH-Filed Notice of Motion and affidavit to inspect and copy certai docs.and for an extension of time until 7/15/70. (Weinfeld |
| 6-17-70 | JAMES V. KEOGH - Deft's motion for discovery and extended time to 7-15-70 to complete certain documents., Dec. Res.     WEINFELD, J. |
| 6-17-70 | JAMES V. KEOGH - Filed Memo Endorsed Re: Deft. motion to inspect.Denied in part, & granted in part. (see memo in file)(mailed notice) WEINF |
| 6-17-70 | JAMES V. KEOGH - Filed Affdvt. in opposition to motion for discovery,b J. Frank Cunningham, Atty. of the Dept. of Justice, Wash. D.C. Filed Respondent's memo of law. |
| 7/10/70 | J.V. KOEGH Filed affidavit and petitioners reply memorandum. to Weinfeld, J. |
| 7-16-70 | Deft. JAMES V. KEOGH - Hearing held. Dec. Resvd., to be decided on counsel's papers.     WEINFELD, J. |
| ~~7-15-70~~ | ~~Filed judgment. Deft. Robert M. Brown is sentenced to one(1) year. Execution of sent is suspended and defendant placed on probation for five(5)years. The Deft. is to fine $5,000.00. Fine is to be paid in one year by 12 equal monthly payments If conditions of payment are not complied with the deft. is to be committed until fine is paid or he is otherwise discharged according to law. XBRXEXX~~ |
| 8-5-70 | Filed U.S.C.A. appendix to appellant's brief. Vol. 1 |
|  | Filed U.S.C.A. appendix to appellant's brief. Vol. 2 |
|  | Filed U.S.C.A. appendix to appellant's brief. Vol. 3 |
|  | Filed U.S.C.A. Exhibits, Vol. 4 |
|  | Filed U.S.C.A. Exhibits, Vol 5 |
| 8-5-70 | James V. Keogh-Filed opinion # 37006, Weinfeld, J. "quotes this is the second application for a writ of error coram nobis by James V. Keogh****** The application is denied in all respects and the petition dismissed. (see file) (mailed notice)    WEINFELD, J. 18/5/70 |

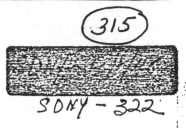

(315)

SONY - 322

*Murphys file copy of Chambers*
*12-8-48 signed statement to FBI*

New York, New York
WC— December 8, 1948 Stmt 1

2 T. Murp

I, Jay David Whittaker Chambers, make the following statement to Thomas G. Spencer and Joseph M. Kelly, whom I know to be Special Agents of the Federal Bureau of Investigation. I understand that any statement that I make can be used against me in a court of law. No threats or promises have been made to me in connection with this statement. I have been advised that I have a right of counsel.

While functioning as a courier for the Communist Party underground apparatus, I was introduced by DAVID CARPENTER to one WARD PIGMAN, and to the best of my recollection, this meeting occurred in 1936. Sometime later, I was introduced to GEORGE PIGMAN, brother of WARD PIGMAN, and this latter introduction probably was made by DAVID CARPENTER, although it is barely possible that WARD PIGMAN may have introduced me to his brother GEORGE. Both at that time, I believe, were employed by the Bureau of Standards, and it was my understanding that both had previously been connected with an underground apparatus, probably one being operated by ELEANOR NELSON.

Subsequent to my meeting WARD PIGMAN and probably in the latter part of 1936 or early 1937, WARD PIGMAN began furnishing me documentary material from the Bureau of Standards, such material being handed over by him to me on the occasion of our meetings, and he continued to do so until the time of my leaving the Communist Party in April, 1938. I had meetings in public places in Washington with WARD PIGMAN approximately once a week, on which occasions he would deliver to me documentary material from the Bureau of Standards.

During this same period, I had personal meetings, perhaps fortnightly or perhaps monthly with GEORGE PIGMAN, but I was never able to activate him as a source of material and never received any material from him.

I want to state that during the above-described period while I was receiving a fairly regular flow of material from WARD PIGMAN, the latter was also meeting DAVID CARPENTER, and on occasion did transmit material to him instead of me. DAVID CARPENTER was doing all of the photographic work in connection with the material received from WARD PIGMAN, and after CARPENTER had reduced such material to film, I would deliver the film to COLONEL BYKOV, having, of course, previously returned the original documents to WARD PIGMAN. Since my leaving the Communist Party in April, 1938, I have never seen either WARD PIGMAN or GEORGE PIGMAN. It is my present recollection that a brief case was employed by WARD PIGMAN

AWZ

EX.122

198

in transmitting documentary material to me, that is he would arrive at the meeting place with the material in the brief case, which I would take when we parted company, and at the next meeting, I would return the brief case with the photographed documents therein. The material made available in the above described manner to me by WARD PIGMAN consisted of documents dealing with a variety of technical subjects, the significance of which was unknown to me, but I do recall that COLONEL BYKOV occasionally complained about the type of material being secured by me from WARD PIGMAN and expressed the feeling that WARD PIGMAN's full potential as a source of material was not being developed. I am reasonably sure that neither WARD PIGMAN nor GEORGE PIGMAN ever met COLONEL BYKOV.

The above-named Agents have this date displayed to me a photograph, the reverse side of which bears the initial "A" and the initials "JK" and "TGS". This photo appears to me to be that of a photographer whom I knew by the name of FELIX. He has visibly matured and seems to have grown heavier and I do not recall he wore glasses at the time I knew him, but the longer I look at the picture, the more certain I am that it is that of FELIX.

With further respect to FELIX, I recall that I met him either in Washington, D. C. or New York City and he was introduced to me by BYKOV, who explained that he was a "technical man," which I understood to mean he was a photographer. To the best of my knowledge, FELIX was not known to DAVID CARPENTER, and vice versa, although they both were Communist Party functionaries. It is my recollection both men received $100 a month for the work they did on behalf of the Communist Party and they also were allowed certain expenses which were incurred in connection with their photographic work, and which also included rent, telephone and medical expenses. It is also my recollection that FELIX was a more proficient photographer than CARPENTER; for that reason, I had occasion to use his services more frequently than those of DAVID CARPENTER. In the event that I desired to use his services, I recall specifically that I had his telephone number and by either calling him or by pre-arrangement, he would come to Washington, D. C. and receive from me documents or other material that I had, would take them to Baltimore where they would be processed by him into negatives, and the documents would be returned to me that same day. In this connection, I would like to state that DAVID CARPENTER did not have a telephone as nearly as I remember, and consequently, my meetings with him were always by pre-arrangement. The developed negatives, which I obtained from FELIX were delivered to BYKOV in the same fashion as the ones I would receive from CARPENTER in the event he did the work.

In connection with the payment of money or the bestowing of gifts on the various people who turned over information to me, I would like to state that no one so far as I know, was actually given any money for the services they rendered. However, I do recall that probably at the end of 1936, BYKOV in one of this conversations with me suggested it might be a good idea to give ALGER HISS, HARRY DEXTER WHITE and A. GEORGE SILVERMAN a gift of some kind. After some discussion, BYKOV thought it might be advisable to present each of them with an expensive rug. I myself was not too keen on the idea. However, BYKOV became somewhat insistent, and as a result, I made inquiries of an Armenian rug dealer in New York City, and arranged for the purchase of three oriental rugs. To the best of my recollection, these rugs cost $600 each. I am rather hazy on the actual amount that was paid for these rugs, but this amount is the price to the best of my present belief. BYKOV furnished me with the money to make this purchase, and as I recall it, the three rugs were sent by the Armenian rug dealer via American Railway Express to the home of A. GEORGE SILVERMAN in Washington, D. C.

Prior to the delivery of the rugs to Washington, I had informed HISS, WHITE and SILVERMAN that they were going to be presented with gifts as a token of gratitude for the activities of the American Communists. WHITE and SILVERMAN were quite pleased with the fact that they were going to receive such a gift. However, HISS was more polite than pleased when he did receive this gift. My recollection of the delivery of the rugs is that SILVERMAN because of his close association with HARRY WHITE, made the delivery of his (WHITE's) rug. In connection with the delivery of the rug for ALGER HISS, I recall one evening by pre-arrangement, SILVERMAN put the rug in his car, drove it to a predesignated point, a restaurant on Route 1 about three or four miles east of College Park, Maryland. I accompanied HISS in the latter's car to this point, and upon arrival there, I got out of HISS' car, got the rug from SILVERMAN's car, and carried it to HISS' car.

I would like to mention another individual with whom I came in contact in 1937. This individual was known to me by the name of KEITH, which I know to be a psuedonym. In so far as I can recall, KEITH was connected with BYKOV in New York City and came to Washington in 1937. KEITH was introduced to me in New York by BYKOV, who related that KEITH was a photographer and that I could utilize his services if I so desired. In my conversation with BYKOV, however, I gained the distinct impression that BYKOV was trying to get rid of KEITH and send him to Washington so that I could handle him and thereby, BYKOV would no longer have to concern himself with KEITH.

In connection with my knowledge of KEITH, I learned either from KEITH or through BYKOV that the former was connected with a White Russian named SVIASHNIKOV (phonetic), who was a ballistics expert employed in Government service in Washington, D. C. It is also my recollection that at the time I met KEITH either in New York or Washington, SVIASHNIKOV was

by them because he had a sister living in Moscow, and I remember KEITH once
described to me how BYKOV used to torture SVIASHNIKOV to the point where he
cried, by saying they were going to put the sister out on the street unless
he produced. So far as I can recall, I never requested KEITH to do any
work for me. I do recall, however, KEITH had an apartment or a room in
Washington, D. C. and that I had at that time in my possession a telephone
number where I could reach him.

It is also my recollection KEITH was connected with one
AZIMOV (phonetic), who was a metallurgist and connected with the University
of California at Berkeley. I also recall subsequently AZIMOV became the
head of the research department at the United States Steel Corporation at
Chicago, Illinois.

Another person whom I met during my work as a courier
for the underground apparatus, was VINCENT RENO, to whom I was introduced
by J. PETERS in Philadelphia, probably in 1937. It is possible DAVID
CARPENTER may have been present on this occasion. RENO had been an
organizer either for the Communist Party or the Young Communist League in
Montana, and had employed the name LANCE CLARK.

At the time I met RENO, he had just commenced employment
with the War Department as a civilian at the Aberdeen Proving Ground,
Aberdeen, Maryland. He resided on the post to the best of my recollection,
and was a mathematician. I had occasional meetings with RENO subsequently
in public places in Washington and possibly Baltimore, and I recall that
on one or two occasions, RENO delivered to me documentary material bearing
upon his work at the Aberdeen Proving Ground on a bombsight project.
It is my recollection that his superior at Aberdeen was COLONEL
ZORNIG.

I would estimate that my meetings with VINCENT RENO
totaled probably five in all; that would include the one or two occasions
on which he handed over material to me. I believe that RENO had been a
member of an underground apparatus operated by ELEANOR NELSON at the
time I was introduced to him.

I would describe VINCENT RENO as probably 27 or 28
years of age at the time I knew him, approximately 5 feet 8 inches,
slender build, sandy hair and eyelashes, blue eyes, and clean-shaven. I
remember one time when I desired to have a meeting with VINCENT RENO, I ascertained that his brother, whose first name I believe is PHILIP, was residing
at a certain address in Washington, and in order for PHILIP to arrange a
meeting for me with VINCENT, I went to that address and for the first time
met PHILIP RENO.

I believe PHILIP RENO, like his brother, had a prior connection with the ELEANOR NELSON apparatus, but he had no connection whatsoever with the work I was doing at that time.

I have read the above statement consisting of this and four previous pages, and to the best of my knowledge and recollection, I declare it is the truth.

JAY DAVID WHITTAKER CHAMBERS

Witnessed:

Thomas G. Spencer,
Special Agent, FBI

Joseph M. Kelly
Special Agent, FBI

# Office Memorandum • UNITED ST...

320

TO : H.B. Fletcher                                    DATE: 12/11/48

FROM : E. Hyatt Mossburg                              8:22 PM

SUBJECT: J. David Whittaker Chambers
Perjury: Espionage-R.

SA Halsey Smith (WFO) telephonically advised that Julian
Wadleigh, whom you will recall was one of the persons named
by Chambers who had furnished him with confidential information,
was calling the field office and desired to furnish information
in connection with the captioned case. SA Smith advised he was
not familiar with the facts in this particular case.

I advised Smith to transfer the call to the bureau and I would
talk to Wadleigh. Smith called back in a couple of seconds and advised
that Wadleigh had been cut off or hung up. I then called Supervisor
Delavaigne in the WFO told Smith to call Supervisor Delavaigne (WFO)
and see that Wadleigh was immediately recontacted.

9:30 PM  Smith subsequently called back and advised that Wadleigh had been
recontacted at once by SA Zander. The substance of Wadleigh's call
was that he wanted to go on record as answering a question previously
asked of him. Wadleigh advised that in 1937 or 1938 he had received
a rug from Chambers as a gift at New Years. Smith was unable to advise
me of who had asked this question of Wadleigh but he advised that a
teletype summary was now being prepared by agent Zander and would be
sent to the bureau and the New York Office.

You will recall that I advised you of the above information.

EX. 123

New York, New York
December 14, 1948

④ Counter Rep

I, HENRY JULIAN WADLEIGH, make the following statement to Thomas G.
Spencer and Francis D. O'Brien, whom I know to be Special Agents of the Federal
Bureau of Investigation. I understand that any statement I may make can be used
against me in a court of law. No threats or promises have been made to me in
connection with this statement. I have been advised that I have a right to counsel.

The following information supplements that contained in my statements
of December 6th and 10th, 1948 made to agents of the Federal Bureau of Investigation. There has been exhibited to me a group of photographs that were contained
on microfilm, as well as a separate group of photographs which appear to be, in
the main, excerpts from cablegrams from the Department of State, as well as five
handwritten notations. I have examined these photographs and my comments are set
forth hereinafter.

Before discussing any particular items in this collection of documents,
I wish to state that my recollections as to particular documents which I received
in late 1937 and early 1938 are no clearer than one would expect after such a
long lapse of time. I can, however, remember in a general way what types of
material I received.

## DOCUMENTS 1 to 48

All this material relates to conversations between the State Department
and the German Ambassador on the possibility of breaking the impasse which existed
in particular relations between the United States and Germany at that time.
Subject to a more thorough and complete examination, this is the only part of
the collection that evokes any recollections at all in my mind, except the names
of persons in the State Department whom I knew, and the names of officers referred
to in some of the other documents.

I recall clearly that during the time that I was in the Trade Agreements
Division until my trip to Turkey, my colleague, Mr. DARLINGTON, made repeated
and, so it seemed to me at the time, rather hopeless attempts to cut the gordian
knot on trade relations with Germany. When I first came into the State Department
he had prepared, I believe in collaboration with Mr. PASVOLSKY, some documents
or document at least as lengthy as the later material contained in the microfilm
collection. I was shown that earlier material and asked to comment upon it.

As to the later material which is contained in this collection, I have
no such recollection. It seems to be probable that this material was not shown
to me, although in my own opinion I was as competent as anyone in the State
Department to give advice on it. I would not make so conceited a remark except
that I feel in this connection I must be perfectly frank. It is possible,
though I think improbable, that I did see the material and paid little attention
to it because I was convinced at the time that nothing would come of it, and in

During my examination by the Grand Jury on Saturday, December 11th, one of the jurors asked me if I was holding in my possession any documents or other objects which might be of interest in connection with the case. I said no. Since then it has come to my recollection that I possess a rug which was given to me as a New Year's present, I believe in 1936-37. It is an 8 X 12 Bokhara rug. I understand it was worth two or three hundred dollars at the time it was given to me and may now be worth around $400. I was given to understand that the rug was presented to me by the authorities in Moscow in appreciation of my collaboration. In 1939, when I moved from the house which I was renting on Quincy Street, Chevy Chase, Maryland, I had this rug stored by NESHAN G. HINTLIAN, Connecticut Avenue, Washington, D.C., a rug dealer. It has never been taken out of storage.

It is my recollection that the rug was delivered to me by CARPENTER, but this recollection is not a certainty. To the best of my recollection it was CARPENTER who told me that the rug was a New Year's present. I recall definitely that the rug was delivered to me in my own car, and by inferential reconstruction of the event I think CARPENTER must have borrowed my car in order to do it.

When the Grand Jury questioned me on December 11th one of the jurors asked me if I possess a typewriter and if I had ever loaned it to Mrs. HISS. I hereby reaffirm the statement I made on that occasion that I never loaned a typewriter to Mrs. HISS, and I add that I never loaned a typewriter to Mr. HISS. However, it is possible, though I think not very probable, that I may have loaned a typewriter to CARPENTER.

Immediately after the hearing I informed Mr. ALEXANDER CAMPBELL that I might have loaned the typewriter to CARPENTER. I also gave him the information that the typewriter in question was sold to Miss MARGARET HARDY, either shortly before or after her marriage to Mr. PITTMAN B. POTTER. I can place the approximate date of the sale of the typewriter by the fact that I sold it because my wife, whom I had just married or was about to marry, possessed a portable typewriter and I saw no need at that time for having more than one typewriter in the family. The date of my marriage was February 15, 1941.

The typewriter was purchased in London in 1928 or 1929. It was a Remington Portable assembled, as I was informed by the salesman, in England from American parts. It had pounds, shillings and pence on the keys instead of dollars and cents.

*I have read this statement consisting of four pages and find it true to the best of my knowledge and belief.*

Witnessed: *[signature]*

*Francis D. O'Brien*

Special Agents, Federal Bureau of Investigation
New York, N.Y.

*Henry Julian Wadleigh*
HENRY JULIAN WADLEIGH

- 4 -

cc: Mr. Fletcher
Mr. Taylor
Supervisor (2)      FBI

MR. H. B. FLETCHER                                December 31, 1948

M. A. TAYLOR, Washington Field Office

JAY DAVID WHITTAKER CHAMBERS, was., etal
PERJURY
ESPIONAGE - R

On the afternoon of December 31, 1948, subject Chambers
was interviewed by Mr. Ray Whearty of the Department and the writer
in the office of Mr. Whearty at considerable length concerning the substance
of his statements to members of the House Un-American Activities Committee
on the evening of December 29, 1948, at his farm near Westminster, Maryland,
which information was subsequently reported in the Washington "Times Herald"
on December 30, and 31, 1948.

The news articles in question attributed most of these statements
to Congressman Karl Mundt and indicated that Chambers had revealed new names,
including some dead individuals and some now operating in other countries,
and had furnished a complete chronology of his activities. Further, that the
figures named did not include any new sources of confidential information.
The articles reported that 52 additional big batches of Top Secret papers,
including data on the Norden bomb sight, had been delivered by Chambers to
secret Soviet agents in New York and that he had related on one occasion
he took a money belt containing $10,000 from New York City to San Francisco
for the purpose of financing West Coast spy operations. Reference was also
made to four costly rugs given as gifts to four of the principal sources
of information in Washington.

Mr. Chambers related the information he had furnished the Committee
began approximately in 1932 when he was introduced into the apparatus of
one Ulrich, who operated an apparatus through the Hamburg-American Steamship
Line and which utilized three New York City apartments and secret writing
and microfilm in their exchange of information and instructions. He mentioned
a number of individuals involved or associated in this matter, naming some
and identifying others by pseudonyms.

Thereafter, he mentioned association with Dr. Philip Rosenbliet,
John Sherman, was.; Maxim Lieber; Hideo Noda, a Japanese; a Finn or Estonian
who held an important position in the Soviet network and who preceded Borris
Bykov. Throughout the interview, Chambers spoke of J. Peters and Peters'
role in making contacts and supplying individuals for the work.

Chambers then related his association with Harold Ware and the
group which Harold Ware had organized, including Alger Hiss, Donald Hiss,
Charles Kramer, Lee Pressman, etc. He explained how the primary objective

MAT:esb

3 p memo Taylor to Fletcher
re WC 12/31/48 int w/ Ray
Whearty

Ex124

F. B. I.
JAN — — 406
WASHINGTON D. C.
ROUTE TO

was placing these men in key positions and how subsequently the principal objective changed to securing information from those who were well placed. He also told about the introduction into the parallel of George Silverman and Harry D. White.

He spent some time discussing Colonel Borris Bykov, listing the persons who had met Bykov on one or more occasions, and stated that Bykov was known well by J. Peters and unknown subject "Keith". He had a new vague recollection that "Keith's" real name may have been Crane, but observed that this was very vague. He mentioned that "Keith" had associated with John Sherman on the West Coast and was certain that "Keith" came from the West Coast by reason of the following incident:

In connection with the news item concerning $10,000 which Chambers allegedly carried to San Francisco, Chambers explained that in 1935, unknown subject "Bill" had sent him to San Francisco with a money belt for the use of individuals on the West Coast. He was not entrusted with the purpose for which the money was sent. He registered at the Golden Gate YMCA as Lloyd Cantwell and by prearrangement was contacted by "Keith", whom he then met as "Pete". Subsequently, "Keith" introduced him to an elderly Jewish man named Volkoff, who was known as the "Old Man" and was connected with the Pan-Pacific Trade Union Secretariat. He did not recall whether he delivered the money belt to "Keith" or Volkoff, but believed it was probably the latter. He mentioned that he understood the Pan-Pacific Trade Union Secretariat was operating a courier system to Japan at the time and he assumed the money was for underground purposes. He stated he did not know the amount of money in the belt and that the news item apparently reflected a casual estimate by him to the Committee that they would not have sent him out there with less than the sum of $10,000.

With reference to the 52 additional batches of secret papers, Chambers stated this was a rough estimate based upon visits every week or ten days with his contacts.

Concerning mention of the Norden bomb sight, Chambers stated that he knew that contact Vincent Reno had been working on a bomb sight and that he may have mentioned the Norden bomb sight, but that he felt this statement must be qualified.

Regarding the four costly rugs mentioned in the news article, Chambers repeated that they were delivered to Harry D. White, Alger Hiss, A. George Silverman and H. Julian Wadleigh.

- 2 -

CONF 3 STNS

WASH AND WFO 25    BALTIMORE 1    FROM NEW YORK

DIRECTOR AND SACS    URGENT

JAY DAVID WHITTAKER CHAMBERS, WAS, ETAL, BRIBERY, ESPIONAGE - R.

DURING THE INTERROGATION OF CHAMBERS IN CONNECTION WITH THE OBTAINING

OF MATERIAL FOR A DETAILED SIGNED STATEMENT CONCERNING HIS ACTIVITIES,

THE MATTER OF HIS PURCHASE OF FOUR BOKHARA RUGS AND THEIR DELIVERY

TO HIS CONTACTS IN WASHINGTON WAS DISCUSSED.    CHAMBERS RELATED THAT

PROBABLY IN THE FALL OF NINETEEN THIRTYSIX WHEN BORRIS BYKOV TOOK

OVER FROM J. PETERS, THE FORMER DISCUSSED AT LENGTH THE WASHINGTON

SETUP.    BYKOV WAS OF THE OPINION THAT AN EXPENSIVE PRESENT SHOULD

BE GIVEN TO THOSE PERSONS WHO PROBABLY WOULD BE MOST PRODUCTIVE

IN THE SECURING OF GOVERNMENT DOCUMENTS.    BYKOV THEN GAVE CHAMBERS

APPROXIMATELY ONE THOUSAND DOLLARS IN CASH AND INSTRUCTED HIM TO PUR-

CHASE FOUR ORIENTAL RUGS SO THAT THESE COULD BE PRESENTED TO ALGER

HISS, HARRY DEXTER WHITE, A. GEORGE SILVERMAN, AND PROBABLY HENRY

JULIAN WADLEIGH.    CHAMBERS RELATED THAT HE HAD NO KNOWLEDGE OF

ORIENTAL RUGS AND SOLICITED THE ASSISTANCE OF DR. MEYER SCHAPIRO,

A PROFESSOR AT COLUMBIA UNIVERSITY AND A PERSONAL FRIEND OF CHAMBERS

OF LONGSTANDING.    CHAMBERS STATED THAT HE EXPLAINED TO SCHAPIRO

WHAT HE DESIRED AND REQUESTED THAT THE FOUR RUGS BE DELIVERED TO

END OF PAGE ONE.

THE ADDRESS OF GEORGE SILVERMAN IN WASHINGTON, D.C.  ON JANUARY TWEN

EIGHT, FORTYNINE, PROFESSOR SCHAPIRO WAS INTERVIEWED IN HIS OFFICE

AT COLUMBIA UNIVERSITY AND RELATED THAT AT CHRISTMAS TIME IN NINETEE

THIRTYSIX, CHAMBERS CONTACTED HIM AT THE UNIVERSITY AND REQUESTED

HIM TO PURCHASE FOUR EXPENSIVE ORIENTAL RUGS.  AT THIS TIME HE TURNE

OVER TO SCHAPIRO SIX HUNDRED DOLLARS IN CASH.  CHAPIRO RELATED THAT

HE  HAD NO INTIMATE KNOWLEDGE OF ORIENTAL RUGS AND HE IN TURN SOLICI

THE AID OF E. SHOEN, AN INTERIOR DECORATOR AND ARCHITECT AND A FRIEN

OF SCHAPIRO.  SHOEN THEREAFTER RECOMMENDED THAT THESE RUGS COULD BE

PURCHASED AT THE MASSACHUSETTS IMPORTING COMPANY, TWO SEVEN SIX FIFT

AVENUE, NYC.  SHOEN GAVE SCHAPIRO A LETTER OF INTRODUCTION IN CONNEC-

TION WITH THE PURCHASE OF THESE RUGS.  AS A RESULT THEREOF, SCHAPIRO

PURCHASED FOUR RUGS.  INVESTIGATION AT THE MASSACHUSETTS IMPORTING

COMPANY REFLECTED A SALES TICKET DATED DECEMBER TWENTYTHIRD, THRITY

SIX, BILLED TO E. SHOEN, FIFTEEN EAST FIFTYTHIRD STREET, FOR FOUR

BOKHARA RUGS AT A COST OF EIGHT HUNDRED AND SEVENTYSIX DOLLARS AND

SEVENTYONE CENTS.  THE SALES TICKET INDICATES A CHECK FOR SIX  HUN-

DRED DOLLARS AND CASH FOR THE BALANCE WAS PAID FOR THESE RUGS.   THIS

COMPANY WAS ALSO IN POSSESSION OF A SALES TICKET DATED DECEMBER TWENT

NINE, THIRTYSIX,  INDICATING DR. MEYER SCHAPIRO, TWO SEVEN NINE WEST

END OF PAGE TWO

PAGE THREE

FOURTH STREET, AS THE PURCHASER AND THE PERSON TO WHOM THESE
RUGS SHOULD BE SHIPPED. THE TICKET DATED DECEMBER TWENTYNINE BEARS
THE SIGNATURE OF MRS. MEYER SCHAPIRO WHICH IS A DEFINITE INDICATION
THAT INSTANT RUGS WERE SHIPPED TO THE SCHAPIRO-S NY ADDRESS. IN
CONNECTION WITH THE ORIGINAL SALES TICKET BEING MADE OUT IN THE NAME
OF E. SHOEN, THE PROPRIETORS OF THE MASSACHUSETTS IMPORTING CO.
ADVISED THAT THE ORIGINAL TICKET WAS MADE OUT TO SHOEN IN VIEW OF
THE FACT THAT SCHAPIRO WAS UNKNOWN TO HIM. HOWEVER, AFTER PAYMENT
FOR THESE RUGS WAS MADE, THE SALES TICKET DATED DECEMBER TWENTYNINE
WAS MADE OUT IN THE NAME OF DR. MEYER SCHAPIRO. THE TICKET DATED
DECEMBER TWENTYNINE, THIRTYSIX, ALSO INDICATES THAT THE RUGS WERE
DELIVERED BY THE MASSIS EXPRESS CO. SCHAPIRO, AS WELL AS HIS WIFE,
HAVE BEEN INTERVIEWED ON SEVERAL OCCASIONS AND ARE WHOLLY UNABLE TO
RECALL THE RECEIPT OF THE RUGS AT THEIR HOME OR THEIR RESHIPMENT.
MRS. SCHAPIRO, AS WELL AS HER HUSBAND, BOTH INDICATE, HOWEVER, THAT
THE SIGNATURE APPEARING ON THE DELIVERY TICKET IS THAT OF MRS. MEYER
SCHAPIRO. INVESTIGATION AT MASSIS EXPRESS COMPANY FAILS TO REVEAL
ANY INFORMATION CONCERNING INSTANT DELIVERY AND AS A MATTER OF FACT
THE EXPRESSMAN WHO DELIVERED INSTANT RUGS IS NOW DECEASED. IT WAS
BELIEVED IN THE ABSENCE OF ANY INFORMATION FROM SCHAPIRO THAT THESE
END OF PAGE THREE

##

PAGE FOUR

RUGS, WHICH WERE DELIVERED TO THE SCHAPIRO HOME, WERE RESHIPPED TO WASHINGTON BY AMERICAN RAILWAY EXPRESS. HOWEVER, OFFICIALS OF AMERICA RAILWAY EXPRESS, NYC, RELATE THAT ALL TANGIBLE EVIDENCE OF THIS DELIVERY HAS BEEN DESTROYED. THEY POINTED OUT THAT IT IS THEIR PRACTICE TO DESTROY DELIVERY INSTRUCTIONS AFTER A PERIOD OF THREE YEARS AND RECEIPTS AT THE OTHER END AFTER A PERIOD OF FOUR YEARS. SCHAPIRO HAS A SOMEWHAT DEFINITE IMPRESSION THAT AT THE TIME HE CONTRACTED FOR THE PURCHASE OF THESE RUGS, HE SPECIFICALLY INSTRUCTED THE RUG COMPANY TO SHIP THEM TO WASHINGTON, D.C. IT IS ALSO HIS RECOLLECTION THAT AT THE TIME OF CHAMBERS-S ORIGINAL CONTACT WITH HIM THAT CHAMBERS TOLD HIM TO DELIVER THESE RUGS TO A MR. SILVERMAN OR SILVERMASTER IN WASHINGTON, D.C. THE OFFICIALS OF THE MASSACHUSETTS IMPORTING COMPANY HAVE BEEN INTERVIEWED ON SEVERAL OCCASIONS AND A DILIGENT SEARCH OF THEIR RECORDS HAS PRODUCED NOTHING OTHER THAN THE ABOVE DISCUSSED SALES AND DELIVERY TICKETS. IF THE RUGS WERE ACTUALLY DELIVERED IN NEW YORK CITY ON DECEMBER TWENTYNINE, THIRTYSIX, IT IS DOUBTFUL THAT THEY WOULD HAVE REACHED WASHINGTON BEFORE SOMETIME IN JANUARY, THIRTYSEVEN. THIS IS OF SIGNIFICANT IMPORTANCE BECAUSE ALGER HISS CLAIMS THAT HE NEVER SAW CHAMBERS SUBSEQUENT TO JANUARY FIRST, THIRTYSEVEN,

END OF PAGE FOUR

1583

PAGE FIVE

~~—————————————————~~

CHAMBERS, WHEN INTERVIEWED, RELATED THAT SOMETIME IN JANUARY OF THIRTYSEVEN, BY PREARRANGEMENT, HE ACCOMPANIED ALGER HISS IN THE LATTER-S AUTOMOBILE TO A PARKING LOT NEAR A RESTAURANT JUST OUTSIDE OF COLLEGE POINT, MARYLAND. THEREAFTER, BY PREARRANGEMENT SILVERMAN DROVE UP TO THIS PLACE IN HIS CAR AFTER WHICH CHAMBERS GOT OUT OF THE HISS AUTOMOBILE, TOOK THE RUG WHICH WAS IN THE SILVER- MAN CAR AND HANDED IT TO HISS. ALTHOUGH THERE IS SOME DISCREPANCY AS TO THE MANNER IN WHICH HISS ACTUALLY PHYSICALLY OBTAINED THIS RUG, HE TACITLY ADMITS HE ACTUALLY RECEIVED IT FROM CHAMBERS. THE WFO IS REQUESTED TO CONTACT THE LOCAL REPRESENTATIVE OF THE AMERICAN RAILWAY EXPRESS TO DETERMINE, IF POSSIBLE, THE INDIVIDUAL IN THAT COMPANY WHO WOULD HAVE HANDLED DELIVERIES TO SILVERMAN-S RESIDENCE IN WASHINGTON, D.C., IN JANUARY OF THIRTYSEVEN SO THAT HE CAN BE INTERROGATED RELATIVE TO ANY RECOLLECTION HE MIGHT HAVE OF THIS TRANS- ACTION OR ANY INDEPENDENT RECORD THAT HE MIGHT POSSIBLY HAVE KEPT IN THIS REGARD. FROM ALL AVAILABLE INFORMATION, ALGER HISS IS STILL IN POSSESSION OF HIS RUG AND THE ONE DELIVERED TO WADLEIGH, ACCORDING

END OF PAGE FIVE

TO THE LATTER, IS IN STORAGE AT THE FIRM OF NESHAN G. HINTLIAN, CONNECTICUT AVENUE, WASHINGTON, D.C., A RUG DEALER. SINCE WADLEIGH HAS BEEN EXTREMELY COOPERATIVE, IT IS FELT THAT HE WOULD HAVE NO OB-JECTION TO TURNING THIS RUG OVER TO AGENTS OF THE WFO. UNLESS ADVISED TO THE CONTRARY BY THE BUREAU, WFO IS REQUESTED TO OBTAIN POSSESSION OF THIS RUG. THE DEVELOPMENT OF THE INFORMATION CONCERN-ING THE RUG WAS AT FIRST BELIEVED TO HAVE SOME BEARING ON THE TESTI-MONY GIVEN BY

IT DOES NOT APPEAR AT LEAST ON THE RECORD THAT            STATEMENTS INDICATE A POSSIBILITY THAT HE PERJURED HIMSELF. HOWEVER, THIS MATTER WILL BE GONE OVER IN DETAIL WITH T. J. DONEGAN AND THE BUREAU WILL BE ADVISED THEREOF. THE INFORMATION REGARDING THE TESTIMONY BEFORE THE GJ WAS RECEIVED ON AN EXTREMELY CONFIDENTIAL BASIS FROM MR. DONEGAN AND THIS INFORMATION IS NOT TO BE DIVULGED TO ANYONE OUTSIDE THE BUREAU.

SCHEIDT

BOTH HOLD PLS

TWO COPIES WFO

# FEDERAL BUREAU OF INVESTIGATION

Form No. 1
THIS CASE ORIGINATED AT NEW YORK                                    FILE NO.

| REPORT MADE AT | DATE WHEN MADE | PERIOD FOR WHICH MADE | REPORT MADE BY |
|---|---|---|---|
| WASHINGTON, D. C. | 3-14-49 | 3/3-11/49 | CARL N. DE TEMPLE    JND:bh |

| TITLE | CHARACTER OF CASE |
|---|---|
| JAHAM | PERJURY<br>ESPIONAGE – R<br>INTERNAL SECURITY – R |

SYNOPSIS OF FACTS:

FLORENCE TOMPKINS, colored maid of ABRAHAM GEORGE SILVERMAN, September 1935 to May, 1945, recalls delivery of three large oriental rugs from New York to SILVERMAN during fall or winter 1936. TOMPKINS aided SILVERMAN in selection of rug for own use. Recalls one rug given to HARRY DEXTER WHITE, later observed by her in WHITE home. Also overheard SILVERMAN mention ALGER HISS as recipient of other rug. She does not recall how rugs delivered or transferred to WHITE or HISS. TOMPKINS described the following people as friends of SILVERMAN: the SILVERMASTERs, HARRY D. WHITE, FRANK COE, CURRIE, PRISCILLA HISS, ULMAN, DOROTHY and IRVING KAPLAN and HAROLD GLASSER. She recalled names of ALGER HISS, BERTHA BLAIR and JERRY GERBACH being mentioned, but could not recognize photographs of ALGER HISS or Mr. and Mrs. CHAMBERS. TOMPKINS stated SILVERMAN often left apartment in evening to go to SILVERMASTERs', taking with him a large envelope, presumed to contain papers brought home from work. Records of Federal Storage Co. examined and reflected storage of 7' 3" x 12' from June 7, 1940, to October 21, 1942. Railway Express records provided no information relative to rug delivery. CLAUDIE CATLETT, maid of ALGER HISS, describes rug in possession of HISS, which may be identical with third rug described by TOMPKINS. VICLA TOMPKINS ABRAMS, SILVERMAN's maid from August, 1934 to late 1935, sister of FLORENCE TOMPKINS, recalls WHITE and CURRIE as friends of SILVERMAN and also overheard Mrs. SILVERMAN speak of SILVERMASTER.

- P -

Bureau file
Bulet to Washington Field dated February 3, 1949

3031

DETAILS: AT WASHINGTON, D. C.

The following investigation was conducted by Special Agents HARRY K. CLAYTON and PHILIP H. WILSON.

FLORENCE TOMPKINS, colored maid, also known as Mrs. FLORENCE PARKS, identified herself to the above-mentioned Special Agents on March 2, 1949, as the former maid of ABRAHAM GEORGE SILVERMAN and family for more than ten years, dating from 1935. She is currently residing at 1212 - 12th Street, Northwest, and is now employed by several families in the apartment building at 2325 - 15th Street, Northwest. She stated that she has been separated from her husband for eighteen years and that she no longer uses the name of PARKS. FLORENCE TOMPKINS said that her employment with the SILVERMANs was terminated a few months before they moved from 2325 - 15th Street, Northwest, to New York City.

With reference to the above statements, it should be noted that according to Mr. C. M. MEDFORD, Maintenance Manager, B. F. SAUL Company, Washington, D.C., the ABRAHAM GEORGE SILVERMANs first paid rent on Apartment 311 at 2325 - 15th Street, Northwest, for the month ending November 1, 1937. The apartment house records reflected that the SILVERMANs moved from the building on June 26, 1947.

FLORENCE TOMPKINS stated that the following persons were friends of the SILVERMANs and visited them at the SILVERMAN home: HARRY DEXTER WHITE, FRANK COE, NATHAN GREGORY SILVERMASTER, "LUD" (probably LUDWIG ULLMAN), LAUGHLIN CURRIE, and PRISCILLA HISS.

A photograph of HENRY HILL COLLINS, JR. was shown to FLORENCE TOMPKINS. She was unable to identify this photograph but believed the person in the photograph seemed familiar. She did not recognize photographs of WHITTAKER CHAMBERS or DAVID SILVERMAN. Photographs of ALGER HISS and Mrs. WHITTAKER CHAMBERS were not available at this interview.

Although she was unable to recall the year, FLORENCE TOMPKINS stated that she definitely recalled three Persian rugs being delivered to the SILVER-MAN apartment on California Street during the "cold weather season," a number of years ago. To the best of her recollection, two of the rugs were disposed of and the other was kept rolled up by the SILVERMANs and not used until they moved to 2325 - 15th Street, Northwest. She further stated that from overhearing conversations of the SILVERMANs, they were to have their choice of the rugs and one of the remaining was to go to HARRY DEXTER WHITE. She stated that she did not know who was to receive the other.

FLORENCE TOMPKINS stated that her sister, ETHEL, now deceased, was a maid of the HARRY D. WHITEs; that she, FLORENCE TOMPKINS, also worked on occasions for the WHITEs. At a later date, she believed that she recognized one of the three rugs containing some orange color in the WHITE household.

- 2 -

8031

She said that she did not know whether or not ALGER HISS received the other rug and that she was unable to state whether or not he had been at the SILVER-MAN home unless she could see a photograph of him. She did not recall anyone who might corroborate her statements, with the possible exception of the former janitor of the building on California Street, THOMAS SMITH, whose present whereabouts she did not know. She believed that he has returned to a farm somewhere in nearby Maryland.

With further reference to THOMAS SMITH, also known as "Pig TOM," it was ascertained on March 8, 1949, from NORMAN CARTER, a friend of THOMAS SMITH, who is currently employed as a Messenger by General Electric Company, Shoreham Building, Washington, D.C., that SMITH and his wife, ROSA, are presently residing at Trappe, Talbot County, Maryland. In this connection, a letter has been directed to the Director, with copies to Baltimore and New York City, requesting interview of THOMAS SMITH.

FLORENCE TOMPKINS stated that as far as she knows, SILVERMAN kept no photographic equipment in his apartment, but she recalls that "UD", who resided with the SILVERMASTERs was a photographer and that he mentioned having photographic equipment set up in the SILVERMASTER home.

FLORENCE TOMPKINS exhibited a willingness to be re-interviewed and arrangements were made to bring her to the Washington Field Office for re-interview on Thursday morning, March 3, 1949.

On March 3, 1949, FLORENCE TOMPKINS was re-interviewed at the Washington Field Office by Special Agent CLAYTON and WILSON. At that time, FLORENCE TOMPKINS repeated the statements set out above and elaborated on them as follows:

With reference to her period of employment by the SILVERMANs, after reflection, she believes it to be about September, 1935, until May, 1945, a period during which the SILVERMANs resided in Apartment 409 at 2138 California Street, Northwest, and Apartment 311, 2325 - 15th Street, Northwest. She recalls that they moved to the latter address during the spring or early summer in 1937.

With reference to SILVERMAN receiving three Persian rugs from New York City in December, 1936 or January, 1937, FLORENCE TOMPKINS stated that during the fall or winter of the year following her initial employment with the SILVERMANs, she recalls that three large "Oriental" rugs, approximately 9x12, were brought to the SILVERMAN apartment at 2138 California Street, North-

3031

west, and placed in the hallway. She said that, to the best of her recollection, this was in the fall or winter of 1936. She recalls that she remembered the SILVERMANs discussing these rugs and that GEORGE SILVERMAN indicated that one of the rugs was for him and he was to have his selection of the three. She also said that the rugs came from New York City, but she did not know who sent them or how they were delivered to the SILVERMAN home. FLORENCE TOMPKINS said that during conversations between GEORGE and SARA SILVERMAN, she learned that one of the rugs was to be delivered to HARRY D. WHITE, a close friend of GEORGE SILVERMAN, and the third rug was to be delivered to a person, whose name she heard at the time but could not recall.

With reference to selecting a rug for themselves, FLORENCE TOMPKINS stated that she distinctly remembered that she assisted the SILVERMANs in selecting one of the rugs to remain in the SILVERMAN home and that the rug picked out by GEORGE and SARA SILVERMAN and herself was a beautiful rug with considerable red coloring and having a heavy fringe of a lighter shade of approximately four or five inches in length. She said that, to the best of her recollection, the other two rugs were the same quality and size.

With reference to the two remaining rugs, she said that she recalled that one was sent to the home of HARRY D. WHITE, although she was not aware as to who selected that rug or how it was delivered to WHITE. These two rugs were of a pattern generally similar and contained some orange coloring. The rug selected by GEORGE SILVERMAN was somewhat different in pattern and design and contained a great deal of red.

With reference to the rugs, FLORENCE TOMPKINS recalled overhearing a conversation somewhat later between SARA and GEORGE SILVERMAN, during which GEORGE SILVERMAN said that he was sorry that he had ever gotten mixed up in the deal (concerning the rugs).

She stated that for a number of years her sister, ETHEL TOMPKINS, now deceased, was employed by ANNE WHITE, wife of HARRY D. WHITE. Some years later, possibly 1940 or 1941, she FLORENCE TOMPKINS, worked on occasions for the WHITEs at 6610 Fairfax Road, Bethesda, Maryland, and during this period, she observed one of the Oriental rugs, described above, on the living room floor of the WHITE residence, which room is located on the left as you enter the front door at this address.

With reference to SILVERMAN's activities, after they moved to 2325 - 15th Street, Northwest, FLORENCE TOMPKINS stated that in contrast to California Street, they often entertained guests at supper parties.

In her previous statement, she mentioned HARRY D. WHITE, FRANK COE, NATHAN GREGORY SILVERMASTER, LAUGHLIN CURRIE, PRISCILLA HISS and an individual known as "LUD." Upon re-interview, from photographs exhibited to her, she identified the above-mentioned persons and also HELEN SILVERMASTER. She identified WILLIAM LUDWIG ULLMAN as the person she knew as "LUD" and she also recalled that ULLMAN was residing with the SILVERMASTERs. She identified photographs of RICHARD SILVERMAN, ANATOLE SILVERMASTER, DOROTHY and IRVING KAPLAN and mentioned that HAROLD GLASSER was a guest at the apartment. She was unable to identify photographs of Mr. or Mrs. WHITTAKER CHAMBERS or ALGER HISS. She recalls the SILVERMANs mentioning the name of ALGER HISS, BERTHA BLAIR and JERRY ORBACH.

- 4 -

8031

During the second interview, FLORENCE TOMPKINS stated that SILVERMAN often left the apartment on 15th Street, Northwest, at night, saying that he was going to the SILVERMASTER's and that when he left, he would take with him a large envelope which she presumed contained papers he had brought home from work. She stated that on no occasion had she examined the contents of these envelopes and that she is not in a position to say what they contained.

She again stated that she is unable to furnish the names of other individuals who would be in a position to give additional information concerning SILVERMAN or to verify the information she has furnished.

The following signed statement was obtained at this interview:

Washington, D.C.
March 3, 1949

"I, FLORENCE TOMPKINS, freely make the following statement to Special Agents PHILIP H. WILSON and HARRY K. CLAYTON who have identified themselves to me as Special Agents of the Federal Bureau of Investigation. No threats or promises have been made in order to obtain this statement from me: I have been advised of my right to counsel and that I do not have to make this statement and that if I do make it, it may be used in a court of law.

"I, FLORENCE TOMPKINS, am 47 years old, having been born June 6, 1901, in Amherst County, Virginia. I now reside at 1812 - 18th Street, N.W., Washington, D.C., and am employed as a domestic by several families in the apartment building located at 2325 - 15th Street, N.W., Washington, D.C.

"I was employed by the ABRAHAM GEORGE SILVERMAN family as a maid from about September 1935 to about May 1945. At the time I was first employed by the SILVERMANs they were residing in Apartment 409, 2123 California Street, N.W. About the spring of 1937 they moved to Apartment 311, 2325 15th Street, N.W., Washington, D.C., at which address they remained until they left Washington to go to New York City in 1947.

"During the fall or winter of the year following my employment by the SILVERMANs, I recall that three large oriental rugs approximately 9 x 12 were brought to the SILVERMAN apartment at 2123 California Street and placed in the hallway. To the best of my recollection, this would be in the fall or winter of 1936. I remember the SILVERMANs discussing these rugs and that GEORGE SILVERMAN indicated that one of them was for him and he was to have a selection from one of the three rugs, also that the rugs came from New York, although I do not know who sent the rugs or how they were delivered to the SILVERMAN home.

"During conversations between GEORGE and SARAH SILVERMAN, I learned that one of these rugs was to be delivered to HARRY D. WHITE, a close friend of GEORGE SILVERMAN, and the third rug was to be delivered to a man whose name I heard at the time, but cannot now recall.

-5-

"With reference to selecting a rug for themselves, I distinctly remember that I assisted the SILVERMANs in selecting one of the rugs to remain in the SILVERMAN home and that the rug picked out by GEORGE and SARAH SILVERMAN and myself was a beautiful rug with considerable red coloring and having a heavy fringe of a lighter shade of approximately four or five inches in length. My best recollection is that the other two rugs were of the same quality and size.

"With reference to the two remaining rugs, I recall that one of these rugs was sent to the home of HARRY D. WHITE, although I am not aware as to who selected the rug or how it was delivered to WHITE. These two rugs were of a pattern generally similar and contained some orange coloring. The rug selected by GEORGE SILVERMAN was somewhat different in pattern and design and contained a great deal of red.

"For a number of years my sister, ETHEL TOMPKINS, now deceased, was employed by ANNE WHITE, wife of HARRY D. WHITE. Some years later, possibly 1940 or 1941, I worked on some occasions for the WHITEs at 6810 Fairfax Road, Bethesda, Maryland, and during this period and later, I observed one of the oriental rugs described above on the living room floor of the WHITE residence at 6810 Fairfax Road, which room is located on the left as you enter the front door at this address.

"I have had this typewritten statement, consisting of two pages, read to me, it is all true. I have sind both pages.

"Signed    FLORENCE TOMPKINS

"Witnessed:
PHILIP H. WILSON
Special Agent, FBI
Washington Field Office

HARRY K. CLAYTON
Special Agent, F.B.I.
Washington Field Office."

On March 7, 1949, FLORENCE TOMPKINS was again interviewed at 2345 - 15th Street, Northwest, at which time she advised that when the rugs were delivered from New York to the apartment on California Street, Northwest, she recalls that SILVERMAN mentioned that ALGER HISS and HARRY D. WHITE were to receive the other two rugs. She stated that she had not previously mentioned HISS as one of the persons receiving a rug since SILVERMAN's conversation was her only basis for believing this. She pointed out that she does not know whether HISS actually received one of the rugs as she has not been in his home. As she has been in the WHITE residence, she actually observed one of the rugs at this residence.

FLORENCE TOMPKINS advised that the SILVERMANs had stored their rug in the summer at the Federal Storage Company on Florida Avenue, Northwest, and that she had signed for the rug on both occasions when it was released to the company and when it was returned by them.

- 6 -

3031

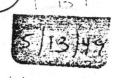

United States Department of Justice

Federal Bureau of Investigation

New York, New York

337

5/13/49

IN REPLY, PLEASE REFER TO

FILE No. _____

1) Exhibit II Rugs
2) AG Silverman

MEMO

May 13, 1949

*[handwritten notes, partly illegible]*
Spincer to form Spincer with regan.
Murphy interview with Tompkins.
AG Silverman's maid, disclosed
rugs delivered to Silverman's home
in the winter of '36

RE:  JAHAM

Re:  FLORENCE TOMPKINS

On May 12, 1949 FLORENCE TOMPKINS, 1812 18th Street, N.W.,
Washington, D. C.; a maid in the residence of ABRAHAM GEORGE SILVERMAN,
2138 California Street, N.W., Washington, D. C. and at 2325 15th Street, N.W.,
Washington, D. C., was interviewed by SAAG THOMAS J. DONEGAN and AUSA
THOMAS F. MURPHY.

Briefly MRS. TOMPKINS related that she recalls that, sometime
in 1936 and during the winter of that year at a time which she stated was
"rug time", upon arriving at the SILVERMAN home one morning she observed
three large rolls in the vestibule of the SILVERMAN residence. A little
later that day she, together with Mr. or Mrs. SILVERMAN, unrolled the
three rolls, saw that they were three 9 X 12 rugs and later learned from
conversation with either Mr. or Mrs. SILVERMAN that the SILVERMANS were
to get one of these rugs and that another of the rugs was to be given
to HARRY WHITE. She has no present recollection of any conversation during
that particular period that would indicate that rug #3 was to be delivered
to ALGER HISS or any other person.

MRS. TOMPKINS recalled that the SILVERMANS retained the rug
with the red background and that the rug that was subsequently given to
WHITE had an orange background. MRS. TOMPKINS related that she is positive
that the WHITES received this particular rug as her sister was a maid at
the WHITE residence in Bethesda, Maryland, and on Sundays, her day off, she
would occasionally visit her sister at the WHITE home and on several of
these occasions recalled seeing the rug with the orange background in the
WHITE residence.

MRS. TOMPKINS recalled that she heard the name of HISS mentioned
in the SILVERMAN household but she could not definitely recall the person

CC - SAAG THOMAS J. DONEGAN
AUSA THOMAS F. MURPHY

*[handwritten: to Spincer for file to Donegan & Murphy]*

*[handwritten: O'Keefe]*

65-14920 - 3376

F. B. I.

MAY 1 1949

N. Y. C.

TGS:MH
65-14920

EX 127

Memo
NY 65-14920

who mentioned it, or the approximate dates or the circumstances attending
the mentioning of this name.

She further stated that the SILVERMANS entertained somewhat
frequently and recalled the following persons as having been guests at the
SILVERMAN residence: SILVERMASTER (NATHAN GREGORY), COE (FRANK), KAPLAN
(IRVING) and ULLMAN (LUDWIG).

She related that none of the HISS investigators or lawyers have
talked to her to date.

THOMAS G. SPENCER, SA

N.Y. 4332

New York, New York
September 16, 1949

MEMO

Re: JAHAM
ESPIONAGE - R

Re: ABRAHAM GEORGE SILVERMAN

Reference is made to the memorandum of SA THOMAS G. SPENCER, dated July 21, 1949, setting forth suggestions for further investigation of instant case for possible use in the retrial of the HISS case.

In the case entitled: "GREGORY, ESPIONAGE - R," ELIZABETH T. BENTLEY, a former member of the Communist Party underground in Washington, D. C. and New York City in the late 1930's and early 1940's, alleged that ABRAHAM GEORGE SILVERMAN was a member of this Communist underground conspiracy. In short, BENTLEY advised that SILVERMAN, while employed as a civilian in the United States Air Force assigned to the Pentagon Building, regularly brought documents obtained in the course of his duties in the Air Corps concerning Air Corps business, to the home of GREGORY SILVERMASTER where they were photographed and photographs turned over to BENTLEY, who passed them on to a superior, JACOB GOLOS, a known Russian agent.

Closely associated with SILVERMAN in this activity were the following individuals, as alleged by BENTLEY:

HARRY DEXTER WHITE
LAUCHLIN CURRY
IRVING KAPLAN
LUDWIG ULLMANN.

Considering the allegations made by BENTLEY, SILVERMAN was interviewed on April 15, 1947 in his office at the Orbach Department Store, New York City.

FJG:MAR
65-14920

EX.128

65-14920-4332

FBI
SEP 1 1953
N.Y.C.

ROUTED TO

In the course of this interview, SILVERMAN set out his background, and was
questioned extensively concerning his Government employment in Washington,
D.C. SILVERMAN denied that he had ever been solicited by any individual to
turn over secret, restricted, or confidential Government documents during
the course of his employment in the Air Corps. SILVERMAN in fact emphasized
that he had been very security conscious during the period of 1940 through
1945, when he left the Government service. He stated that he had never taken
Government documents from his office to his home at any time.

SILVERMAN advised of his relationship with NATHAN GREGORY SILVERMASTER
and denied any knowledge that the latter was engaged in obtaining information
for the Communist Party or any foreign Government. He described SILVERMASTER
as progressive minded, but did not know whether or not he was a Communist or
sympathetic with them.

SILVERMAN denied that he had ever been a member of the Communist
Party or had ever been solicited for membership in the Communist Party. He
disclaimed any knowledge of Communist Party activities in the District of
Columbia. SILVERMAN stated that he became acquainted with LUDWIG ULLMANN
while both were employed in the United States Treasury Department, Division
of Monetary Research under HARRY DEXTER WHITE, who was described as SILVERMAN'S
closest personal friend. SILVERMAN claimed that he saw little of ULLMANN
until he commenced his duties at the Air Force. He also denied any knowledge
of espionage activities on the part of ULLMANN and illegally securing and
transmitting information to unauthorized persons. SILVERMAN has stated that
he has seen ULLMANN on various visits to the SILVERMASTER residence. He was
aware of the fact that ULLMAN was interested in photography; however, he did
not know of the presence of photographic equipment in the basement of the
SILVERMASTER home.

SILVERMAN described his duties in the Air Force as being in the
Research and Statistical Field in handling of logistical problems with respect
to the development of the B-29 program.

SILVERMAN denied the allegations that he supplied information to
SILVERMASTERS concerning any aspects of the B-29 program or any other information obtained in the course of his employment at the Air Corps.

SILVERMAN admitted a close personal relationship with IRVING KAPLAN of the War Production Board with whom he had discussed on occasions various phases of the Government's war time activity. He denied ever transmitting information given to him by KAPLAN to the SILVERMASTERS.

SILVERMAN also stated that he was acquainted with SOL ADLER and FRANK COE, having met the latter through his brother, who was at Brown University with SILVERMAN. This brother is believed to be identical with CHARLES COE, an alleged Communist Party member.

SILVERMAN, in the course of the interview, described himself as a middle-of-the-road follower and insisted any admiration he had for Russia is outweighed by his loyalty to United States. He declined to give a signed statement.

On September 11, 1947, SILVERMAN testified before a Special Grand Jury sitting in the Southern District of New York. At that time, he testified as to his eduction, background, and employment with the Federal Government. He related in detail his duties with the Air Corps as Civilian Chief of the Analysis and Reports Branch of the Material and Service Section. He related substantially the same information as obtained in the course of his interview with agents. He related his association with SILVERMASTER and how their relationship was founded on a common interest in unemployment insurance and labor problems.

SILVERMAN admitted that he was a long-standing friend of HARRY DEXTER WHITE, and also of DAVID WEINTRAUB. He had lived with WEINTRAUB in New York City in late 1946 or early 1947, when he had taken a position in New York and was attempting to locate a place to live. He admitted that WEINTRAUB had introduced him to a Russian in 1945 who was believed to be in charge of a section in UNRRA and who wanted SILVERMAN to take a position with UNRRA.

SILVERMAN stated that he had considerable to do with ULLMANN being assigned to the Air Corps since he believed ULLMANN to be a very good statistician, and on learing that ULLMANN was attending OCS, attempted to get him assigned to the Air Corps. SILVERMAN has denied any undue influence on the

part of SILVERMASTER, with whom ULLMANN resided, to place ULLMANN in the Air
Crops. It will be noted here that SILVERMAN, at the time he was interviewed
by agents, did not mention the fact that he had assisted ULLMANN in being
assigned to the Air Corps.

SILVERMAN also testified that he was acquainted with IRVING KAPLAN
and that they were close friends. He stated that he had discussed with
KAPLAN his interview by the FBI since KAPLAN also had been interviewed.
However, he denied that this discussion went into great detail. He also
denied that he had ever discussed with KAPLAN classified Government information pertaining to his position. He also testified to his acquaintanceship
and friendship with FRANK COE, SOL ADLER, LAUCHLIN CURRY, HARRY MAGDOFF.

SILVERMAN testified that he was not a Communist or a contributor
to the Communist Party or its front organizations.

On September 17, 1947, SILVERMAN was recalled as a witness before
this same Grand Jury and clarified certain points in his previous testimony.
He stated that it was during December, 1946 and January, 1947 that he had
roomed with DAVID WEINTRAUB. He also qualified his testimony concerning
the handling of documents in the Air Force which were of a classified nature.
He stated that he often took such documents when going between other Government offices in the Air Corps in the course of his official duties. However,
he denied ever taking such material to the home of the SILVERMASTERS.
SILVERMAN testified that he did not recall having in his possession top
secret material, but, however, it was quite possible such material came to
his attention. He stated that on occasions, he had taken home Air Corps
documents which he described as being of a non-classified nature and pertaining to strictly administrative matters as compared with information of a
restricted nature. He denied ever showing HARRY DEXTER WHITE restricted information; however, he stated that he may have shown such material to
LAUCHLIN CURRY in the latter's capacity as United States representative of
the U. S.-Canadian Production Board.

At this time, SILVERMAN testified that SILVERMASTER might have
spoken to him concerning ULLMANN and may have displayed some interest in his
future. SILVERMAN also testified that he assisted IRVING KAPLAN return to
the United States from Germany while the latter was in the Service. SILVERMAN

denied that he had ever met ELIZABETH BENTLEY in the kitchen of the SILVER-
MASTER home and denied recognizing a photograph of her. He stated that he
may have discussed the B-29 Program on occasion at the home of the SILVER-
MASTERS; however, he believes that his discussion would be confined to
information contained in newspaper articles.

SILVERMAN was represented at this time by ISRAEL OSEAS, 55 Liberty
Street, New York City.

On December 22, 1947, SILVERMAN was interviewed in connection with
another Bureau investigation, and on that occasion he was asked if he were
willing to make a full disclosure of his activities in connection with the
subject's of the GREGORY case. SILVERMAN expressed some indignation at the
fact that the espionage matter was again being brought up and declared that
he would not answer any questions without the benefit of consulting with his
attorney, ISRAEL OSEAS.

On August 12, 1948, SILVERMAN testified before the House Committee
on Un-American Activities and refused to answer any direct questions on the
grounds that he was excercising his consititutional privileges against self-
incrimination under the Fifth Amendment.

In the above captioned case, WHITTAKER CHAMBERS has alleged that
SILVERMAN in 1936 was a member of a Communist espionage group in Washington,
D.C. CHAMBERS also alleged that he introduced SILVERMAN to Colonel BYKOV
in addition to HARRY DEXTER WHITE, HENRY HILL COLLINS, and ALGER HISS.

SILVERMAN, at this time CHAMBERS stated, was an employee of the
Railroad Retirement Board, and although he was not in a position to supply
him with confidential Government documents, was utilized by this espionage
group to keep HARRY DEXTER WHITE "in line" in view of the fact that WHITE
was a very close friend of SILVERMAN.

CHAMBERS also stated that in 1936, BYKOV, CHAMBERS' superior in
the espionage group, suggested that a gift of rugs be made to ALGER HISS,
HARRY DEXTER WHITE, and GEORGE SILVERMAN. Arrangements were subsequently
made for these rugs to be delivered to SILVERMAN in Washington, D. C. and,
therbafter, the rugs were presented to HARRY WHITE and ALGER HISS.
SILVERMAN is alleged to have delivered a rug to HARRY WHITE, and also
delivered a rug to CHAMBERS in the outskirts of the District of Columbia

MEMO
NY 65-14920

which rug was transmitted by CHAMBERS to the car of ALGER HISS. This meeting was pre-arranged by CHAMBERS and SILVERMAN.

CHAMBERS also alleged that prior to breaking with the Communist Party, he was assisted in obtaining a Government position with the National Research Project by SILVERMAN and IRVING KAPLAN, who was in Philadelphia with the National Research Project at that time.

An attempt was made to interview SILVERMAN concerning the above allegations in December, 1948 at which time SILVERMAN declined to answer any questions without advice of his counsel.

Information set out below is a brief summary of SILVERMAN'S testimony before the Grand Jury in the Southern District of New York made available for review by a confidential source.

On December 15, 1948, SILVERMAN testified that he was residing at 255 West 23rd Street, New York City, and that he was unemployed at that time. SILVERMAN was represented at this time by Attorney BERNARD JAFFEE, 52 Broadway, New York City.

SILVERMAN testified briefly as to his various Government positions especially during the period of 1936, 1937, and 1938, when he was employed with the Railroad Retirement Board. It will be noted that this is the last position SILVERMAN held prior to his joining the Army Air Force in a civilian capacity. He advised that in 1937 and 1938, he lived in Washington at 2138 California Street and also 2325 Fifteen th Street. At the outset of his testimony, SILVERMAN refused to answer questions concerning ALGER HISS and WHITTAKER CHAMBERS on the grounds that he might tend to incriminate himself and on the advice of counsel. A discussion took place as to his reason for not answering questions and this resulted in a consultation between SILVERMAN and his attorney. After this conference, SILVERMAN returned to the Grand Jury Room and expressed his desire to cooperate with the Grand Jury without urging any privilge.

SILVERMAN testified that he was acquainted with WHITTAKER CHAMBERS and had first met him in late 1936 as DAVID WHITTAKER. At that time, SILVERMAN was Director of Research at the Railroad Retirement Board, and CHAMBERS visited him at his office, advising that he was a free-lance writer

MEMO
NY 65-41920

desiring information on the Railroad Retirement Act and its constitutionality.
SILVERMAN did not recall giving CHAMBERS any information at this time. He
testified that he saw CHAMBERS on numerous occasions after this meeting in
Washington and understood that CHAMBERS was from New York City. These various meetings took place at dinner or luncheons. In the course of this
relationship, it was discovered that they had a common interest in art and
discussed the French write DeSTENDAHEL. SILVERMAN testified that they also
may have discussed politics. He stated that he was never acquainted with
CHAMBERS' real occupation as an underground operator for the Communist Party.
SILVERMAN stated that CHAMBERS may have visited his home; however, he denied
ever being acquainted with Mrs. CHAMBERS.

SILVERMAN testified that he was not acquainted with ALGER HISS and
had first met him in the Grand Jury anteroom when both were waiting to testify.
He believed that HISS approached him and introduced himself after SILVERMAN
had been identified to him by his attorney. SILVERMAN testified that he had
never seen HISS prior to that time.

SILVERMAN also testified that during his acquaintance with CHAMBERS,
the latter had borrowed various small amounts of money amounting to total of
over $75.00. SILVERMAN testified that this money has not been repaid as
such; however, SILVERMAN related that he had bought two rugs from CHAMBERS
sometime in 1937. He described these rugs as imported orientals. It was
SILVERMAN'S understanding that CHAMBERS had an import connection and was
ale to get these rugs. Since CHAMBERS owed SILVERMAN money, these rugs were
taken by SILVERMAN and paid for by him. SILVERMAN testified that he recalled
he gave CHAMBERS two or three hundred dollars in addition to what CHAMBERS
owed SILVERMAN. This was to be considered payment for the rugs. SILVERMAN
testified that he gave one of these rugs to HARRY DEXTER WHITE who was a
long-standing friend of his over twenty-six years. He explained that he
gave this rug to WHITE in return to WHITE'S hospitality when SILVERMAN lived
with him for a period of two months when his wife was away, and WHITE would
not accept any money for this. SILVERMAN recalled that when the rugs were
delivered, there were four rugs and that he picked out two for himself and
the remaining two were taken by CHAMBERS at a later date. SILVERMAN denied
that he had ever put a rug in his car and drove to a point outside of
Washington and delivered a rug to CHAMBERS. SILVERMAN said that he had
accepted delivery of the four rugs at the request of CHAMBERS and recalled
this to be about 1936 or 1937.

SILVERMAN also testified that he was not a Communist nor had he ever been active in Communist Party circles. He also stated that HARRY WHITE was not a Communist to his knowledge. He denied every speaking to WHITE concerning CHAMBERS. SILVERMAN described himself as an "easy touch" and, as a result, CHAMBERS often borrowed money from him. SILVERMAN stated that he has been unemployed since his appearance before the House Committee on Un-American Activities, as a result of which he resigned his position with Orbach Department store.

SILVERMAN also testified briefly at this time concerning the allegation of ELIZABETH BENTLEY. SILVERMAN also testified that he had been contacted by a Mr. ROSENWALD, who he understood to be council for Mr. HISS and advised that he had visited ROSENWALD at his home to discuss his giving a deposition in favor of HISS concerning HISS' Baltimore libel suit. SILVERMAN also denied that he had ever talked to CHAMBERS about keeping HARRY WHITE in line.

In connection with SILVERMAN'S testimony before the Grand Jury in 1947, it is to be noted that Mayor WILLIAM O'DWYER of New York City contacted T. VINCENT QUINN, Assistant Attorney General, who was handling the Grand Jury at the time and advised that he was interested in SILVERMAN and had been approached on his behalf by JEROME K. ORBACH of Orbach Department Store. O'DWYER inquired if QUINN would be interested in having SILVERMAN make a complete and detailed statement concerning his part in instant case, furnishing all details, regardless of whether or not they were detrimental to himself or his friends. As a result of this, arrangements were made for SILVERMAN to appear before Mr. QUINN and Mr. T. J. DONEGAN to make a complete statement.

In this connection, SILVERMAN secured the services of Judge EDWARD LAZANSKY, former Presiding Judge, Appellate Division, New York Supreme Court. At the time stated, SILVERMAN appeared to make this statement and advised that he had come to answer any questions, and claimed that he had no information which he had not already given to Bureau agents.

Inasmuch as this was a radical change from the contemplated attitude of SILVERMAN, this interview was brought to a close. It was apparent that SILVERMAN had talked to someone and suffered a change of heart.

MEMO
NY 65-14920

It will be noted that SILVERMAN has testified before the Grand Jury as not having been previously acquainted with ALGER HISS. In this connection, attention is directed to the case file of SILVERMAN in which it is set forth on Page 118 a signed statement by Mrs. VIRGINIA OLMSTEAD McINTYRE, who advised that she identified a picture of PRISCILLA HISS as identical with a woman she had seen on several occasions in the company of Mrs. SARAH SILVERMAN. Mrs. McINTYRE from August, 1937 until June, 1945 was employed as a resident manager of the Garden Towers Apartment located at 2325 Fifteen Street, Washington, D. C. In connection with her relief duties at the telephone desk in the lobby of the Garden Towers, which was the residence of SILVERMAN, she also recognized a photograph of ALGER HISS as a person observed in the company of SILVERMAN.

Also contained in the file mentioned above, which is Serial there is set forth on Page 126, a signed statement by STEVEN M. WALTER, who advised that he resided at the same address above from late 1937 to late 1938. He also was aware of the fact that SILVERMAN lived on the same floor as his own apartment. He also stated that he was acquainted with ALGER HISS, having first come in contact with him during 1933 at the Agricultural Adjustment Administration. He advised that during the period 1937 to 1938, he recalled meeting ALGER HISS in the elevator and after recognizing him, spoke to him casually. However, this greeting was not returned. Mr. WALTER also advised that HISS got off the elevator on the third floor, however, he did not determine which apartment he entered.

It is set out in Serial 3 in the file 100-95971, which is the case file of CHAIRMAN, the signed statement given by WILLIAM MARSHALL BATCHLOR, a former employee of 2325 Fifteen Street, for a period of six months during 1937 or 1938. BATCHLOR recognized a photograph of ALGER HISS as an individual whom he had seen visiting someone in the apartment building.

It would appear from the above information set forth that there is a possibility SILVERMAN was acquainted with ALGER HISS and has not told the truth before the Grand Jury when he denied knowing HISS. It is also set forth in the above-mentioned Serial 3 that HELEN RINGE is a former girlfriend of SILVERMAN, which acquaintance dates back to 1931. HELEN RINGE has been interviewed at length by the San Francisco Office when she was visiting San Francisco as a delegate to the YWCA Convention. HELEN RINGE is an official of the YWCA in New York City and resides in New York City.

105

MEMO
NY 65-14920

At the time RINGE was interviewed in San Francisco, she expressed her desire to conclude the interview and to consider a future interview upon her return to New York City. However, she has not contacted this office since her return from the West Coast. It will be noted that RINGE after being interviewed and having an appointment the following day with agents of the San Francisco Office, contacted the local office of the Civil Liberties Union which in turn contacted the San Francisco Office concerning the interview of RINGE on the previous day. During the interview RINGE admitted a close personal relationship with SILVERMAN, indicating that she might be the girlfriend of SILVERMAN. RINGE denied being a Communist; however, it will be noted that her sister, IRMA MAY RINGE was a Communist Party member in 1935, having left the Party in 1940.

The investigation concerning SILVERMAN indicates that he has been extremely distressed as a result of the investigation and has been unable to obtain employment since leaving the Orbach Department Store.

The above information is being set forth as a brief summary of SILVERMAN'S activities and statements in order to determine whether or not further interview of SILVERMAN should be conducted.

                                        FRANK J. GALLANT, SA

106

Silverman

(349)

(Dict. by HR)

January 12, 1949

Memorandum of Conference
with Mr. Bernard Jaffe.

This afternoon I had a long conversation with
Mr. Bernard Jaffe, 52 Broadway, who is counsel for Mr. A.
George Silverman.

At the outset, I told Mr. Jaffe that we would
like to know anything that Mr. Silverman may know concerning
our case and that, of course, we might want to call Mr.
Silverman as a defense witness if his information had any
value.  I told Mr. Jaffe that we were particularly interested
in the truth or falsity of Chambers' allegations that Silverman
was a member of the same Communist apparatus as Hiss and that
Silverman's chief function was to hold Harry White in line.
I told him we were also interested in Chambers' story that
Silverman had assisted Chambers in getting his position
with the Railroad Retirement Board.

Mr. Jaffe stated that Mr. Silverman would not make
a very good witness for us chiefly because of his temperament
and personality.  I told Mr. Jaffe that I knew perfectly well
that Mr. Silverman is an extremely nervous person and that he
suffers an emotional collapse any time that the entire subject
of his alleged Communist activities is mentioned.  Mr. Jaffe
stated that in addition to this difficulty, Mr. Silverman
might be subject to damaging cross examination.

EX. 129

Mr. Jaffe stated that he did not want Mr. Silverman to testify under any circumstances if it could be prevented. I asked him whether he would be willing to have him testify in an examination before trial in the libel action but added that we would want him to testify in the criminal case if we thought his testimony in his deposition in the libel action might have some value for us.

I received no definite answer to this suggestion from Mr. Jaffe.

I then talked about Chambers' testimony with respect to Mr. Silverman and I told Mr. Jaffe that we intended to examine Chambers further in the near future. He then asked whether he could see the entire deposition of Chambers which has already been taken. I told him that I would recommend to Mr. McLean that he be permitted to see this deposition if he wanted it for the purpose of determining whether or not he would permit Silverman to testify voluntarily in the criminal case. He said that he would keep an open mind but repeated his objection to any further testifying by Silverman. I intimated as gently as possible that we could, of course, subpoena Silverman as a defense witness or in the libel action and that we could challenge any claim of privilege that he might make. However, I assured him that we would much prefer to have Mr. Silverman testify voluntarily.

I got the definite impression that Mr. Jaffe is not trying to protect Mr. Silverman from divulging any criminal conduct on his part but that he is distrustful of the authorities

in connection with this entire matter. From my own knowledge
of Mr. Silverman and his alleged activities, I rather doubt
whether he has done anything wrong although he may well have
been indiscreet.

My final arrangements with Mr. Jaffe were as
follows:

1. Subject to the approval of Mr. McLean, we will
send him as soon as possible the entire deposition of
Chambers in Baltimore. This will be used by Mr. Jaffe only
for the purpose of reaching a final decision as to whether
or not he will permit Silverman to testify.

2. Mr. Jaffe offered to tell us the entire story
concerning Silverman's activities if we would agree not to
challenge any claim of privilege that Mr. Silverman might
make, either on direct or indirect examination as a witness
for the defense. I told Mr. Jaffe that I doubted very much
whether we could make such an agreement but that I would discuss this with Mr. McLean and let him know our decision.

I should add that we will have no assurance whatsoever that Mr. Jaffe will permit Mr. Silverman to testify for
us after he has carefully considered the deposition. Nevertheless, I see no harm in letting him have the deposition.

H. R.

(Dict by HR)

HISS PERSONAL 2395                    March 21, 1949

## Memorandum re A. George Silverman

About Wednesday of last week, I called Mr. Bernard Jaffe and told him that we would like to talk to Mr. Silverman on the terms prescribed by Mr. Jaffe which are set forth in my earlier memorandum. Mr. Jaffe suggested that I have a preliminary talk with him and I went to see him that afternoon.

In a preliminary discussion, I told Mr. Jaffe that I had understood that we would be allowed to talk to Mr. Silverman if we agreed not to call him as a witness without the consent of Mr. Jaffe. Mr. Jaffe said that we would be able to talk to Mr. Silverman if we wanted to but that such a conversation might be unnecessary. He said that he thought that it would be preferable for him to tell me what Silverman knew. I agreed to this, reserving our right to talk with Mr. Silverman himself but agreeing that in no event would we compel Silverman to testify except with the approval of his counsel.

I should note that our agreement to Mr. Jaffe's terms was based in large measure on the impression that Silverman probably had a fairly good claim of privilege. I believe we had been told by Lee Pressman, who presumably got it from Jaffe, that Silverman had refused to testify before the Grand Jury with respect to the matters involving Whittaker Chambers.

At the outset, Mr. Jaffe told me that Silverman did testify fully and freely before the Grand Jury when he was called there recently. This would mean that he probably waived any privilege he may have ever had. I merely note this in the event that Jaffe should act unreasonably in refusing to agree to Silverman's testifying and attempt to hold us to our agreement not to compel him to testify or to challenge any claim of privilege he might make. I think it is quite possible that we entered into the agreement with Jaffe on the basis of a false impression which was fairly deliberately offered to us by Jaffe both directly and via Lee Pressman.

Silverman knew Whittaker Chambers during the general period 1935-37 in Washington. He does not remember the circumstances under which he met Chambers and recalls him as just one of the people he happened to know. From time to time he had lunch with Chambers. He recalls that they talked about art and music. Both of them were interested in Pieter Breughel.

Chambers borrowed money from Silverman from time to time and ran the debt up to $100 or $200. Subsequently, Chambers told Silverman that he could get rugs in New York at a substantial saving and that he would like to get some of these rugs for Silverman and have Silverman apply his claim against Chambers in part payment for the rugs. Silverman agreed to this and later received four rugs from New York. He does not remember the date of this transaction.

Silverman accepted two of the rugs and paid Chambers $200 or $300 and cancelled his claim against Chambers. He gave one of the rugs to Harry White and kept the other for himself. Chambers' story concerning delivery of one of the rugs by Silverman to Hiss at a restaurant on the Baltimore Road is completely false.

Nothing like it ever happened. Chambers picked up the remaining two rugs at Silverman's home. Silverman's reason for giving a rug to the Whites was that he was greatly indebted to them for many favors and wanted to give them a present.

Silverman has never been and is not now a member of the Communist Party. He was never a member of any Communist apparatus in Washington or elsewhere. He did not endeavor to hold Harry White in line in any such apparatus. He says that Harry White was not the kind of a man who can be held in line. The relations between Chambers and Silverman have nothing whatever to do with any left-wing political activities of any nature.

Silverman knew Chambers under the name of Whittaker Chambers. He has never met Mrs. Chambers. He never visited Chambers at his home. Chambers did not visit Silverman except on the occasion when he came to get the two rugs.

Silverman had a long and close professional and social relationship with Harry White. They were both economists and frequently consulted on matters of interest to either or both of them. They gave advice to each other concerning their separate economic problems.

Silverman does not remember whether he helped Chambers to get a job. He thinks it is possible that he may have done so. He knew that Chambers was hard up and was always borrowing money. He thought he might have even called Irving Kaplan and says that he knew Kaplan. He knows that he did not get Chambers an important position because Chambers was not qualified to do any important work. However, he might have helped him get some clerical position of a routine nature.

Silverman does not know Alger Hiss. He also does not
know Donald Hiss, Richard Post, Yost or Trueblood.

I told Mr. Jaffe that I thought Silverman's testimony
would be of great value to us particularly with respect to the
rug and the denial of his participation in the parallel apparatus.
Mr. Jaffe did not question the value of such testimony. However,
he did discuss with me at some length the deficiencies of
Silverman as a witness about anything. Having observed Silverman's
conduct when he was under investigation by the Grand Jury last
summer, and having talked with him one evening a few months ago,
I share the view of Mr. Jaffe concerning Silverman as a witness.
He is pretty neurotic even when he discusses these matters. He
looks somewhat like my idea of a Russian professor. He will be on
the verge of hysteria even when testifying truthfully concerning
a routine fact. I told Mr. Jaffe that I agreed with everything
he said about Silverman's personality but that nevertheless, we
might want to call him. I told him that we were not in a position
to pick and choose among possible witnesses and that we had to
use people who were familiar with the facts. I told him that we
would probably agree to advise him concerning persons who would
be testifying for the defense, so that he would have some assurance
that Silverman would not stand alone. This seemed to lift Mr.
Jaffe's spirits considerably.

We concluded the conference with the following understanding: If Mr. McLean desires to talk with Mr. Silverman, Mr.
Jaffe will arrange for such an interview. I am strongly of the
opinion that this should be done as soon as possible.

H. R.

(356)

2 FBI Investig

FBI 1/18/49
3/15/26
1059

JAN 18 1949

TELETYPE

WASHINGTON AND WFO   FROM NEW YORK   84

DIRECTOR AND SAC       URGENT

18 tele

JAY DAVID WHITTAKER CHAMBERS, WAS, ETAL, PERJURY, ESP. R.   WASHINGTON
FIELD IS REQUESTED TO ADVISE IF THE CHECK OF ALGER HISS-S BANK ACCOUNT
IN WASH. DC, REFLECT ANY TRANSFER OF FUNDS TO A BANK IN NYC.   SUTEL.

1059

EX. 130

① FBI Investig

1-2-4-49

WASHINGTON AND NEW YORK FROM WASH FIELD      24      3:30 PM

DIRECTOR AND SAC, NEW YORK

J. B. WHITTAKER CHAMBERS, WAS, ET AL, PERJURY, ESP - R, IS - R.
RETEL JANUARY TWENTY, LAST. ALGER HISS HAS OPEN BANK ACCOUNT AT THE
FARMERS AND MECHANICS BRANCH, RIGG'S NATIONAL BANK, WISCONSIN AVENUE AND M
STREET, NW, DC. CONFIDENTIAL INFORMANT OF THIS OFFICE ADVISES THAT NO
PERMANENT RECORDAK IS MAINTAINED OF WITHDRAWALS FROM BANK ACCOUNTS AT RIGGS
BANK. IN ORDER TO ASCERTAIN IF TRANSFER OF FUNDS WAS MADE OTHER THAN BY REGULAR
CHECK, IT WOULD BE NECESSARY TO CHECK ALL CORRESPONDENCE FILES AND ALL CASHIERS'
CHECKS. OFFICIALS OF RIGGS BANK ARE RELUCTANT TO FURNISH SUCH INFO WITHOUT A
SUBPOENA DUE TO PUBLICITY THIS CASE HAS RECEIVED AND THE POSSIBILITY OF
INFO GIVEN BY THEM WITHOUT A SUBPOENA BECOMING PUBLIC. SUGGEST THAT YOU CONTACT
SPECIAL ASSISTANT TO ATTY GENERAL, MR. T. J. DONEGAN, RE ADVISABILITY OF
ISSUANCE OF A SUBPOENA TO JOHN McCORMACK, VICE PRESIDENT AND CASHIER OF RIGGS
NATIONAL BANK, MAIN OFFICE, FIFTEENTH AND PENNSYLVANIA AVENUE, NW, TO PRODUCE
ALL THE CORRESPONDENCE AND ALL PERTINENT RECORDS INCLUDING CASHIERS' CHECKS,
RECORDAK FILMS, ETC., TOGETHER WITH SUPPORTING LEDGER CARDS, OF ALGER HISS'
ACCOUNT. UNLESS ADVISED TO CONTRARY, NO FURTHER ACTION WILL BE TAKEN BY THIS
OFFICE IN REGARD TO THE BANK ACCOUNT OF ALGER HISS.

- 1240

HOTTEL

p telex re Wash office investig H bank accounts

EX. 131

# Office Memorandum • UNITED STATES

**DATE:** January 27, 1949

1382

**TO** : Director, FBI

**FROM** : SAC, New York

**SUBJECT:** JAY DAVID WHITTAKER CHAMBERS, was., et al
PERJURY
ESPIONAGE - R
INTERNAL SECURITY - R

Re Washington Field teletype to the Bureau and New York January 24, 1949, and New York teletype to the Bureau and Washington Field January 26, 1949, re issuance of a subpoena duces tecum for use in examining the bank account of ALGER HISS at the Farmers and Mechanics Branch, Riggs National Bank, Wisconsin Avenue and M Street NW, Washington D.C.

Mr. T. J. Donegan was consulted concerning the advisability of securing such subpoena and after concluding that it would be appropriate, he on this date caused a subpoena to be issued to that bank for the purpose of examining all correspondence and pertinent records in the bank's possession concerning the ALGER HISS account. The original and copy of this subpoena, addressed to JOHN McCORMACK, Vice President and Cashier, are being transmitted herewith for the Washington Field Office.

Mr. Donegan pointed out that undoubtedly the Washington Field Office enjoys close liaison with the Riggs National Bank and that it would be more satisfactory for Agents to handle the service of the subpoena.

Mr. McCormack should be advised that his appearance before the Grand Jury in New York City on the day specified in the subpoena is not required, and that if it later becomes necessary to call him he will be so advised.

2 cc Washington Field (Encs. 2) - REGISTERED MAIL

JMK:AG

1382

EX.132

# FEDERAL BUREAU OF INVESTIGATION

| FORM No. 1 THIS CASE ORIGINATED AT NEW YORK | | | | FILE NO. |
|---|---|---|---|---|
| REPORT MADE AT | DATE WHEN MADE | PERIOD FOR WHICH MADE | REPORT MADE BY | |
| WASHINGTON, D. C. | 3-14-49 | 1/19,24,27-31; 2/3-7,10-14,16-18; 3/2-7/49 | J. BERNARD COOK (A) vda | |

| TITLE: | CHARACTER OF CASE |
|---|---|
| JAY DAVID WHITTAKER CHAMBERS, was, et al | PERJURY ESPIONAGE – R INTERNAL SECURITY – R |

SYNOPSIS OF FACTS:

Subpoena served on Riggs National Bank
January 31, 1949 for the accounts of
ALGER and PRISCILLA HISS. Photographs
of accounts of ALGER and PRISCILLA HISS
and related documents obtained and being
forwarded to New York City. Analysis of
savings accounts reflect account opened
November 4, 1936 at Farmers and Mechanics
Branch, Riggs National Bank with deposit
of $300. Present balance $3,441.82. On
November 19, 1937 PRISCILLA HISS withdrew
$400 from savings account, leaving balance
of $40.46. Withdrawal slip for this amount
being forwarded to the New York Office.
Ledger sheets and deposit slips of checking
account on ALGER and PRISCILLA HISS analyzed from June, 1934 to February, 1949.
Balance in this account as of February 4,
1949 amounted to $2,433.45. This analysis
reflects deposits from May, 1936 to September, 1945 of approximately $22,405 in checks
from National Bank of Norwalk, Norwalk,
Connecticut, most of which deposits were in
form of monthly checks of $100 each. Details
of other deposits set out. Checks deposited
not available for review as bank does not retain recordak film. Bureau Laboratory reports
that two typewritten deposit slips of ALGER
HISS were not identical with known specimens
of Woodstock and Royal typewriters. PRISCILLA

| APPROVED AND FORWARDED: | SPECIAL AGENT IN CHARGE | DO NOT WRITE IN THESE SPACES |
|---|---|---|

HISS maintained safe deposit box at Riggs
National Bank from October 14, 1935 to sometime subsequent to October 14, 1946, at which
time last rent payment made.  Loan made by
ALGER and PRISCILLA HISS through Riggs National Bank on October 6, 1943 for $6,000.
Remaining balance of $3,641.26 on November 14,
1947 paid off in full on that date.  A signed
power of attorney in the name of ALGER HISS
dated July 28, 1938 submitted to Bureau Laboratory for handwriting examination.  During February, 1949 $500 paid to HAROLD ROSENWALD and
$2,500 to PAUL STRYCKER from the checking ac-
count of ALGER and PRISCILLA HISS.

- P -

REFERENCE:  Bureau file

Teletype to Bureau January 24, 1949.

Teletype from New York January 26, 1949.

New York letter to Bureau January 27, 1949.

Letter to Bureau February 10, 1949.

Teletype to New York February 14, 1949.

2 - Chicago
2 - Cleveland
2 - Kansas City
2 - Los Angeles
2 - New Haven
2 - Philadelphia
2 - San Antonio
2 - San Diego
3 - Washington Field

2-14-49

J. D. W. CHAMBERS, WAS., ET AL, PERJURY, ESP DASH R. SUBJ HAS ADVISED
THAT AROUND NINETEEN THIRTY FIVE HE PURCHASED FORD SEDAN, THIRTY ONE
OR THIRTY TWO MODEL, TAN IN COLOR WITH FUNDS PROVIDED BY J. PETERS.
CAR BOUGHT NYC AND ORIGINALLY REGISTERED HERE UNDER NAME DAVID BREEN.
CHAMBERS EXPLAINED CAR PURCHASED FOR HIS USE IN WORK AND PRIMARILY
FOR TRAVEL BETWEEN NY, BALTIMORE AND WASHINGTON. BELIEVES HE SECURED
NEW YORK PLATES IN NINETEEN THIRTY SIX. WHEN HE MOVED TO AUCHENTERLY
TERRACE, BALTIMORE IN EARLY NINETEEN THIRTY SEVEN HE BELIEVES HE SOLD
CAR TO HIMSELF AS JAY CHAMBERS OR POSSIBLY TO HIS WIFE, MRS. JAY CHAM-
BERS. AT THAT TIME HE SECURED MD. PLATES. STATES THAT ON ARRIVAL
OF COL. BYKOV, LATTER FORBADE HIM TO USE ANY CAR IN HIS WORK AND ACCOR-
DING TO CHAMBERS HE WAS NOT AWARE OF FACT CHAMBERS HAD THIS CAR. SUBJ
STATES WHEN HE BEGAN TO PLAN HIS BREAK HE DECIDED A CAR WAS ESSENTIAL
AND HE FINALLY PERSUADED BYKOV THAT HE, CHAMBERS, NEEDED A CAR. HE
ASKED BYKOV FOR FIVE HUNDRED DOLLARS. LATTER SAID HE DID NOT HAVE THAT
AMOUNT ON HAND. CHAMBERS THEN INDICATED HE COULD BORROW MONEY FROM
ALGER HISS AND BYKOV SAID HE SHOULD DO THAT AND THIS WOULD BE PAID
BACK. CHAMBERS STATES HE ASKED ALGER FOR MONEY AND LATER RECEIVED
SAME.

INDEXED - 135
RECORDED - 135
MAR 15 1949
2354

See p 2

2-p telex on WC statements about 1934-1937 Ford cars

2354

EX.133

PAGE TWO

HAS RECOLLECTION THAT PRISCILLA HISS SAID SHE HAD TO CLOSE OUT HER
ACCOUNT TO GET THIS MONEY FOR HIM.  THIS WOULD HAVE BEEN IN EARLY
NINETEEN THIRTY EIGHT.  CHAMBERS BELIEVES HER ACCOUNT WOULD HAVE BEEN
IN THE RIGGS NATIONAL BANK, MAIN OFFICE OR DU PONT BRANCH.  A FEW
DAYS AFTER HISS GAVE HIM MONEY, MRS. CHAMBERS TURNED IN AFOREMENTIONED
FORD AT THE SCHMIDT MOTOR CO., RANDALLSTOWN, MD. AND GOT NEW NINETEEN
THIRTY SEVEN FORD.  LATTER CAR STILL IN CHAMBERS POSSESSION.  HE
ADMITS HE NEVER PAID HISS BACK THE FIVE HUNDRED DOLLARS BUT BELIEVES
LATTER WAS PROBABLY REPAID BY BYKOV THOUGH HE HAS NOTHING TO SUBS-
TANTIATE THIS.  REQUEST BALTIMORE CHECK FOR ANY DETAILS AVAILABLE AT
SCHMIDT MOTOR CO. AND AT MD. BUREAU OF MOTOR VEHICLES.  REQUEST WFO
CHECK FOR BANK ACCOUNTS OF PRISCILLA HISS TO DETERMINE IF SHE MADE
ANY SUCH WITHDRAWAL IN EARLY NINETEEN THIRTY EIGHT.  2354

FEDERAL BUREAU OF INVESTIGATION
U. S. DEPARTMENT OF JUSTICE
COMMUNICATIONS SECTION

DEC 3

TELETYPE

FBI 12/3/49
1/13/76
file HISS-Bank Acct

(orig. FORD 1937)

4297

CONF WASH AND WASH FLD FROM NEW YORK   2

DIRECTOR AND SAC          URGENT

9-p teley summarizing

*ALGER*

...AHAM. DURING THE COURSE OF THE HISS TRIAL, DEFENSE ATTORNEY CLAUDE

B. CROSS BROUGHT OUT THE FACT THAT A SUBPOENA, DATED JANUARY THIRTY

FIRST FORTY NINE HAD BEEN SERVED ON THE RIGGS NATIONAL BANK AND ATT-

EMPTED TO LEAVE THE INFERENCE WITH THE JUDGE AND JURY THAT THE FBI

HAD SUBPOENAED THESE RECORDS AND HAD MADE THEM AVAILABLE TO WHITTAKER

CHAMBERS, AFTER WHICH CHAMBERS KNOWING THAT HAD ADMITTED PURCHASING

A NINETEEN THIRTY SEVEN FORD AUTOMOBILE, INDICATED THAT HISS HAD LOANED

HIM FOUR HUNDRED DOLLARS IN NOVEMBER OF THAT YEAR. IT IS NOTED IN

THE REPORT OF SA J. BERNARD COOK /A/, MARCH FOURTEEN, FORTY NINE,

THE WITHDRAWAL OF FOUR HUNDRED DOLLARS WAS MADE IN NOVEMBER, THIRTY

SEVEN.    THE INFORMATION CONCERNING THE WITHDRAWAL OF THIS FOUR HUNDRED

DOLLARS WAS OBTAINED FROM WHITTAKER CHAMBERS ON FEBRUARY FOURTEEN,

FORTY NINE, AT WHICH TIME HE STATED THAT HE HAD RECEIVED FIVE HUNDRED

DOLLARS FROM ALGER HISS TO PURCHASE AN AUTOMOBILE AND IT WAS CHAMBERS

OPINION THAT HE HAD TOLD COLONEL BYKOV THAT HE COULD OBTAIN THIS MONEY

FORM HISS AND BYKOV HAD AGREED THAT HE SHOULD OBTAIN IT FROM HISS.

IT IS NOTED THAT CHAMBERS CLAIMS HE RECIVED XXXX RECEIVED FIVE HUNDRED

DOLLARS WHEREAS THERE IS ONLY A RECORD OF FOUR HUNDRED DOLLARS BEING

END OF PAGE ONE

PAGE TWO

WITHDRAWN FROM THE BANK. AUSA T. J. MURPHY HAS REQUESTED THAT THE FILES

OF THE WFO BE REVIEWED AND A MEMO PREPARED STATING THE DATES   THE

RIGGS NATIONAL BANK WAS CONTACTED IN CONNECTION WITH THE ALGER HISS

CASE, THE PURPOSE OF THESE CONTACTS, THE NAMES OF THE OFFICIALS

IN THE BANK WHO WERE INTERVIEWED, ALSO WHETHER OR NOT THE BANK HAS

A RECORD OF THE DATES THAT THE AGENTS MADE THE CONTACTS.  IT IS DE-

SIRED THAT THE NAMES OF THE AGENTS WHO MADE THE ORGINAL CONTACTS BE

MADE AVAILABLE IN THE EVENT IT IS NECESSARY TO SUBPOENA AN AGENT TO

TESTIFY TO THE PURPOSE OF THE ORIGINAL CONTACT AT THE RIGGS NATIONAL

BANK.  THE REFERENCED REPORT OF SA ,. BERNARD COOK /A/  REFLECTED THAT

TWO TYPEWRITTEN SPECIMENTS OF DEPOSIT SLIPS BY HISS WERE FURNISHED

TO THE FBI LABORATORY FOR COMPARISON PURPOSES.  THEREFORE, IT IS BELIEVED

THAT THE ORIGINAL CONTACT WITH THE BANK WAS MADE IN ORDER TO OBTAIN

TYPEWRITING AND HANDWRITING SPECIMENS.  EXPEDITE.

        SCHEIDT

HOLD                                           4297

STANDARD FORM NO. 64

# Office Memorandum • UNITED STATES GOVERNMENT

TO      :  DIRECTOR, FBI                           DATE:  December 5, 1949

FROM    :  GUY HOTTEL, SAC, WASHINGTON FIELD

SUBJECT:  JAHAM

Retel from New York Office dated December 3, 1949.

All contacts with the Riggs National Bank in connection
with this case were made by Special Agent (A) J. BERNARD COOK of this office.

The first contact with the Riggs National Bank with regard
to the account of ALGER and PRISCILLA HISS was made on January 24, 1949, at
which time the New York Office requested the Washington Field Office to
check the account of ALGER and PRISCILLA HISS at the Riggs National Bank.
On January 24, 1949, Mr. JOHN McCORMICK, Vice President and Cashier, was
contacted by Special Agent COOK in regard to the examination of the account
of ALGER and PRISCILLA HISS. Mr. McCORMICK stated that in accordance with
the policy laid down by the officials of the Riggs National Bank, no information whatsoever could be given by the bank to this office without the
issuance of a subpoena duces tecum.

The above information was transmitted by teletype dated
January 24, 1949, to the New York Office and a request was made at that
time that a subpoena duces tecum be issued to the Riggs National Bank for
the account of ALGER and PRISCILLA HISS and all related correspondence.

Information was received by the Washington Field Office on
or about January 27, 1949, that a subpoena duces tecum would be issued by
the Grand Jury at that time sitting in New York City. On January 30, 1949,
a subpoena was received by the Washington Field Office and upon authority
of the Bureau, this subpoena was served on a Mr. JACK COCHER, Assistant
Cashier of the Riggs National Bank, Washington, D. C., at approximately
9:49 A. M.

EX. 135

4319

DIRECTOR, FBI                                         December 5, 1949

    This subpoena was served on Mr. COOKER inasmuch as Mr.
JOHN McCORMICK, the Vice President and Cashier, Riggs National Bank,
was absent on that particular day.  It is to be noted that this subpoena
was served at the main office of the Riggs National Bank located at
15th and Pennsylvania Avenue, N. W., Washington, D. C.

    Immediately upon receipt of this subpoena by Mr. JACK
COOKER, he noted thereon the time it was received and initialed this
subpoena.  He then called Mr. THEODORE COWGILL, Assistant Manager and
Assistant Cashier, Farmers and Mechanics Branch, Riggs National Bank,
Wisconsin Avenue and M Street, N. W., Washington, D. C., and informed
him in the presence of Agent COOK that a subpoena had been received by
the Riggs National Bank calling for the account of ALGER and PRISCILLA HISS
and all related correspondence.  Mr. COOKER requested that in compliance
with this subpoena that this information should be obtained from the
records of the Farmers and Mechanics Branch of the Riggs National Bank
and made available to Agent COOK.

    It is to be noted that all the records concerning this
account were maintained at the Farmers and Mechanics Branch of the Riggs
National Bank where ALGER and PRISCILLA HISS maintained their account.

    Contact was again made with the Riggs National Bank on
February 3, 1949, along the general lines of obtaining the records.  However, the records were not made available to this office until February
7, 1949, at which time they were photographed by Agent COOK and the originals remained in the files of the Farmers and Mechanics Branch of the
Riggs National Bank.  This method was used so that the original records
would not have to be brought to New York and laid before the Grand Jury
by an officer of the bank.

    On February 14, 1949, a teletype was received by the
Washington Field Office requesting information concerning the withdrawal
of $400.00 from the savings account by PRISCILLA HISS sometime in Novem-
ber 1937 or early part of 1938.  At this time the Washington Field Office
had in its possession the photographs of all the ledger cards, together
with the savings, withdrawals and deposit slips obtained as a result of
the issuance of the subpoena.  No particular significance had been attached to this withdrawal of $400.00 by the Washington Field Office prior
to February 14, 1949.  Immediately upon receipt of this teletype from the
New York Office on February 14, 1949, an analysis was made of the savings
account of PRISCILLA HISS and complete information concerning the $400.00
was furnished to the New York Office by teletype dated March 2, 1949.  At
the date of this teletype there was no information in the Washington Field
Office files indicating that any prior information or documents had been
furnished to the New York Office regarding this transaction.

-2-

DIRECTOR, FBI                                          December 5, 1949

On February 16, 17 and 18, 1949, the Riggs National Bank was again contacted by Agent COOK of this office with reference to one ledger card that was missing and had not been located.

On March 4, 1949, the original power of attorney was obtained from the Farmers and Mechanics Branch of the Riggs National Bank by Agent COOK and this power of attorney was returned to the bank on March 8, 1949.

On March 11, 1949, the Riggs National Bank was contacted at the request of the New York Office in an effort to ascertain the officer of the bank who should be subpoenaed and who would be qualified to introduce the records of the bank. As a result of this contact, Mr. LYNN DeLASHMUTT, Assistant Vice President and Manager of the Friendship Branch of the Riggs National Bank was designated by the officials of the Riggs National Bank as the person most qualified to handle this particular assignment.

On March 16, 1949, the Riggs National Bank was again contacted in the person of Mr. LYNN DeLASHMUTT at the request of the New York Office in order that he might identify a photograph of ALGER HISS.

The Riggs National Bank has no record whatsoever as to the dates that contact was made with officials of the Riggs National Bank by agents of this office concerning the ALGER HISS case with the exception of the original subpoena which was issued on January 31, 1949. It is to be noted that no information concerning the accounts of ALGER HISS was obtained prior to January 31, 1949.

The two typewritten specimens of deposit slips of the account of ALGER HISS which were furnished to the FBI Laboratory for comparison purposes were obtained subsequent to January 31, 1949, at the time that the original records of ALGER HISS were being photographed, namely, on or about February 7, 1949. In analyzing these deposit slips, it was found there were two typewritten deposit slips which might be of some use to the Bureau for comparison purposes and therefore, these deposit slips were transmitted to the Bureau Laboratory.

It is to be noted that the photographs of the ledger cards of the account of ALGER and PRISCILLA HISS, together with all related correspondence, were first submitted to the New York Office with the report of Special Agent (A) J. BERNARD COOK dated March 14, 1949. This report was dictated on March 3, 1949, between the hours of 9:00 A. M. and 10:00 A. M., and had as enclosures all the photographs which were obtained from the Riggs National Bank pursuant to the subpoena issued on January 31, 1949.

-2-

DIRECTOR, FBI                                    December 5, 1949

     Inasmuch as the information concerning the withdrawal of
the $400.00 was obtained from WHITTAKER CHAMBERS on February 14, 1949,
and the Washington Field Office received notification of this by teletype
on the same date and the Washington Field Office answered this teletype
on March 2, 1949 and submitted the documents with the report of Special
Agent (A) J. BERNARD COCK dated March 14, 1949, to the New York Office,
it is not probable that the New York Office would have any information,
particularly the documents in question, in their possession as of February 14, 1949.

# *APPENDIX*

## Amendment to the
### *Coram Nobis* Petition

UNITED STATES DISTRICT COURT
SOUTHERN DISTRICT OF NEW YORK

-------------------------------------x

In Re                    :    78 Civ. 3433 (RO)

ALGER HISS,               :    <u>NOTICE OF MOTION</u>

Petitioner.          :

-------------------------------------x

PLEASE TAKE NOTICE that upon the annexed affidavit
of Victor Rabinowitz, duly sworn to on the 31st day of October, 1979, the petitioner will move this court before the
Honorable Richard Owen, United States District Court, United
States Courthouse, Foley Square, New York, New York, for an

ORDER granting leave to the petitioner to amend the
petition herein by adding thereto the allegations set forth
in Exhibit A attached hereto, and

for such other and further relief as may be just
and proper.

Dated: New York, New York
       October 31, 1979

Respectfully submitted,

VICTOR RABINOWITZ, Esq.
RABINOWITZ, BOUDIN, STANDARD,
  KRINSKY & LIEBERMAN
30 East 42nd Street
New York, New York 10017
  (212) 697-8640
Attorneys for Petitioner

TO:
     Robert B. Fiske, Jr., United States Attorney
        Att: Mary C. Daly, Assistant United States Attorney

UNITED STATES DISTRICT COURT
SOUTHERN DISTRICT OF NEW YORK

-----------------------------------x

      In Re           :    78 Civ. 3433 (RO)

    ALGER HISS,        :      AFFIDAVIT

        Petitioner.   :

-----------------------------------x

STATE OF NEW YORK  )
                  : ss.:
COUNTY OF NEW YORK  )

      VICTOR RABINOWITZ, being duly sworn, deposes and

says:

      I am the attorney for the petitioner in the above

matter and make this affidavit in support of an application

for leave to amend the petition herein by adding the allega-

tions set forth in Exhibit A attached to the Notice of Motion.

      The amendment has been made necessary as a result

of research into the facts and by the disclosure of certain

materials submitted by the United States Government under the

Freedom of Information Act which has supplied evidence tend-

ing to support the allegations of the amendment.

No prejudice to the defendant will result in the granting of this relief.

The defendant, in its answer, assigned numbers to the paragraphs of the petition herein which had not been previously numbered. We have, in the proposed amendment, adopted the defendant's suggestion and have numbered the paragraphs to follow in sequence the numbering proposed by the defendant.

_____
VICTOR RABINOWITZ

Sworn to before me, this
31st day of October, 1979.

_____
Notary Public

BETTY S. VERDEJO
NOTARY PUBLIC, State of New York
No. 03-4608901
Qualified in Bronx County
Commission Expires March 30, 19__

## Amendment To Coram Nobis Petition

141.  Extensive surveillance of persons suspected
of disloyalty, espionage or "subversive activities" was a
part of the program and practice of the FBI and the CIA in
the period between 1940 and 1953, and thereafter.  Wiretaps,
other forms of electronic surveillance, mail covers and inter-
cepts, programs of infiltration into political organizations,
wide spread use of informers, burglaries and similar activities were a standard part of the technique of government investigative and police agencies during this period.

142.  Although occasional instances of such activity became public information prior to 1975 (as in the case
of the 1949 disclosures that the FBI had intercepted telephone calls between Judith Coplon and her attorney), the investigation carried on by the Select Committee of the United
States Senate to Study Government Operations with Respect to
Intelligence Activities, 94th Cong., 1st Sess. (the Church
Committee), resulted in the exposure of many of these activities.  The findings by the Committee were supplemented by
evidence disclosed in a great many cases litigated in the
federal courts all over the country in the past several years
- cases like United States v. Ellsberg (burglary); Socialist

Workers Party v. Attorney General (burglary, infiltration and other assorted activities); Lamont v. United States of America (mail cover); Birnbaum v. United States of America (mail cover); Halpern v. Kissinger (wire-tapping), etc. Much of this activity has not been denied by the DBI when discovered, though the Bureau denies that such is any longer its policy.

143. Petitioner was one of the subjects of government surveillance beginning in 1941 and continuing with little interruption in the years following. The surveillance took many forms such as mail covers (including the opening of mail) by the FBI, investigation of toll calls by the same agency, and the copying of petitioner's desk calendar and mail by the State Department. In addition, the petitioner's telephone was tapped by the Washington field office of the FBI from November 30, 1945 to September 13, 1947, when it was discontinued because petitioner moved from Washington to New York.

144. The field office of the FBI in New York contends that it has destroyed some of its files connected with the Hiss case, which may have included logs of telephone taps. Despite this effort to destroy evidence of violations of the Fourth Amendment, some concrete written evidence of surveillance has survived. See, for example, Ex. CN 13 attached to this petition which the government concedes in its

response was found in the files of the United States Attorney for the Southern District of New York. Attached hereto as Ex. CN 84 is a letter dated December 17, 1951 from Paul Willert to Chester Lane, then attorney for petitioner, also found in government files. There is much further evidence of mail openings, covers on petitioner's toll calls and telegraphic communications and similar forms of surveillance of the petitioner between 1947 and 1953.

145. Petitioner's telephones and those of his attorneys were tapped at various times between 1947 and 1953 and other forms of electronic surveillance of the petitioner and his counsel were engaged in by the FBI or other state or federal governmental agencies, in violation of applicable law. As a result of such surveillance, evidence or leads to evidence were obtained for use by the government in the 1948 and 1949 prosecutions of petitioner.

(376)

14 Halsey Street,
London, S.W.3.

17th December, 1951.

Mr. Chester T. Lane,
Beer, Richards, Lane & Haller,
70 Pine Street,
NEW YORK 5., N.Y.

Dear Mr. Lane,

Your telegram reached me a few days after returning from
Spain. I had in the meantime collected in Paris a copy of your letter
addressed to me here. I must apologise for the delay.

My difficulty in the whole of this tortuous business, as I told
our mutual friend, is that I have no documentary evidence to support
my own memories as to when I met Chambers and when he told me that he
had definitely left the Communist Party and was in fear of his life.
It would appear to me, from my own recollection and from the date of
the publication of Dr. Gumpert's book, that these meetings must have
been just before or after Christmas 1937-8. It would be difficult, as
you will understand, for me, lacking documentary evidence, to swear to
this impression in a court of law. The best I could do would be to
repeat that fatal phrase "to the best of my recollection".

However, there is one way in which to support my memories one way
or the other; that is, to ask Dr. Gumpert on what date he handed back
his manuscript to me to be retranslated, or - and much more important -
to ask the then editor of the Oxford University Press, Philip Vaudrin,
when he first discussed this translation with Whittaker Chambers. It
was Philip Vaudrin who brought Chambers to my office for the purpose
of translating Dr. Gumpert's book. It would seem to me that these two,
far more important than myself, are in a position to state what date
Chambers began his work. It was during his work on the translation
that he told me of his fear of being murdered by the O.G.P.U. and
went into hiding in a way which embarrassed us very much. This would
be sufficient evidence to show when he said he had broken with the
Communist Party.

I am indeed sorry not to be more helpful and hope very much that
you will have some success with Gumpert and Vaudrin. I hope you
will not think that I am being uncooperative.

*65-1642-1900*

Yours very sincerely,

C.N. EX. 84